Women in Korean History

Women in Korean History

Lee Bae-yong

Translated by Lee Kyong-hee

Ewha Womans University Press

Foreword

Do women have a history? What have been the contributions of women? These are basic questions that would face anyone who seriously examines women's history. Yet, one finds that women have been pushed to the remote corners of written history. Why, then, have historians ignored women so unjustly?

Ironically, these questions lead to the self-evident conclusion that the study of women's history should focus explaining why women have been jettisoned from mainstream history and reassembling the forgotten bits and pieces about the lives of women in the past. The ultimate objective should be to awaken not only women themselves but society in general to the fact that women are as important creators of history as men and that future society should be led by both men and women together.

Women account for half of the world's population. Human history has evolved on the two wheels turned by men and women. Without cooperation of the two genders the stream of human history would have been halted; the existence of mankind itself would have been impossible. However, spotlight has focused on one wheel, leaving the other in darkness. Women's roles have been excluded from historical writings and fallen into oblivion in male-centered history.

It is the time for women's history to be illuminated to open an era of gender equality. A truly humane society can be realized only when men and women coexist as equal partners turning the two wheels of history side by side along its long valley.

The history of Korean women differs greatly from conventional thought. Even those who believe they are knowledgeable about Korean history often have stereotypical views of Korean women centuries ago — the chaste and virtuous women of the Joseon Dynasty (1392-1910). It means their historical knowledge is limited to the latter part of the Joseon period, when Neo-Confucianism became firmly entrenched as the ruling ideology exerting far-reaching influence on the behavior of the whole society.

In much of ancient Korean society women played vital roles in meeting the basic subsistence needs beyond childbirth and child-caring. In marriage and economic activity they were as much independent and self-supportive as men. Women's rights to succeed the family lineage and inherit property were widely recognized. Thus the Silla period (57 B.C.-A.D. 935) could have three reigning queens over a millennium ago.

Historical records show that during the Goryeo period (918-1392) women faced little discrimination in inheriting family assets and pedigree as well as rights to hold ancestral rites. Goryeo women lived under the influence of both Confucianism and Buddhism: the former as the basic governing principle of state and the latter as the means for mental and spiritual cultivation. Barred from any opportunity to participate in politics, women naturally were more influenced by Buddhism. As funerals and memorial rites for ancestors were held at Buddhist temples, monks supervised the events while the children paid the expenses. It was one reason the ancestral rites were not monopolized by the eldest son; all his siblings could serve in turns. Daughters and sons-in-law, or even their children performed the ancestral rites in families without sons.

Therefore, few families adopted sons to continue the lineage through the eldest son. Particularly, women enjoyed advantages from the time-old custom of holding weddings at their homes. The groom lived with the bride's family until their children reached a certain age.

The founders of the Joseon Dynasty fortified the patriarchal family system, as they regarded the family as the essential unit for smooth governance under Confucian ideology. To keep women inside the boundaries of the family, they introduced various moral doctrines such as banning them from remarriage, promulgating "Seven Evils" to justify divorcing a wife, and promoting the "Three Obediences," which demanded women obey their father, husband and son, and the rule of gender segregation. But it was not easy to change the people's lifestyle overnight. In the early Joseon period, women's social and economic position was not as weak as perceived today. Family assets were divided in more reasonable ways than now. Women lived in a relatively free atmosphere.

In the latter part of the Joseon period, however, women's rights were reduced and immaculate virtues were demanded to confine them within the boundaries of home as part of the policy to reinforce the Confucian mantle over society. Nonetheless, Joseon women made more conspicuous achievements in cultural areas than their forebears of any era. Though they were denied any formal education many women left behind great literary and artistic works or excelled in academic realms such as Neo-Confucianism and Practical Learning (*Sirhak*). They overcame the repressive Confucian ideology with deep insight and strong determination.

In the modern period, Catholicism and Eastern Learning (*Donghak*), a homegrown religious thought, both advocating gender equality, contributed remarkably to Korean women's awareness and intellectual development. With the establishment of modern educational institutions for women doors opened for women to have jobs and advance into society. The Gabo Reform of 1894, in particular, brought about epochal changes to women's life by lifting the ban on remarriage and the law of gender separation, and abolishing premature marriage. Feminist groups were organized to debate women's position and humanization. Amid the waning national fortune women joined the struggle for independence to be reborn as vital participants of historical change.

The Japanese colonial rule (1910-1945) placed Korean women under the multiple yokes of racial discrimination, gender discrimination and class discrimination. Their prospects for the future were extremely murky. However, they never gave up their struggle to secure basic rights as human beings and sowed the seeds for national liberation as well as women's liberation. Thus they helped lay the groundwork for an advanced society.

The 21st century is expected to be an era of unprecedented use of female human resources. There cannot be more valuable information than historical experiences in assessing the present and planning the future. In this context, the author has intensively studied the history of Korean women with the aim of shedding light on the dynamic life of those who defied numerous feudalistic barriers to assume pioneering roles in modernization as well as in transmission and development of traditions.

This book was compiled with articles written with such an aspiration and contributed to various newspapers and magazines over the years. The articles were designed to present a fresh insight into the diverse lives of women who stood out in Korean history by depicting how they actively overcame the tides of time in different eras.

It is my great pleasure to see this book published in English. At the same time, I feel a greater sense of responsibility. I hope this humble volume will help arouse greater interest in the history of Korean women around the world. It will be all the more gratifying if readers warmly open their hearts toward Korean history and culture. I earnestly hope that this book will provide momentum to rediscover the wisdom and strength of Korean women and contribute to creating a history of women that will enrich the future of mankind.

Lee Bae-yong

Contents

Chapter 8 Women of the Modern Period

Part III Historical Records and Sites Related with Women

Chapter 9 Korean Women as Seen Through Historical Records and Sites

Part I
Women's Life during the Joseon Dynasty

Chapter 1

Confucianism and Women's Life

Women's Response to Confucian Family Ethics

Marriage System and Women's Status

Property Inheritance and Women's Status

Law on Gender Segregation

Doctrine of Absolute Chastity

Education of Women

Women and Crimes

Women's Response to Confucian Family Ethics

The Joseon Dynasty (1392-1910) reinforced patrimonial institutions rooted in the family as the basis of smooth governance under Confucian ideology. In order to prevent deviation from the patrilineal family structure, various moral regulations were introduced to segregate the sexes, forbid women from remarrying, and confine women to rigid prescriptions for ethical behavior such as the "Seven Evils" or "Three Obediences." A father who had an unmarried daughter over 30 years old was subject to government punishment on the grounds that she could eventually end up wandering around without a family to rely on and thereby cause social problems. In the Confucian moral standards, women had to remain perpetually dependent upon men — their fathers, husbands and sons.

Joseon women largely complied with government policies and social institutions. The annals of the dynasty have numerous accounts of women commended by the state for faithfully accomplishing their moral obligations as daughters, mothers, wives and daughters-in-law. They were from all social classes, suggesting that women from the commoner class had a strong desire to emulate upper-class culture.

Not a few daughters considered it their filial duty to sacrifice their lives to save their parents from danger. A tale of a brave girl who fought a tiger while searching for her parents' bodies vividly illustrated the moral principles during Joseon. Stories about exemplary daughters-in-law who devotedly supported their parents-in-law in adverse circumstances also abounded.

Another deeply ingrained ethical principle was chastity. Many women killed themselves to keep their chastity from enemy troops. Many a widow committed suicide to follow their husbands in death. This practice increased in the latter part of Joseon because the principle of chastity became so widespread and deep-rooted that women could only draw attention through such an extreme act.

Mothers taught their children to devote themselves to academic pursuit and service to the country, which would help enhance their family reputation. The outstanding enthusiasm of Joseon mothers for their children's education derived largely from their family ethics and sense of duty to promote their family prestige as well as their personal desires for vicarious satisfaction in a male-centered society dominated by Confucian values.

Still, the rigid Confucian order did not go unchallenged. Generally, women who tried to break out of their defined role either ended up as criminals or achieved intellectual growth and self-cultivation. Typical "crimes" committed by women included running away and adultery. They were probably the only alternatives available to Joseon women — breaching the unforgiving doctrine of chastity and fleeing ethical obligations toward their family.

Intellectual challenge was a far more affirmative and productive response. Joseon had no formal institutions for women's education. Therefore, women had to be content with attaining a minimum education at home to demonstrate their intellectual potential. Still, many talented women overcame the institutional limitations to attain remarkable levels of self-cultivation and play important roles. These self-taught women greatly contributed to the cultural and artistic advancement of Joseon. Sin Saimdang (1504-1551) and Heo Nanseolheon (1563-1589) were the two most prominent women in this respect. Many other women also left their names in history through their paintings and poems.

Other women distinguished themselves in scholarly research. Some families with renowned traditions in Neo-Confucian philosophy and Practical Learning (*Sirhak*) produced prominent female scholars, too. Im Yunjidang (1721-1793) was distinguished in the study of Neo-Confucian philosophy emphasizing the supremacy of *gi* (energy) over *i* (reason); Seo Yeongsuhap (1753-1823) showed unusual talent in poetry and mathematics; and Yi Bingheogak wrote *Women's Encyclopedia* (*Gyuhap chongseo*) containing practical knowledge for home keeping in various areas in 1809.

The Korean script, Hangeul, invented in early Joseon gave women the means to scholarly pursuit. Women were avid readers of Chinese textbooks and novels translated into Korean. They also wrote in Korean, immensely contributing to the advancement of Korean literature while men generally preferred the Chinese letters.

Through their intellectual activities these women secured firm positions in their respective areas and further encouraged changes to societal perceptions of women's roles. Though they fell short of completely vanquishing conventional views of gender, the voice they gave to women's intellectual ability and equality with men sowed the seeds of gender view and feminist movements in the next era.

On another plane, women strongly challenged the Confucian social order by participating in religious and social movements such as Western Learning (*Seohak*), referring to Catholicism, and the homegrown Eastern Learning (*Donghak*). Despite severe government persecution, Catholicism radically changed women's lives. Female converts came out of their home to propagate their faith, defying norms of gender separation, and Bible studies offered them access to a new world of knowledge. Moreover, women gained hope and courage from Christian scriptures that proclaimed all human beings are equal before God.

The ideology of Donghak advocated the unity of all humans and God: both women and men and the Supreme Being were one and the same. It called for reform of the corruption-ridden world and the realization of paradise on earth. Donghak respected the role of woman in conceiving and delivering man, the innately good and genuine Supreme Being that serves God. Such a deferential view of woman and the female believers' active missionary activities had a profound influence on modernization movements in Korean society, including education for women, abolition of premature marriages, approval of remarriages and social participation.

Marriage System and Women's Status

In Korea old bachelors are often asked, "When do you get into *jangga*?" The word *jangga* literally means a man's father-in-law's house. The expression stems from the Goguryeo period (37 B.C.-A.D. 668), when weddings were held at the bride's home and the couple lived there with the wife's family until their children reached a certain age. Then they moved to the husband's home.

"Accounts of the Eastern Barbarians" (*Dongyizhuan*, or *Dongijeon* in Korean) from *Records of Wei* (*Weizhi*, or *Wiji*) of the *Records of Three Kingdoms* (*Sanguozhi*, or *Samgukji*), an ancient Chinese source, said, "In Goguryeo, once a marriage has been arranged, the bride's parents build a small house for the groom at the back of their house, called *seo-ok*, meaning the 'son-in-law's house.' The groom arrives at the bride's house late in the evening on the wedding day. He gives his name outside the gate, kneels down and bows, asking that he would be allowed to stay with his bride. He repeats this a few times before the bride's parents give their permission."

Conversely, the Chinese weddings were held at the groom's home and the bride lived with her in-laws from that day on. China was a patrilineal society, which confined inheritance of family property to sons. Daughters had no economic rights and were married off to live

"Wedding" from "Pictures of a Man's Life" by Kim Hong-do (1745-?). The groom heads to the bride's home for a wedding ceremony. (National Museum of Korea)

with their husband's family.

Ancient Korea initially had a non-patrilineal family structure. There was little discrimination between sons and daughters, and they equally inherited family property. The equal inheritance influenced the life of daughters even after marriage as they continued to live with their parents up until the early Joseon period. Thus, the maternal parents maintained much closer relations with their sons-in-law and daughters' children.

The differences between Korea and China also were reflected in formal mourning periods for one's grandparents, maternal grandparents and wife's parents. In Korea, until the early Joseon period, they were all mourned equally for one year following their death. The mourning periods differed in China: they mourned for one year for grandparents, five months for maternal grandparents, and three months for wife's parents.

In Korea, a son-in-law or a daughter's son could hold ancestral rites for those who died without a male offspring. Sons-in-law enjoyed greater advantage in official recruitment than brothers or grandsons. Also, they were regarded guilty by association along with sons in cases of treason.

Neo-Confucianists criticized the traditional wedding practices. In the late Goryeo Dynasty (918-1392), Neo-Confucian bureaucrats such as Jeong Do-jeon asserted that women tended to lack deference to their husband because they remained under the protection of their parents after marrying. The debate intensified as Confuciansm made a deeper impression on the values of the Joseon Dynasty. Many scholars called for change in the wedding custom which they insisted made the *yang* (male) follow the *yin* (female), not the other way round. They contended it was improper for the Koreans not to follow the Chinese wedding customs when they had accepted Chinese ways in most other rites.

Amid solid support from bureaucrats, Princess Suksin, a daughter of King Sejong (r. 1418-1450), was married in a ceremony held at her husband's home and stayed on with his family. But a custom with history of more than 1,000 years could not be changed overnight. Most of the literati class continued to marry their children in the traditional style.

With Neo-Confucianism taking firm root in Korean society in the mid-Joseon period, the wedding custom eventually found ways to reach a compromise. The wedding was held at the bride's home but the couple stayed there for only a few days before moving to the groom's home. Even today, newlywed couples first pay a visit to the bride's home when they return from their honeymoon.

The shortened stay of newly married couples at the brides' homes prompted considerable changes to family life and women's status. In the latter half of the Joseon period, women were no longer considered members of their maiden family once they were married. Daughters were discriminated against in property inheritance and the eldest sons were given the largest portion because they were responsible for holding ancestral rites. Formal mourning periods were differentiated between paternal and maternal grandparents; mourning garments were worn for five months for maternal grandparents and three months for wife's parents.

Those who had no son adopted a son rather than have their son-in-law or a daughter's son observe ancestral rites. Thus a patrilineal family system was firmly established. The prevailing mindset was that a proud man would not depend on his wife's family even in dire circumstances.

Confucian scholar bureaucrats of the Joseon period also prohibited women from remarrying. They contended that women should not remarry but live under the principle of Three Obediences: obey their father, husband and son. They insisted that a woman should remain

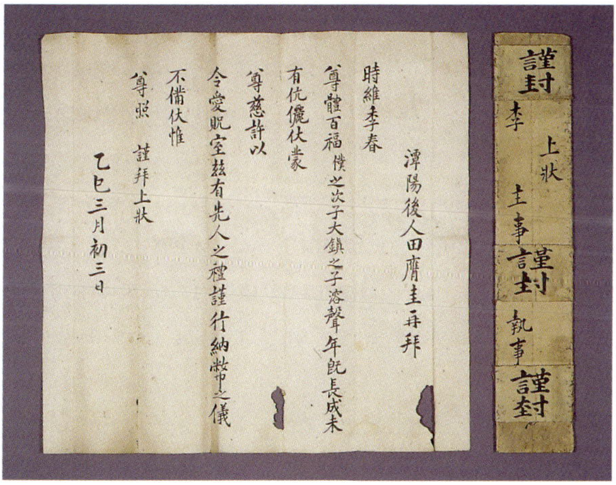

謹封
李 上狀
主事 謹封
執事 謹封

潭陽後人田膺圭再拜
時維季春
尊體百福僕之次子大鎭之子溶聲年旣長成未
有伉儷伏蒙
尊慈許以
令愛貺室玆有先人之禮謹行納幣之儀
不備伏惟
尊照 謹拜上狀
乙巳三月初三日

Marriage letter (*honseo*) Prior to wedding the groom's family sent a letter to the bride's family along with some gifts. (National Folk Museum of Korea)

Wooden goose (*mogan*) The groom presented a wooden goose to the bride's mother when the wedding ceremony began. (National Folk Museum of Korea)

faithful to her dead husband and continue rearing their children. This served the patriarchal family system and helped prevent potential problems of remarriages, such as conflict between children and their stepfather, and adoption of another surname. Thus the patriarchal lineage was protected.

Remarried women faced disgrace and punishment in that their children were disqualified from taking state examinations for public service. Thus their children were denied a chance of attaining a decent career and social excellence in Joseon society. The law banning women's remarriage was introduced during the reign of King Seongjong (1469-1494) amid much controversy. The majority of officials proposed banning women from marrying only a third time. They argued that a young widow would have no choice but to remarry when both of her parents were dead, or some parents would not leave their young widow daughters to live alone all their lives. However, the king endorsed the minority opinion that "losing chastity was a bigger issue than dying of hunger."

Remarriage became a taboo among not only women of the upper class but commoner women as well in the late Joseon period, when Neo-Confucianism became the entrenched norm across all social strata, imposing severer restrictions on women and weakening their status even more.

Property Inheritance and Women's Status

The custom of equal inheritance of family property among sons and daughters continued to be practiced until the mid-Joseon period. The basic statute of Joseon, *Grand Code for State Administration* (*Gyeongguk daejeon*), completed in 1485, the 16th year of King Seongjong, prescribed in detail the equal property inheritance among male and female offspring. It provided that all children born of a legitimate wife were entitled to equal inheritance regardless of gender or seniority, with the one responsible for ancestral rites given an additional one-fifth of his due. The law stipulated that children born of a concubine from the commoner class would be alloted one-seventh of that for legitimate children, and those of a lowborn concubine only one-tenth, regardless of gender. In other words, the social class of mothers mattered while gender or seniority did not.

The Annals of the Joseon Dynasty (*Joseon wangjo sillok*) have no reference to disputes concerning the equal inheritance of family property among male and female offspring until the years of King Seongjong (r. 1469-1494). The royal household as well as private families followed the custom recognizing women's rights of inheritance. In the year of his accession, King Sejong (r. 1418-1450) issued an ordinance to "sternly punish those who are reluctant to equally divide

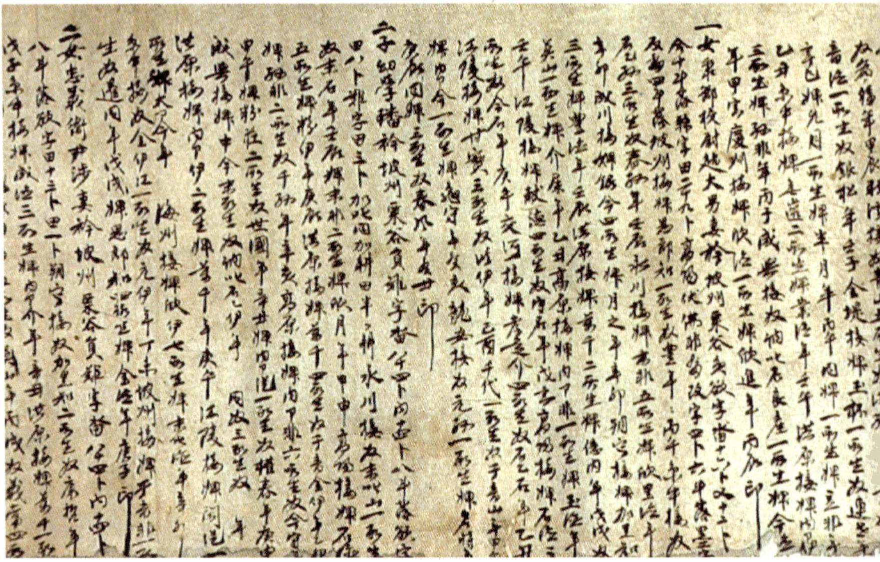

family assets, including slaves, for married female siblings after their parents pass away."

While the law protected the inheritance rights of married daughters, it was difficult for government to actually intervene in asset disposal among private families. More often than not the social norm and custom provided the guideline. Still, inheritance deeds from the early Joseon period show that in most cases family property was equally divided among sons and daughters.

During early Joseon, women could keep their own property from the confines of their marriage. The court annals of Joseon have various references to personal property of married women, such as "slaves of so and so, who is the wife of so and so," indicating that women could own slaves in their names, which they were able to trade or present to others as gifts on their own. For example, an entry in March of the eighth year of King Sejong says, "Second State Councillor (*jwaeuijeong*) Yi Won purchased a slave, named Kim Jang, from the

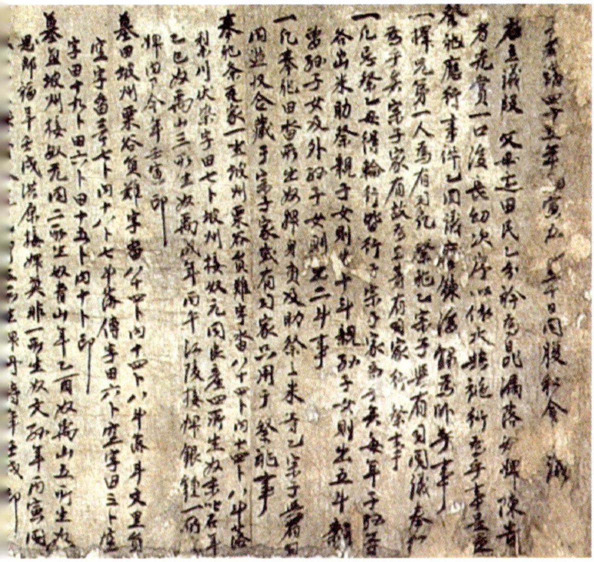

Inheritance deed of Yi I's family The document shows Yi I (1536-1584) and his siblings equally divided their parents' property regardless of gender or seniority. (Konkuk University Museum)

wife of Kim Do-ryeon when his family already possessed not a few slaves."

When a married woman died, her personal property was evenly divided among her children. If she had no children, her property was often returned to her maiden family. If her widowed husband inherited her fortune, he had to return it to her maiden family if he remarried. In a sense, married women during early Joseon were ensured greater rights to property than today's women.

Many women filed lawsuits or requested government mediation to keep their fortune. There are records about a mother who sued her son who had expended her fortune and a daughter who sued her mother for what she considered an unfair division of assets.

An equal property inheritance implied an equal division of duties. Children of both genders were equally obliged to do their best to support their parents. When their parents passed away, both sons and daughters shared the duties to observe memorial rites on their death anniversaries. In many cases during the early years of Joseon, both sons and daughters took turns conducting the ancestral rites.

Land and slaves constituted the main family assets inherited through generations. Houses, cattle and horses as well as gold, silver and all articles of daily use, including kettles and farming tools, were also passed down. Slaves were widely regarded as personal property and valuable means of the ruling class to maintain their social prestige and exhibit wealth. During Joseon, one slave equaled 10 *bu* of farmland in value for exchange. Slaves were distributed in consideration of their age and working ability. Ownership of slaves was clarified among family members as "belonging to" the father, mother, or wife. Farmland was evaluated according to space, fertility and crops.

In the latter half of the Joseon period, women's property inheritance rights were considerably reduced as Confucian ethics spread widely across the nation. The family system changed to emphasize the patriarchal lineage and the role of the eldest son in ancestral rites and property inheritance. The equal inheritance rights existed only as a nominal code as the eldest son was accorded an increasingly important position while daughters faced discrimination. The eldest sons eventually inherited most of the property as they were regarded as successors to the family lineage and shouldered the full responsibility of performing ancestral rites.

Law on Gender Segregation

The Confucian-oriented rulers of Joseon imposed rigid moral doctrine upon women. They considered family as the basic unit of society and the conduit to social stability under well-managed patriarchal order. Therefore, the rulers of Joseon made strenuous efforts to incorporate Confucian ethical norms, stressing distinction between classes and sexes and elaborate family rituals, into the daily life of the people. They believed women needed to be regulated to maintain order in individual households and the family-based social structure.

As a result, boys and girls as young as seven years of age were taught not to mingle with one another. Women had to hide their faces when they went out of their house. Unlike under Goryeo, they were no longer allowed to visit Buddhist temples or ride horses.

The strict rule of sex segregation was defined as *naeoebeop*, literally the "law separating the outside and inside." Men and women, and even husband and wife, were strictly distinguished and had to adhere to a code of etiquette with each other. More specifically, naeoebeop required males and females to "not contact one another and keep distance." The idea derived from the Chinese classic, *Book of Rites* (*Liji* or *Yegi* in Korean), which provided in its chapter on "Pattern of Family" that "men and women should neither sit nor eat together when they have become seven years old."

Accordingly, upper-class homes segregated men and women into walled sections connected with gates. They passed through the gates to other quarters only when necessary. Women of the noble class were not supposed to speak directly to men other than their family members. When it was inevitable, they could only speak indirectly in the form of addressing to a third person even if there was nobody else around.

The Annals of the Joseon Dynasty contain various appeals from courtiers to regulate the daily life of women. Some petitioned for a ban on women at Buddhist temples. Some demanded that women hide their faces on outings, and others called for banning women from riding palanquins or playing games. In December of the fourth year of King Taejong (r. 1400-1418), there was an appeal that "women should not be permitted to attend any memorial rites, including those for their parents, held at Buddhist temples to set straight public morality, because there are endless streams of women at temples despite the law banning their visit." The king accepted the appeal.

The ban on visiting Buddhist temples imposed on women derived from a fear that they might lose their chastity. At the same time, women's outings in general were unwelcome because their contacts with society outside their homes might influence their thinking. In spite of the stern rule, the age-old practice of women visiting temples did not disappear. In November 1412, the 12th year of King Taejong, a decree was issued with the king's approval making it mandatory for women "to hide their faces on outings and not to pull up the cloth to reveal their faces." In 1429, the 11th year of King Sejong, wooden signs were put around the capital announcing a ban on women's access to temples. Monks were forbidden to visit homes of widows.

In March of the third year of King Sejo (r. 1455-1468), the court annals say, there was an appeal from courtiers lamenting the loosened regulations that led women to "unashamedly play drums and flutes,

Covered palanquin (*okgyo*) Women of the families of high-ranking officials used covered palanquins to avoid contact with men. (National Palace Museum of Korea)

dancing, and leading parades of clowns, and have the clowns perform their feats on the street in broad daylight." Thus the royal court banned women from joining games in public or attending festivals outside their homes.

An entry in April of the same year has it that "shamanic rites are widespread around the capital, where women drink, sing and dance in groups along with men, and return home only after dark." It further notes that "even women of noble families have big tents pitched up and gather their daughters-in-law to compete in luxuriousness. They have this outdoor activity mostly in the spring when azaleas are in full blossom, so they call it *jeonhwaeum* (enjoying flower cakes and drinks)."

These records became the basis for the provision in *Grand Code for State Administration* that "those women who go up to Buddhist temples, and those women of noble families who engage in merry-making in the valleys or by the streams, or attend outdoor rites for ancestors, mountain spirits or shamanic deities, shall be given 100 floggings." The law later applied to women of all social classes.

Under such stifling circumstances, women were left with a short list of opportunities to see the world outside their homes. They included public holidays — New Year's Day, the day of the year's first full moon (Daeboreum), the spring festival on the fifth of the fifth lunar month (Dano), and the autumn festival on the 15th of the eighth lunar month (Chuseok). On these days, women could enjoy such games as jumping seesaw (*neol ttwigi*), treading bridges (*dapgyo nori*), swinging (*geune ttwigi*), and circle dancing (*ganggang suwollae*). Other occasions included the king's processions and street parades for foreign envoys, seeing off male family members leaving on a trip, and greeting relatives visiting from the countryside. No doubt women had to cover their faces, with coats or skirt-like veils, without fail during all of the outings.

Doctrine of Absolute Chastity

"Lady Bak married Yi Dan-pyo at age 15, during the years of King Sukjong (r. 1674-1720). When her husband died of illness while on a trip, she sent equipment for his funeral and hung herself but was rescued immediately. She then ate poisonous herb but failed to die again and then she jumped into a well twice but only to fail each time. Refusing to quell her suicidal urge, she jumped down from a high place but only suffered multiple injuries. With her parents mounting an around-the-clock vigil, she could only refuse to eat or drink anything to achieve her goal. She became haggard and as she neared death, she told a servant to bring her a mourning garment. She could barely rise but put on the garment, made four deep bows toward her husband's portrait, and took her last breath."

This is the story of a woman cited for her fidelity toward her husband during the Joseon period. There also are records about dutiful wives and sons awarded by the government during the Goryeo period. But Joseon had a far greater number of women recognized for fidelity as institutions coerced women to fulfill their obligations toward their spouses far more strongly.

With Neo-Confucianism as its ruling ideology, Joseon accepted clan rules that emphasized the patriarchal family lineage. For a woman the

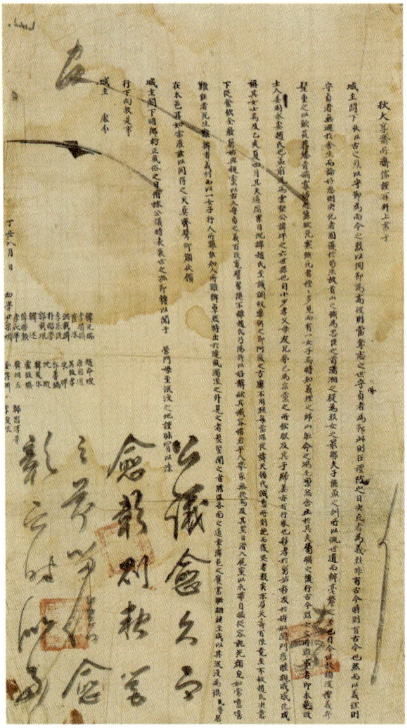

A petition of Confucian scholars
The scholars recommended a virtuous wife for government award. (National Museum of Korea)

primary purpose of marriage was to serve her parents-in-law and give birth to sons who would continue the family lineage of her husband. Women's chastity was regarded to be of utmost importance in order to keep a pure patriarchal blood line.

The government employed both awards and punishments to encourage women to remain chaste. Every year the government cited women who had shown exemplary deeds as a "virtuous wife," or *yeollyeo*. A red spiked gate was erected before the home of an honored woman, grain was awarded, and her family was exempted from corvee labor. It was therefore a great honor and privilege to have a virtuous woman in the family. Naturally, women were explicitly pressured by their families to remain chaste whatever the personal sacrifice. Stories of virtuous women were made into books and translated into the

Korean script so that women could read them and follow the examples.

On the other hand, women who failed to preserve their chastity were severely punished, mainly because it was difficult to keep pure patriarchal lineages when married women committed adultery. The Joseon penal code, *Daemyeongnyul*, or the *Great Ming Code* (*Da Ming Lu*), prescribed 90 lashes for women who had illicit affairs though such punishments were seldom executed. In some extreme cases, female adulterers were ordered to stand in a marketplace for three days before being beheaded because they were regarded to deserve "improbable punishment for an impossible crime." Those who committed adultery also were put on the list of "promiscuous women" and their children were forbidden from all government posts or even sitting for civil service examinations. Since the examinations were the only official entryway to government posts, it constituted a serious threat to the whole family not to mention the future of children of the disgraced women.

Gate of honor (*jeongmun*) King Jeongjo presented the gate to Princess Hwasun in recognition of her virtuous deed.

Upper-class families took it for granted that their women would maintain their chastity in all circumstances and, as years passed, remarriages of women were regarded as a crime of sort. Not only remarried women but those who arranged a remarriage also faced punishment. During the years of King Seongjong, an official named Hong Gi-ho was tried for corrupting public morals after marrying the widow of a man named Gang Gye-suk. A central government official named Jeong under the reign of King Jungjong (1506-1544) was fired after the remarriage of his young widowed daughter. A law for punishing the heads of families with remarried women was introduced in the 23rd year of King Jungjong.

As women's chastity was emphasized ever more strongly, it grew increasingly harder to attain recognition as a "virtuous woman." A widow could be regarded as virtuous simply by not remarrying during the early years of Joseon when the law banning remarriage of women had yet to be introduced. In late Joseon, however, only those who killed themselves following the death of their husbands could claim honors as virtuous women. Chastity was such an overwhelming obsession that one would even hack her shoulder with an axe simply because a man touched it. In another outstanding case, a woman wrapped herself with a skirt and jumped into the river when a ferryman held her hand to help her get onboard. Some women went so extreme as to remain single and chaste until death if they were betrothed and their fiancé died before their marriage.

Preserving chastity was mostly an obligation of upper-class women during early Joseon. But many commoner women and even those of lower classes followed suit as years went by, probably because they could afford to think of morals and etiquette as their economic condition improved. Also, Neo-Confucian ethics was disseminated from the literati to the broader public across the country owing to the invention of Korean script in the 15th century. From nobility down to

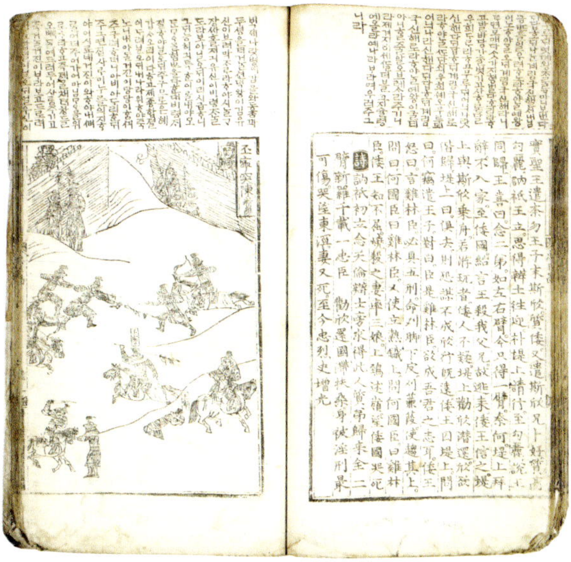

Conduct of the Three Bonds (*Samgang haengsildo*) This book illustrated the basic moral decorum of Joseon society. (National Museum of Korea)

the commoners, the entire Joseon society became obsessed with the dogmatic moral principle of immaculate chastity and virtue of women.

War brought about changes to the perception of virtuous woman. Many women fully demonstrated their deeply entrenched moral awareness at the expense of their lives during the long wars with Japanese and Manchu invaders. During the Japanese invasions of 1592-1598, the Joseon government cited a total of 67 dutiful sons, 11 loyal subjects and 356 virtuous women. Not only the conservative Confucian scholars but noted scholars of Practical Learning (*Sirhak*) such as Yi Ik (1681-1763) and Bak Ji-won (1737-1805) boasted that the nation deserved credit for its unique tradition of cherishing chastity, which they said was found nowhere else under heaven.

While there were many suicides to preserve chastity, a greater number of women paid a price for not taking their lives. Hundreds of thousands of them ended up being taken away by Chinese troops of Qing Dynasty. When war ended, their families searched for them and paid fortunes for their return. But many men of the literati class asked for divorce on the grounds that their wives had lost their chastity. Many repatriated women, called *hwanhyangnyeo*, suffered condemnation, though the government did not endorse their divorce. There were simply too many of them. Eventually, the moral concept of Joseon began to change bit by bit. But the misery of the returned women still resonates in the derogatory word *hwanyang*, derived from *hwanhyang* (homecoming), which means "loose morals."

The extreme concept of chastity often led to tragic acts by individuals. Some women had to throw away their babies born out of wedlock because there was no way to raise them legally. Noblemen could have as many concubines as they wanted but widows had to live alone and poor bachelors found it difficult to get married. Like the heroine in Bak Ji-won's novel, "A Virtuous Woman: Lady Bak from Hamyang" (*Yeollyeo hamyang bakssi jeon*), many a young widow had to live alone in tears until death. Some scholars like Jo Heon (1544-1592), Yi Geung-ik (1736-1806) and Jeong Yak-yong (1762-1836) pointed out problems with coercing women to abide by the inhumane moral doctrine. They said it was "wrong to praise the suicide of young widows when they were already sufficiently pitiable to have become widows at young age." The Donghak peasant revolutionaries included remarriage of young widows in their plan for governance reform. The Gabo Reform of 1894 legalized remarriage of women. The traditional view of virtuous woman collapsed amid modern reform movements.

Education of Women

Not only government leaders but the intellectual community at large had reservations about educating women. They believed too much education would lead women to neglect their household and family duties. Since no formal educational institution for women existed, they were educated at homes and the sole subject was moral education.

During a lecture meeting with high courtiers in 1437, the 19th year of his reign, King Sejong said: "In China women are literate so they sometimes get involved with political affairs to ruin the country. In our eastern nation, however, women are not literate so they have no opportunities to participate in state affairs. But we should mind that, though they do not actually take part in politics, women can still disturb the minds of the king and his subjects, and some of us may be ill-advised to listen to them and misrule the nation."

King Sejong was not alone in believing it was fortunate that Korean women were illiterate. Society at large shared his view and most *Sirhak* (Practical Learning) and Confucian scholars expressed similar opinions. Even a prominent thinker of Practical Learning in the late Joseon period, Yi Ik (1681-1763), wrote in his basic work, *Trivial Discourses of Seongho* (*Seongho saseol*): "Reading and lecturing are men's work. Women should serve their families, hold ancestral rites and entertain guests. Given these roles, how can women spare time for reading books? Throughout history there have been numerous women who were well versed in history and debate on etiquette but failed to put their knowledge into practice, thereby causing immense harm."

Education of women during early Joseon tended to stress correcting women's lax morals by teaching Confucian ethical decorum and promoting the image of virtuous woman rather than instructing moral obligations in everyday life. Various textbooks for women's education, mostly translations of Chinese classics, were published under government supervision, particularly under the reign of King Sejo (1455-1468).

Queen Sohye, the eldest daughter-in-law of King Sejo, compiled *Instructions for Women* (*Naehun*) based on four Chinese classics — *Biographies of Women* (*Yeollyeojeon* or *Liunuzhuan*), *Lesser Learning* (*Sohak* or *Xiaoxue*), *Lessons for Women* (*Yeogyo* or *Nujiao*) and *Precious Mirror of the Clear Heart* (*Myeongsim bogam* or *Mingxin baojian*). It was the first Korean textbook for teaching moral decorum and manners to women. Textbooks for women continued to be published under state policy until the mid-Joseon period. In later years, however, individual scholars wrote books for women based on their personal experiences and opinions. Among outstanding books from this period were *A Lady's Handbook* (*Gyujung yoram*) by Yi Hwang (1501-1570), *Book for Instructing a Daughter* (*Gyenyeoseo*) by Song Si-yeol (1607-1689) and *The Scholar's Seasonal Ways* (*Sasojeol*) by Yi Deok-mu (1741-1793).

These books generally aimed at indoctrinating women to practice moral behavior on their own instead of coercing them by legal provisions. Women were taught to feel ashamed when they failed to follow the teachings. In a way it was a far more forceful means of regulation. All this may indicate that although Joseon had adopted Confucianism as its governing ideology, the Confucian moral teachings were yet to be internalized and practiced in everyday life by the general public.

The situation changed notably during the latter part of Joseon. Most of all, individual scholars wrote textbooks for women's education. Unlike translations of Chinese classics, these books contained practical and detailed instructions necessary for the daily life of Korean women.

The texts overwhelmingly stressed chastity and good manners. Unmarried daughters were taught to fulfill their filial duties in gratitude to their parents. Filial duties comprised obeying one's parents and respecting their wishes even after their death, not to mention supporting one's parents while they were alive. Further, maintaining harmony and peace among siblings and relatives was also considered an important filial obligation.

As a daughter-in-law, the Joseon woman was taught above all else to serve her parents-in-law with all her heart and soul, and maintain peace

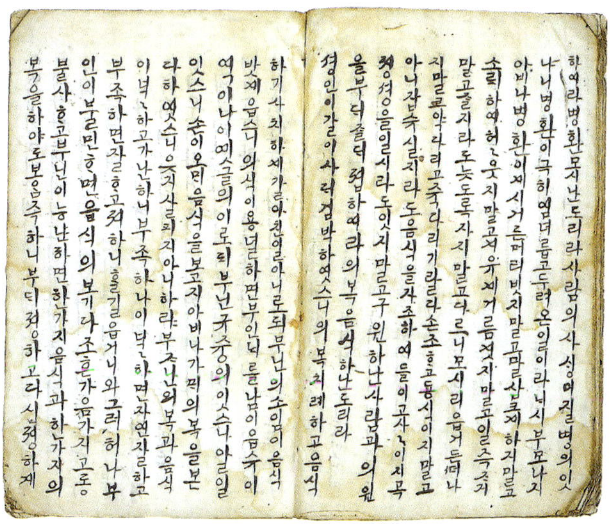

Book for Instructing a Daughter (*Gyenyeoseo*) Song Si-yeol, a famous scholar official of the 17th century, wrote this book for his daughter before her marriage. (National Folk Museum of Korea)

and harmony with relatives of her husband, including her sisters-in-law. Song Si-yeol, a prominent Confucian scholar, authored *Book for Instructing a Daughter* ahead of his eldest daughter's marriage to a Gwon family. He wrote, "Serve your parents-in-law like your own parents, paying heed to their every movement, every word and every matter." He repeatedly stressed that peace and harmony in the family depended heavily on women.

Women were taught to look up to their husbands like heaven all their lifetime. Based on the theory of *yin* and *yang*, men were supposed to be strong and women to be frail, their roles also divided according to their gender characteristics.

Nonetheless, the role of mothers was greatly emphasized because it was believed that families could either prosper or perish depending on the education of children and mothers were mostly responsible for educating their children. *A Lady's Handbook* and *The Scholar's Seasonal Ways* said proper education of women was crucial because a poorly educated daughter would ruin others' families while an ill-taught son would only ruin his own family. The widespread belief that children would eventually resemble their mother indicated the vital role of mothers in children's education.

Women were thus required to take a backseat as assistants who should quietly and obediently sacrifice themselves for peace and stability in their families. They were also expected to acquire necessary etiquette and skills for holding ancestral rites and entertaining guests, not to mention doing household chores and practicing frugality.

Education of women during Joseon was more aimed at motivating women to contribute to the Confucian social order than teaching them knowledge. However, not a few women dared into the world of intellectual learning and surmounted tough restrictions to achieve considerable academic growth, outperforming men.

Women and Crimes

Women's activities in Joseon society, except a small number of those engaged in a few special occupations, were confined to their homes. Therefore, female criminals were seldom detained unless they committed adultery or felonies deserving of death sentence. Unless they were related to the royal court or socially controversial, all other crimes involving women also tended to be concealed.

Criminal records of the Joseon period have few cases of women punished for thefts but there were numerous murder cases. In murder cases involving women, husbands killed by their wives accounted for the largest number of victims, followed by slaves killed by their female owners, masters killed by their female servants, and infants. Female slaves murdered by their mistresses were mostly the concubines of their masters. But female servants who murdered their masters were mostly driven by problems of social classes rather than gender issues. Famine caused most infant murders, while some newborn babies were killed to conceal sexual misconduct or for medicinal use.

Adulteries always invited stern punishment during Joseon for the sake of public sexual morality as well as to protect women of the noble class and reduce moral misdemeanors in the elite class.

Crimes by career women such as court ladies (*gungnyeo*), shamans (*munyeo*) or entertainers (*ginyeo*) occurred mostly in the course of performing jobs. Court ladies who served the royal family were often embroiled with political conflicts, putting a curse on someone or something, or cases of homosexuality or adultery. Female shamans were often charged for agitating the public or untoward curses. The female entertainers, also called *gisaeng*, often became a cause for fighting among their male adorers. Those who became concubines of married men set off scandals because their lovers mistreated their wives or they became jealous of their lover's legitimate wife.

Let us look a little deeper into adulteries, husband murders and crimes involving wives and concubines.

First, the Joseon society had a different notion of adultery, or *gantong*, from these days. Adultery today means a voluntary extramarital sexual relationship between a man and woman, with at least one of them married. Sex involving an unmarried man and woman is not considered an act of adultery. In Joseon, however, all sexual relationships out of marriage were seen as adultery subject to punishment.

The Joseon criminal code, *Daemyeongnyul*, or the *Great Ming Code*, prescribed 80 lashes each for a man and woman who committed adultery voluntarily, but 90 lashes for the woman when she had a husband. The code provided different penalties for married and unmarried women accused for adultery, while it did not care whether men were married or not. It indicates that the responsibility of keeping marriage rested mostly with the wife.

The Joseon government used the legal provisions governing adultery for protecting the chastity of women in the noble class. It remained relatively lenient toward adultery until the reign of King Jeongjong (r. 1398-1400), the second ruler. But the succeeding monarchs, Taejong (r. 1400-1418) and Sejong (r. 1418-1450), ordered severe punishment of adulterers as a strong admonition against loose morals among women of the literati class. King Taejong had a woman named Jeseokbi, wife of mid-level official Yun Su, beheaded for committing adultery with a Buddhist monk. During the reign of King Sejong, Lady Yu, wife of Yi Gwi-san, a former governor, was ordered to stand in a marketplace for three days before decapitation for having an affair with Jo Seo-ro.

But adultery by noble women continued to take place. Particularly, Yu Gam-dong, the discarded wife of Choe Jung-gi, magistrate of Pyeonggang, had sexual relations with 39 men. Her partners varied in their social status from Public Works Minister Seong Dal-saeng and Yi Hyo-rye, a secretary at the Office of the Inspector-General (*Saheonbu*), to a craftsman, as well as her husband's nephew and brother-in-law. According to law, she was flogged and made a slave for a government office in a remote region. Two other noble women, Geumeumdong and Dongja, faced similar punishments for committing adultery with their male relatives.

In the 11th year of King Seongjong (r. 1469-1494), the sex scandal of Eoeuludong, who had relations with numerous men, including royal relatives, court officials and slaves, rocked the country. The scandal ended with a death penalty meted out to the famously promiscuous woman of noble birth. In the seventh year of King Jungjong (r. 1506-1544), there was a legal revision providing death by hanging for noble women who committed adultery and their sex partners.

Next, husband murderers faced death by dismemberment, a severer punishment than other murderers. On the contrary, husbands who beat their wives to death were sentenced to death by hanging, which was a relatively lighter punishment than other perpetrators of homicide.

In the fourth year of the founding monarch King Taejo (r. 1392-1398), a woman named Jungbo was hanged for murdering her husband, Choe An-jong. It was during the reign of King Taejong, the third ruler, that death by dismemberment was introduced for women who killed their husbands. Naeungai was the first woman executed by having her limbs and head torn apart by carts. Like adulterers, husband killers also came to face harsher punishments under King Taejong.

Conflict between wives and concubines was sometimes so fierce as to invite state intervention. In case a concubine, out of confidence in her man's love for her, slandered or beat his wife and her children, the husband was punished by the government for failing to maintain order between his women. The concubine also faced punishment commensurate with her crime and in more serious cases, the husband was ordered to stay away from her. On the other hand, wives who abused their husbands' concubines faced relatively milder penalties. It was because their relationship as servant and owner was considered to outweigh one as concubine and wife. Still, the changing penal procedures showed that the position of concubines was improving.

The penal code concerning crimes occurring between wives and concubines was apparently intended to define a proper relationship between the lawful wife and concubines as well as between the mistress and her servants. At the same time, the wife's obligations toward husband were also emphasized ever strongly.

Looking into the criminal code governing crimes by women, it can be gleaned how the Joseon government tried to control individual families. It aimed to establish the moral superiority of the ruling elites over other social classes by protecting the chastity of upper-class women by means of legal punishment. Harsh penalties on husband killers were aimed at delineating the position of wives as subservient beings. The Joseon rulers intended to define relations between wives and concubines, and between masters and servants, through sternly punishing concubines humiliating wives but minimizing penalties on wives who maltreated or killed concubines of their husbands.

Chapter 2

Activities and Roles of Joseon Women

Queen Consorts' Political Participation as Regents

It wasn't easy for women to play any significant political role in the rigid Confucian society of Joseon. Women's ability and rights were not duly recognized and most women were cut off from all social contacts. But some women found ways to access political power, mainly through their relationship with men.

Though limited in scope, the kings' wives could officially participate in state affairs as regents. Regency by queen dowagers, or young monarchs' mothers or grandmothers, was referred to as "rule behind the bamboo screen" as the strict Confucian norms of gender segregation banned face-to-face contact between men and women. Unofficially, the queen consorts incessantly intervened in the investment process of crown princes, which was one of the most sensitive issues among royal consorts. Regency by queen consorts prevented usurpation of the throne and thereby contributed to the longevity of the Joseon Dynasty.

King Taejo, the founding monarch of Joseon, named his youngest son, Bang-seok, as crown prince in disregard of the rule of royal lineage providing that the king's eldest legitimate son would succeed the throne. Behind his controversial decision was tearful entreaty from his second consort, Queen Sindeok. Historian Yi Geung-ik wrote in

The Narratives of Yeollyeosil (*Yeollyeosil gisul*) that King Taejo defied advice from courtiers such as Bae Geuk-ryeom and Jo Jun in favor of his youngest son. When the king called them to an inner court room to discuss the matter, they told him to "appoint a legitimate son in peacetime but a meritorious one when the nation is in chaos." Then they heard the queen weeping outside. The king was moved by her appeal and appointed her son, Bang-seok, as his successor, eventually triggering two rounds of bloody conflict among his sons. As a result of the brutal bloodbath, the king's fifth son Bang-won, who was born to his deceased first wife, grabbed power and ascended the throne. He was King Taejong, the third monarch of Joseon.

Queen Wongyeong, the consort to King Taejong, also intervened frequently in state affairs. She was a smart and ambitious woman with astute political intuition. Her useful counsel helped her husband steer his way to the throne, and as soon as he was seated, she urged him to appoint their eldest son, Prince Yangnyeong, as crown prince. Considering that her husband was a noted womanizer, she was worried that he might sire more children and favor other sons to repeat her father-in-law's mistakes. She also believed that she had to secure a firm position looking ahead to possible court intrigues.

In the 18th year of his reign, King Taejong eventually replaced Yangnyeong with his youngest son, Chungnyeong (later King Sejong), as his successor. Queen Wongyeong incessantly intervened in his political decisions and her jealousy toward his other women displeased him. Finally, Taejong had her younger brothers executed to hold the political ambitions of her relatives in check.

King Sejong established the rule of royal succession but his eldest son, King Munjong, was in feeble health and died two years after he came to the throne. His son, Danjong, ascended the throne at 12 in 1452. With nobody in his direct lineage to protect the young monarch (his grandmother, Queen Soheon, passed away in 1446 and his mother,

Queen dowager's birthday party The painting depicts Queen Sunwon's 60th birthday party, held in 1848, the 14th year of King Heonjong, on the grounds of Tongmyeongjeon Hall. (National Museum of Korea)

Queen Hyeondeok, even earlier in 1441), his uncle, Prince Suyang (later King Sejo), usurped the throne and sent him into exile. The ensuing bloody persecution of supporters of the dethroned boy king showed how women's regency contributed to shielding the throne from reckless power struggle in the royal family.

Queen Jeonghui (1418-1483), consort to King Sejo (r. 1455-1468), was the first queen dowager of Joseon who acted as a regent. Upon Sejo's death, King Yejong ascended the throne at 19. He was too young as a monarch though he had already been looking after state affairs on behalf of his ailing father. The queen dowager was asked to be a regent, with the high state councillors Sin Suk-ju and Han Myeong-hoe supporting her as decision makers. Queen Jeonghui accompanied the king at all meetings on state affairs. Though her power was limited, she was the first woman to actively influence the political process as the most senior member of the royal family in Joseon.

King Yejong died one year later, however. He was succeeded by 13-year-old Prince Jasan, who would be known as King Seongjong, the ninth ruler of Joseon. Prince Jasan was the second son of posthumous King Deokjong, the eldest son of King Sejo, who had died prematurely as a crown prince. The queen dowager picked Prince Jasan as the new king and continued her regency.

The second most notable female regent of Joseon was Queen Munjeong (1501-1565), the third consort to King Jungjong and the mother of King Myeongjong. She became a regent for his young son and demonstrated enormous power when her younger brother, Yun Won-hyeong, purged their political rivals led by Yun Im, another faction of the Yun clan, who were the in-laws of the deceased King Injong. Her power far exceeded that of Queen Jeonghui, with many of her relatives in important government posts. As a woman with no academic or political connections, she had to rely on support from her relatives. She also depended on the counsel of Buddhist monk Bou and greatly promoted Buddhism in defiance of strong opposition from students of Seonggyungwan, the National Confucian Academy.

Other Joseon queen dowagers who performed regency were: Queen Insun during the years of King Seonjo (r. 1567-1608), Queen Jeongsun during the years of King Sunjo (r. 1800-1834), Queen Sunwon during the years of King Heonjong (r. 1834-1849) and King Cheoljong (r. 1849-1863), and Queen Sinjeong during the years of King Gojong (r. 1863-1907). Particularly, Queen Sinjeong, who is also known as Queen Dowager Jo, played a decisive role in the accession of King Gojong and ending the so-called in-law government of the Kim clan from Andong.

Economic Activities of Women

An old Korean saying goes, "A widow would have three jars of silver while a widower should have three jars of lice." It obviously indicates that a single woman can be nicely self-sufficient but a single man is most likely to suffer poverty. The old saying may apply to all women in general not just widows. Even these days, most of those who make headlines by donating their lifetime savings of billions of won to schools or welfare organizations are women. Most of these women worked hard, sewing or peddling after losing their husbands at a young age. Korean women are strong and frugal. They work hard and save assiduously.

Joseon was an agrarian society. Many women joined men in the farm fields in addition to doing all the housekeeping chores and rearing their children. They also engaged in weaving, the second most important industry after farming. It was necessary for supplying clothing and fabrics were also used as currency for commercial transactions at marketplaces.

Cotton farming, spinning and weaving became especially important to farm households as a means to generate income. Goryeo envoy Mun Ik-jeom introduced cotton to Korea when he brought back some cotton seeds from China in the 14th century, during the reign of King

"Picture of Farming and Weaving"
The painting depicts women growing silkworms at the bottom. (Collection of Gertrud Krassen in Germany)

Gongmin. Since cotton provided both the fabric and padding for garments, cotton farming was actively promoted by government decree. By the years of King Seongjong in the late 15th century, it had spread across the country except the northern regions of Hamgyeong Province. With rapid increases in cotton production, cotton fabrics became a most popular material for clothing and were used as currency as well. Weaving silk, hemp and ramie was also a valuable source of income generated by rural women, contributing to the agrarian family economy.

The government also encouraged growing mulberry trees by law. *Grand Code for State Administration* (*Gyeongguk daejeon*), completed in 1485, the 16th year of King Seongjong, classified all private households into three grades and assigned different numbers of mulberry trees to be grown at each household: 300 trees for "large households," 200 trees for "middle households" and 100 trees for "small households." Jamsil, or the Silkworm Nursery, was installed near Seoul to distribute new breeds of silkworms and mulberry seedlings and teach skills for silkworm raising. (Jamsil was the main venue site of the 1988 Seoul Summer Olympics and is now a booming part of the capital.)

During the reign of King Seongjong, the queen consort led silkworm raising ceremonies in the palace in March of 1477 and 1493 to demonstrate the importance of the industry. Earlier, in June of 1412, the 12th year of King Taejong, Ha Ryun composed eight songs praising peasantry, four on farmers and four on weaving women. The government emphasized silkworm cultivation in all agricultural policy instructions, commending the efforts of women weavers and their high productivity. The government collected silk yarn as a tax in kind and surplus product was sold in markets.

Not only cotton (*mumyeong*) and silk (*myeongju*) but hemp (*sambe*) and ramie (*mosi*) were also useful means for women's economic activities. Before cotton was introduced, hemp had been the primary clothing material for commoners. Therefore, growing hemp was important for acquiring clothing material of family members as well as an income source for many farming households. The best hemp in all Korea was produced in Yukjin, Hamgyeong Province. It was called *bukpo*, meaning the "northern hemp," and was so fine that it was said a whole roll could be put in a bowl. Prices of hemp cloth varied depending on the denier of the yarn. The top quality hemp was produced by women and products from Andong area in Gyeongsang Province, called *andongpo*, and Gangwon Province, called *gangpo*, were most highly valued. Ramie, the fine gauze popular for luxurious summer wear, was also woven by women. The best ramie fabrics came from Hansan, Chungcheong Province.

Women also gathered wild vegetables in the spring and sold simple foods they cooked at home in markets for extra family incomes. The annals of King Jungjong (r. 1506-1544) describe a debate among officials on banning markets, where they also mentioned women's commercial activities. They said, "Markets began to appear recently.

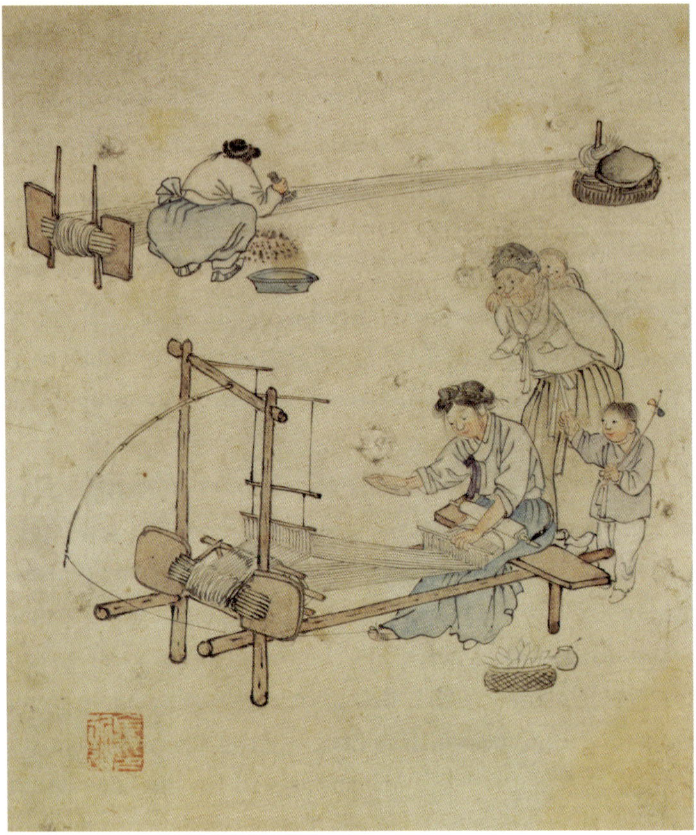

"Weaving Women" by Kim Hong-do (National Museum of Korea)

On market days, men and women prepare drinks and meat, and sell them to make profits." In his *Diary of a Refugee* (*Swaemirok*), written during the Japanese invasions of 1592-1598, civilian nobleman Oh Hui-mun wrote in the entry for March 11, 1594: "My wife intended to sell the rice cakes she made at the market today. But she couldn't go to the market as it rained. We ate the cakes with our children, only to waste precious rice." It seems women did not care about their social status when they could earn a little money to support their family in hard times.

"Fish Vendor" by Sin Yun-bok (1758-?) (National Museum of Korea)

There were also women engaged in rare types of economic activity, such as the famed female divers of Jeju Island who gathered sea food. Sin Gwang-su (1712-1775, pen name Seokbuk), a scholar official during the reign of King Jeongjo, wrote "A Song for Women Divers" (*Jamnyeoga*). It went, "*Lassies of Tamna* (an old name of Jeju) *swim so well. Ten-year-olds learn to swim playing in the streams. They swim even after they marry, to their parents food and clothes are no worry...*" The song attests to the active economic activity of women divers in Jeju.

Another famous Jeju woman, Mandeok was a rich *gisaeng*, or an artist entertainer, during the reign of King Jeongjo. The annals of King Jeongjo says in its entry for November 25, 1796, the 20th year of his reign: “The magistrate of Jeju reported that a local gisaeng named Mandeok spent her fortune to save the starving people. The government offered an award for her but she refused it and hoped instead to have a trip across the sea to the capital and visit Mt. Geumgang. Her trip was allowed and villages along her way were instructed to serve her food.” Mandeok was probably the first known woman in Korean history who returned her earnings to society. Though her profession was not highly regarded, she set a prominent example as a female entrepreneur.

Literary World of Female Writers

For most Joseon women it was practically impossible to express their thoughts and feelings through literary works, engage in any activity as professional writers, or form organizations for literary exchanges. The prevalent thought in society was that even those women with some writing talents should refrain from writing any literary pieces because their works might leak out and eventually end up being sung by entertainers and prostitutes.

Nevertheless, some women wrote about life and discontent with reality. Among outstanding works by female writers of the Joseon period that are known today are such essays as "Seven Friends of a Woman" (*Gyujung chiru*) and "Funerary Address for My Needle" (*Jechimmun*), and song cycles like "An Old Spinster's Song" (*Nocheonyeo ga*), "Song of a Widow" (*Gwabu ga*) and "Ode on the Lady's Proper Conduct" (*Gyujung haengsil ga*). The writers of these essays kept their identity hidden, apparently to protect themselves from social scorn. As the titles suggest, they personified everyday objects and observed them with their uniquely sensitive and subtle insight and imagination.

There are also prominent prose works depicting events in the royal palace, such as *The Memoirs of Lady Hyegyeong* (*Hanjungnok*), *The Diary of Gyechuk Year* (*Gyechuk ilgi*), and *A Biography of Queen*

Inhyeon (*Inhyeon wanghu jeon*). All these works were written in refined Korean to chronicle turbulent events in the palace in memoir styles. *The Diary of Gyechuk Year* is a record of the tragic suffering of Queen Inmok, consort to King Seonjo, and her son, Prince Yeongchang, amid the power struggles of 1613. *A Biography of Queen Inhyeon* depicts the conflict between Queen Inhyeon, consort to King Sukjong, and his favorite concubine, Lady Jang. *The Memoirs of Lady Hyegyeong* is an autobiographical record of Lady Hyegyeong, consort to Crown Prince Sado, who was brutally killed by his father, King Yeongjo. She depicts how her husband faced his tragic death and her family subsequently fell victim to factional strife. The writers displayed their unusual literary gifts while faithfully recording major historical events in the royal court.

Some women writers succinctly expressed their emotions through simple verses. Short poems and *sijo*, the native Korean literary genre born in mid-Goryeo and fully developed toward the end of the Goryeo period, served as useful outlets for women who had to restrain personal expression under Confucianism. With their limited education, women were probably unable to write lengthy and erudite pieces. Instead, poems written by Joseon women were brief but deeply intensive.

Most poems written by women dealt with everyday life, but some women also pursued their individual ideals and thoughts. Two distinct features characterized verses written by noble women. First, they stressed the feminine virtues taught in Confucianism. Second, they rebuked the societal and family discrimination heaped on women. Sometimes raw emotions spewed from the poems, but more often, they expressed longings for nature or a utopian world, or a lover. The two famous female writers, Sin Saimdang and Heo Nanseolheon, deftly expressed their frustration in refined language.

Sin Saimdang (1504-1551) was an example of a virtuous woman — a supportive wife faithfully assisting her husband who was less able than herself and a wise mother devoted to the education of her children. What is worthy of note is that she constantly looked back at her childhood and maiden home in her poetry while she tried to be perfect as a wife and mother in her real life. Through her poems and paintings on her favorite motifs from nature, she could probably sublimate the deep remorse in her heart.

Heo Nanseolheon (1563-1589) expressed her distressful life through her poetry. She had to face endless frustration as she couldn't fully demonstrate her ingenious literary talent amid the fall of her maiden family, conflict with her in-laws and her husband having an affair, and death of her children. Her last poem read, "*As the blue phoenix mingles with colorful peers, the blue water seeps into the sea of beads*; *As twenty-seven red lotus flowers fall, the cold moonlight shatters on the frost.*" After composing the poem, she burned all her poems and books that filled her room and then took her last breath. She was 27. A few works of hers that escaped the flames were gathered by her younger brother, Heo Gyun, and published later in Ming China.

Poetry was a favored literary genre among concubines and *gisaeng*, the artist entertainers, who were pained by their social status. Unfulfilled love was the most popular theme of their poems. They lamented parting with their lovers and deplored the passing of time, an allegory of their stressful situation and veiled criticism of reality. At times, however, they also expressed mature contemplation and even masculine boldness with liberty allowed for them by their relatively freer status.

In the 19th century, five concubines of high-ranking officials formed a poetry club. They gathered at Samhojeong Pavilion in Yongsan in southern capital to enjoy reciting poems, hence they were called "Samhojeong Sidan," or the Samhojeong Poetry Club. They were all daughters of noblemen born to their concubines, so they also were not qualified for legitimate marriage. Through poetry meetings they could share their frustration as well as their critical views about class and gender discrimination.

Poems by gisaeng, such as Hwang Jin-i, Cheongeum, Gyesaeng and Sohong, went beyond aloof contemplation to poke fun at a world they regarded to be full of absurdity and confusion. Particularly, Hwang Jin-i rivaled distinguished men of letters of her time with her literary talent. She mocked Byeokgyesu, a royal relative, for his tepid attitude in her famous poem: "*The blue stream in the valley of green mountains, boast not of your flowing fast. Once you dash to the vast sea, it should be hard to return. All over the mountains the moon shines bright, so how about resting for awhile*?" Her life and artistic gift was as much shrouded in mystery as her birth. It appears that even her widely adored beauty and talents could not help her overcome the limitations of her social status. Looking forward to her death, she willed that her body not be placed in a coffin but left in the open to be eaten by black kites as a warning to all women under heaven to guard against gisaeng. She probably felt acutely the vanity of all the frivolity she had enjoyed with her aristocratic lovers. In another poem she confessed her sadness: "*Mountains are the same old mountains, but nor is water. Flowing day and night, how can water remain the same old one? As once gone they never return, eminent men are just like water.*"

Among female writers of the Joseon period were not only high-born ladies but those of lowly classes such as illegitimate daughters, concubines and entertainers. Despite gaps in their social status, the female writers shared similar frustration as women born in a patriarchal society. They probably resorted to literary writing in an effort to overcome their conflict between reality and ideals.

Life and Role of Court Ladies

Court ladies, or *gungnyeo*, officially referred to all women in court below the major first rank (*jeong ilpum*), the highest official rank accorded the consorts of kings and princes. But court ladies actually meant women serving the royal family in the palace. They were so-called female public servants, also called *gunggwan*, *naegwan* or *yeogwan*. *Grand Code for State Administration* (*Gyeongguk daejeon*), the main statute of Joseon, referred to them as *naemyeongbu*, meaning "ladies of the court." They were given varied titles and ranks in accordance with their duties and positions.

The regulations concerning court ladies were introduced in the sixth year of the founding monarch King Taejo (r. 1392-1398). The detailed ranks, titles and positions were determined in the 10th year of King Sejong (r. 1418-1450), and included in the *Grand Code for State Administration* when the statute was promulgated in 1471, the second year of King Seongjong.

The court ladies from the major fifth rank (*jeong opum*) to the minor ninth rank (*jong gupum*), called *yeogwan* or *nain*, were assigned to serve in various quarters of the palace. They were recruited through different procedures and given different titles depending on their duties. In the early Joseon period, court ladies were chosen from

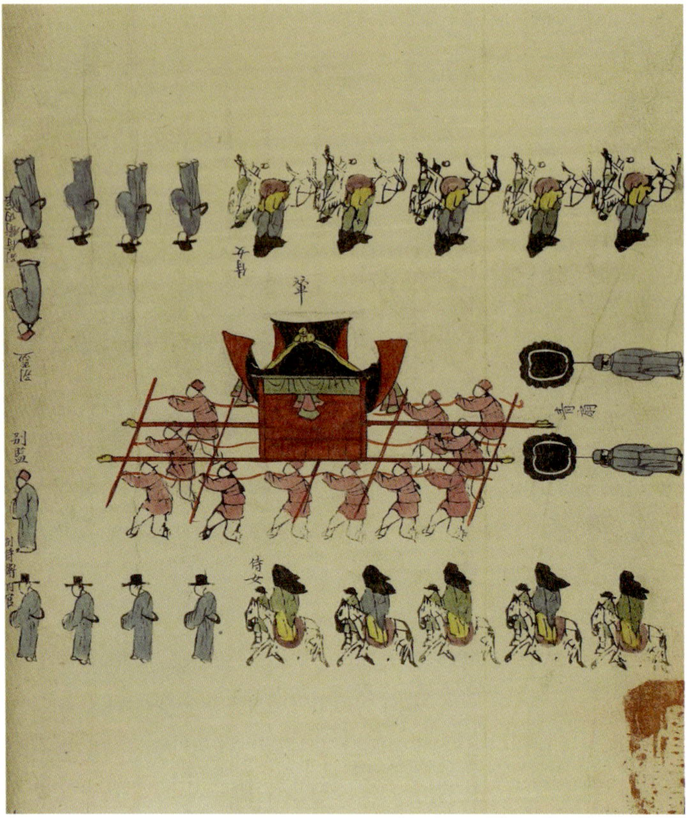

The wedding procession of King Sukjong and Queen Inwon, as recorded by a court painter. The queen's palanquin is flanked by court ladies on horseback, with their faces covered with black cloth. (Kyujanggak Institute for Korean Studies)

among female servants working for public offices or daughters of *gisaeng* concubines. As well-born daughters of respectable families began to be recruited as well, many parents married off their little daughters prematurely to avoid their selection as court ladies. Therefore, recruitment of well-born daughters of good families was banned in the latter part of the dynasty. *Supplement to the Grand Code for State Administration* (*Sok daejeon*), compiled during the years of King Yeongjo (r. 1724-1776), provided that only the servants at public offices would be recruited as court ladies but not other girls born to good families. However, the rule probably applied only to court ladies of lower ranks, not those serving on the personal staffs of the king or the queen.

Young girls of about four to 10 years of age were recruited and trained as court ladies. Those who were to closely serve the king were chosen with recommendation from senior court ladies, called *sang-gung*, or through personal connections. Candidates were interviewed by the senior court ladies of the concerned quarters, and those who passed were presented clothes and instructed to enter the palace on a chosen day. Parents of young girls chosen to become court ladies were honored but felt sad because their daughters would have to live in confinement in the palace the rest of their lives.

The trainees for the king's personal staff entered the palace at the youngest age of four or five, those to serve in the sewing and embroidery rooms at six or seven, and those for other members of the royal family at 12 or 13. Young trainees aged seven or eight began to learn Korean script and read the *Thousand Character Classic* (*Cheonjamun*) and the *Lesser Learning* (*Sohak*, or *Xiaoxue* in Chinese), the Confucian primer for youths. They also learned the court vocabulary, manners and writing in decent Korean in court style calligraphy, as well as sewing and em-broidery. The trainees began working around the age of 11 or 12. When they turned 18, a coming-of-age ceremony, practically combining with a symbolic wedding, was held to mark their becoming a regular palace attendant.

The highest-ranking court ladies were *sanggung*, and they were headed by the *jejo sanggung*, the chief lady-in-waiting. There was one chief lady-in-waiting, and she was responsible for managing court properties at the orders of the queen and commanding the entire court ladies. She had two personal servants and a secretary. Those court ladies who always accompanied the king and the queen, called *jimil sanggung*, had tremendous power. Kim Gae-si (?-1623) was probably the most notorious among all political court ladies of Joseon. As a court lady waiting upon King Seonjo, she approached his son Gwanghaegun and earned his favor. When the prince ascended the throne, she wielded enormous influence through her intimate relations with powerful courtiers. When King Gwanghaegun was ousted and replaced by King Injo in a coup, she was executed in front of a large audience. The court ladies who waited upon the king had access to confidential information, so they easily became vulnerable to political upheaval.

Winning the king's heart and serving him at night was the greatest wish for most court ladies who had no other opportunities for romance. In reality, however, it was extremely difficult to grab the king's attention. Therefore, the whole palace was excited when a certain court lady succeeded in earning the king's favor and became pregnant. When any court lady had a baby of the king, she was ensured of all the luxury and comfort as a royal consort. She was awarded the title of *sugwon* of minor fourth rank and her quarters would bear her name. It did not simply mean her personal glory but often opened the path for her relatives to powerful public posts. There were ample reasons that so many court ladies strived to catch the king's interest.

The rivalry and jealousy among women in court often created uncomfortable situations, however. Not a few royal consorts and court ladies lost their lives amid such turmoil. King Taejong (r. 1400-1418), the third ruler, is known to have had 10 consorts, the largest number among all Joseon monarchs. He was followed by King Seongjong (r. 1469-1494), the ninth ruler, who had nine. But the noisiest scandal surrounding an overambitious royal consort occurred during the years of King Sukjong (r. 1674-1720), the 19th ruler. Lady Jang Huibin bore him a son, who succeeded the throne as King Gyeongjong (r. 1720-1724), but she eventually received a death sentence and was handed poison to drink.

King Sukjong also made a court maid pregnant. She was a kitchen hand with the family name Choe, but was awarded the title of *sukbin* after giving birth to a prince. Her son later became King Yeongjo (r. 1724-1776). But all the court ladies who won the king's favor were not given such coveted titles or experienced rapid changes in their status. Without delivering a prince or a princess, they just remained as court ladies, though of higher ranks.

Then, how many court ladies were there in the Joseon royal palace? During the reign of King Seongjong, there were 29 court ladies at the place of the queen grandmother, 27 at the queen dowager's place, and 49 at the king's quarters. As the result of gradually increasing court ladies, however, there were as many as 684 court ladies in the 18th century Joseon palace, according to *Trivial Discourses of Seongho* (*Seongho saseol*), an encyclopedic book dealing with various subjects, written by Yi Ik (1681-1763). In the waning decades of Joseon, the bureaucracy was restructured under King Gojong (r. 1863-1907) and the number of court ladies fell to 480. They included 100 each for the place of the king, the queen and the queen dowager, 60 for the crown prince's palace, 40 for the crown princess's palace, 50 for the grand heir's palace, and 30 for the palace of the consort to grand heir.

Once they entered the palace, court ladies were supplied all articles necessary for their daily life. Their wages depended on the financial condition of the state, and they also received special awards on holidays and felicitous occasions. They were given 20 days of annual leave so they could visit their families or attend birthday parties of relatives with approval from supervising senior court ladies. But only the elderly court ladies were allowed to attend any wedding ceremony outside the palace.

The court ladies worked in two shifts; they read, practiced calligraphy or made ornamental knots during off-duty hours. *The Diary of Gyechuk*

Year (*Gyechuk ilgi*) and *A Biography of Queen Inhyeon* (*Inhyeon wanghu jeon*), both recognized as major literary works of Joseon women and important records of palace history, were authored by anonymous court ladies. Although they were supposed to spend the rest of their lives inside the palace, some were released in a bid to harmonize *yin* and *yang* energies. For example, severe droughts were among the few occasions when court ladies were freed from the palace. It was believed the droughts would be eased by freeing the court ladies, a symbolic gesture of appeasing the resentful spirits of women who died unmarried. Still, even those who happened to be released from the palace were far from completely free to lead the kinds of lives they desired.

All in all, the court ladies were unique professionals who played crucial roles in preserving and passing on the culture and lifestyle of the royal household as well as an indigenous genre of court literature. It also need be remembered that these women helped sustain the dynasty through their roles in facilitating smooth political operations.

Life and Role of Medical Ladies

The strict gender separation during Joseon created the need for female medical personnel for sick women. In March of the sixth year of King Taejong's reign (1400-1418), an official at the Public Welfare Agency (*Jesaengwon*), named Heo Do, advised the king: "Many ailing women die because they put off getting medical help because they regard it as a shameful act to see male doctors. Therefore, I would like to recommend teaching a few scores of young maidservants at the Royal Office of Supplies (*Changgo Gungsa*) how to feel pulse and apply acupuncture so they would be able to heal patients. It will contribute to Your Majesty's virtuous rule benefiting the people."

The king accepted his proposal and instructed the Public Welfare Agency to train female medical personnel for the first time. It apparently seemed like a measure for saving women's lives but, looking deeper, it was intended as another institutional device to keep women from contacts with men.

Medical ladies were initially recruited from among maidservants at public offices in the capital. During the years of King Sejong (r. 1418-1450), recruiting was extended to provincial offices to meet rising demand for female medical personnel. One reason servants at public offices were recruited for medical ladies was that they had to assist

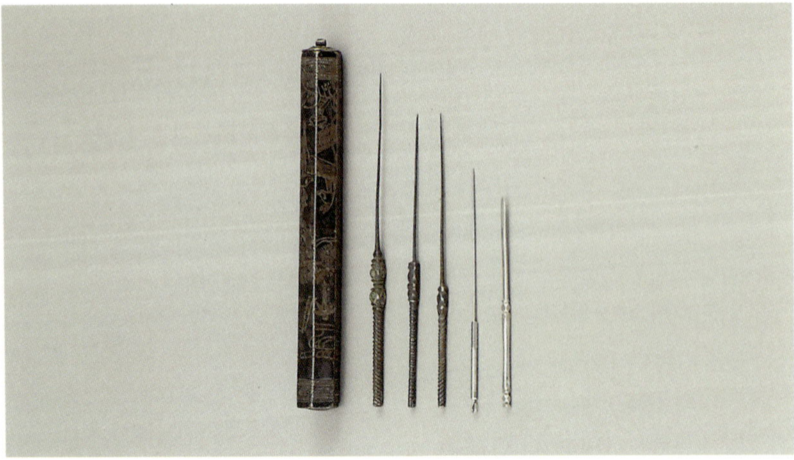

Acupuncture and case Medical ladies often carried acupuncture cases by tying them on their jacket ribbon. (National Folk Museum of Korea)

male doctors. The lowly status of all technicians in Joseon society aside, it was unthinkable for upper-class women or even commoner women to work with male colleagues.

Despite their lowly social status, medical ladies were among the most educated women. Ahead of acquiring skills for nursing and acupuncture, they had to read Chinese textbooks for general cultural education, such as *Thousand Character Classic*, *Classic of Filial Piety* and *Jeongsokpyeon* (*Zhengsubian* in Chinese), a classic for moral education. Special regulations were introduced to encourage academic learning and reading among medical ladies and the regulations were included in the *Grand Code for State Administration* (*Gyeongguk daejeon*) during the reign of King Seongjong (1469-1494). As they dealt with human lives, medical ladies were required to be equipped with virtuous character. So they also read the popular Confucian textbooks such as the *Analects of Confucius*, *Mencius*, the *Great Learning*, and the *Doctrine of the Mean*.

As the number of medical ladies continued to increase, they were divided into those serving in the royal palace and those for the Public Dispensary (*Hyeminseo*). Twelve medical ladies were assigned to the palace to tend the queen, the queen dowager and other women in the royal family. Seventy medical ladies worked for the Public Dispensary, treating women of various social classes.

Medical ladies accompanied male doctors and diagnosed female patients for the male doctors, who waited outside because they were not supposed to face the patients themselves. Medical ladies were not allowed to write prescriptions, but they treated boils or toothaches of women because they had to touch the patients. Feeling the female patient's pulse and applying acupuncture were likewise the job of medical ladies. They also assisted birth as midwives.

Some medical ladies displayed outstanding skills and earned fame. Jangdeok, in Jeju Island, was widely known for curing abscess and toothaches. There are records of her reputation spreading to Seoul, where various noble families tried to recruit her. She grew even more famous after death because her servant Gwigeum, whom she taught her secret skills, did not properly teach the two medical ladies assigned to her by the government.

The annals of King Seongjong reflected his deep concern about the capabilities of medical ladies. An entry for June 14 of the third year of his reign recounts the questioning of Gwigeum, who was summoned before the throne: "The king said, 'Two medical ladies were assigned to accompany you. But you hid your skills and did not teach them. Is that because you want to monopolize the benefits? If you dare to hide your skills to the end, you will be tortured and interrogated. So speak.' Gwigeum said, 'I began to learn the skills at seven but could not master them before I was 16 years old. It isn't that I did not teach them wholeheartedly but they failed to learn.' "

The role of medical ladies changed significantly under King Yeonsangun (r. 1494-1506), who mobilized them as musicians for parties in the palace. Yeonsangun was a notorious pleasure-seeking monarch and wanted medical ladies rather than *gisaeng* to entertain at his parties because the medical ladies were better educated and displayed finer skills in poetry and calligraphy. He ordered newly recruited gisaeng to learn how to read and write and medical ladies to play music, so he could enjoy the company of scores of them at each banquet. Hence medical ladies began to be called *yakbang gisaeng*, meaning the "pharmacy entertainers." They performed both roles for a considerable time. With the enthronement of King Jungjong in a coup in 1506, the government encouraged them to focus on medical service but could not root out the ill-advised practice overnight.

Thanks to their good education, medical ladies were given an additional role as investigators. In the eighth year of King Yeonsangun, medical ladies were mobilized for investigation of the homes of aristocrats charged for preparing excessively luxurious dowry. They also investigated and arrested suspects in criminal cases involving women in the royal palace or noble families. Delivering poison to female convicts sentenced to death continued to be an important duty of medical ladies.

According to *The Diary of Gyechuk Year* (*Gyechuk ilgi*), an old court lady implicated to an alleged conspiracy surrounding Prince Yeongchang (1606-1614) protested, "How come you've had me arrested by patrolmen not medical ladies. I do not deserve such a disgrace." This is evidence that investigation and arrest of women by medical ladies was considered as a matter of fact, or even desirable, in the royal court or among nobility.

Life and Role of Entertainers

Female musician-dancers entertaining at banquets in the royal palace or noble households were called *ginyeo* or *gisaeng*, or sometimes *haeohwa*, meaning "flowers understanding words." These female entertainers officially belonged to public offices. They were of the lowly social class easily accessible to men and were occasionally recruited for medical or sewing staffs. But the young and pretty ginyeo had an important role of entertaining noble bureaucrats, borderline troops and visiting foreign envoys. Therefore, they were gradually identified as men's playthings, or prostitutes, rather than artists or technicians.

There was active debate on abolishing the official operation of the ginyeo system from the early years of Joseon because the Confucian-oriented dynasty advocated high moral standards. But the idea did not materialize. The logic of proponents of the system was that these women were properties of public offices legally available for noble bureaucrats. They insisted that these women were needed and otherwise many able men might end up facing punishment for assaulting women of ordinary families. Also, it was not easy to do away with ginyeo, who were indispensable for encouraging troops serving in border areas. *Grand Code for State Administration*

(*Gyeongguk daejeon*), the main statute of Joseon, notes that "150 ginyeo were recruited from across the country once every three years." The number of ginyeo only increased as years went by.

The reign of King Yeonsangun, 1494-1506, was the heyday of court entertainers. Ginyeo serving at local public offices were renamed *unpyeong*, and those who served in the royal palace were called *heungcheong*, *gyepyeong* or *sokhong*. Those who entertained the king near him were named *jigwa heungcheong*, and those especially favored by the king *cheongwa heungcheong*. Officials exclusively responsible for recruiting beautiful and talented young women from across the country were called *chaehongsa* or *chaecheongsa*. In the early years of Yeonsangun there were about 100 young female entertainers in the royal palace. By his later years the number had exceeded 10,000. The huge expense of keeping these women was extracted from farmers and craftsmen around the country, causing serious problems.

Ginyeo were allowed to have a husband in the mid-Joseon period as it would be useful for keeping the census and help to stabilize their livelihood. Husbands of ginyeo were usually men of low birth except in very special cases. The popular expressions, "a lucky man like a gisaeng's husband" or "a dandy like a gisaeng's lover," indicate that there were men married to or living with these women.

Female entertainers exclusively serving at public offices, or *gwangi*, over 30 years of age retired to do other jobs. They were supposed to bring in their daughter or niece to fill their place. It implies that the status of female entertainers for public offices was hereditary in a sense. Their names were listed on the roster of entertainers and servants throughout their lifetime. To be freed they had to pay a certain amount of money.

Young gisaeng trainees had harsh education beginning at 15. They studied music and dancing, and some talented ones were taught calligraphy as well. The annals of King Sejong (r. 1418-1450) said that education of gisaeng at public offices took place twice a year, from February to April and from August to October, every other day. Dancing and playing the Chinese lute were compulsory subjects for all ginyeo. They had to choose another instrument for elective course.

Hwang Jin-i was a famous gisaeng during the years of King Jungjong (r. 1506-1544). For her stunning beauty and ingenious talents in poetry and singing, she was adored as one of the three beauties of Songdo, the present-day Gaeseong. She looked so attractive that she could even steal the heart of the revered monk, Zen Master Jijok. Her poem for the monk remains well known today. Yi Mae-chang, of Buan, during the reign of King Gwanghaegun (r. 1608-1623), was well known as a poetess. She belonged to the local magistrate's office but left behind various episodes about her relations with renowned scholars.

Some gisaeng became noted for their patriotic deeds. During the Japanese invasions of 1592-1598, Nongae of Jinju and Gyewolhyang of Pyongyang sacrificed themselves to kill Japanese generals. Gimseom and Aehyang, both retired ginyeo who became concubines of Dongnae Magistrate Song Sang-hyeon and the local navy commander Jeong Bal, respectively, died while trying to rescue their husbands from enemy territory. Manhyang of Hamheung was renowned for devotedly looking after her parents.

But not all ginyeo were so heroic. Some men ruined their families and lost their fortune in disgrace, victims of wily ginyeo tricks. Rich merchants cohabited with ginyeo only to be stripped of their whole fortune and then abandoned, some even ending up as a servant for their former lover. Gossipers whispered that a truly prominent and capable ginyeo should know how to make her man expend all his fortune for her.

Ginyeo had certain privileges as well. In the first place, they never lacked in food and clothing, and they could wear silk dresses and jewelry like noble women. *Grand Code for State Administration*

"Sword Dance" by Kim Jun-geun (1753-1822)

provided that even prostitutes, or *changgi*, might adorn themselves with gold and silver accessories and fine silk garments. Their luxurious lifestyle was justified by their profession and, more often than not, by their role as bread winners for their families. Some needy fathers went so far as to sell their daughters as gisaeng. These women were free to go anywhere; they were not subject to the rule of gender separation that confined most other women at their homes. In a way it was a great privilege.

A significant role of ginyeo was in demonstrating their artistic talents rooted in their local cultural traditions. For example, those in Andong area were good at reciting *The Great Learning* (*Daehak*, or *Daxue* in Chinese), a Chinese Confucian classic. No doubt Andong has a long tradition as the regional hub of education. Second, the ginyeo in

Gwandong region, or Gangwon Province, enjoyed singing the "Songs of Gangwon Scenes" (*Gwandong byeolgok*), written by famous poet Jeong Cheol (1536-1593). Thus they could promote the prominent natural scenary of their home province. Third, the ginyeo of Yeong-heung region in Hamgyeong Province proudly sang the "Songs of Flying Dragons" (*Yongbi eocheon ga*). The song praises ancestors of the Yi royal family of Joseon who came from the region. Fourth, the ginyeo in Pyongyang area often recited "Mountains and War Horses" (*Gwansan yungma*). Fifth, those of Jeju, Euiju and Bukcheong were famously adept at horse riding. Particularly, the ginyeo of Euiju were excellent at sword dance.

Ginyeo were luxury slaves of a patriarchal society. But their role as guardians of the arts, including traditional music, dance and poetry, should be properly recognized.

Life and Role of Shamans

The history of shamanism in Korea dates back to remote ancient times. As intermediaries between man and gods, shamans have performed rites appeasing gods so they would chase away evil spirits and invoke blessings for humans. Shamans are called *mudang* or sometimes *mansin*, literally "ten thousand gods," denoting that they worship numerous gods. Female shamans are called *munyeo*. Male shamans are usually called *baksu*.

Women of the Joseon period, harshly confined to their homes, found comfort through their faith in Buddhism or shamanism. They visited Buddhist temples to offer prayers or invited shamans to their homes to perform rites or tell fortunes.

The Joseon Dynasty, however, condemned and suppressed all religious activities other than Confucian rituals. Critical debate on so-called "impure rites," or *eumsa*, began as early as the reign of the founding monarch, King Taejo, and became more active under King Taejong (r. 1400-1418) and King Sejong (r. 1418-1450). The impure rites included outdoor rites held within the capital, rites held at shamanic shrines in the countryside or mountains, commissioning shamans to hold ancestral rites, and believing and following shamans.

All the shamans living in the capital were driven out during the reign of King Sejong. In July of the 13th year of his reign, the sage king approved a proposal from the Office of the Inspector-General (*Saheonbu*), which read: "In the olden days, shamans, both male and female, used to live apart from ordinary people far away from the capital, so there has long been a place named Mugyeok-ri, or the village of male and female shamans. But they have recently moved into the capital and mingled with other people, causing much discomfort. Therefore, we would like to propose that the shamans would be ordered to move out of the capital and live among their own kind." In January of the third year of King Seongjong (r. 1469-1494), the Office of the Inspector-General banned all "impure rites." When a family in mourning held a rite at a shaman's house, the head of the family and the shaman were both punished.

While shamanic activities among the public were legally prohibited, shamans were occasionally mobilized for government events. Particularly, shamans as well as Buddhist monks were invited to oversee rain-making ceremonies. The annals of King Taejong say that during a severe drought in the 11th year of his reign, 74 female shamans were gathered at the national altar to pray for rain. As rain came, the king presented one *seok* (a large sack) of rice to each of them. A total of 22 rain-making ceremonies were held during the years of King Taejong and King Sejong alone, and even more ceremonies were held in later years of the dynasty.

The government also assigned male and female shamans to heal patients at two public dispensaries in the eastern and western areas of the capital, named *Dongseo Hwarinseo*. In March of the 11th year of King Sejong, the Ministry of Rites (*Yejo*) proposed that shamans who lived near public offices and private houses be permitted to treat diseases. It was proposed that magistrates order doctors and shamans to visit fever patients to diagnose and heal them, and punish them immediately if the patients did not recover. Many people were cured and those shamans who contributed to their recovery were given tax cuts or exempted from corvee labor. In April of the 18th year of King Sejong, it was recommended that female shamans be assigned to the public dispensaries as healers. Hence a considerable number of female shamans became public health workers.

But these shamans began to perform various rites once they moved into the capital. Therefore, in the 12th year of King Jungjong (r. 1506-1544), all of these female shamans as well as male shamans working for the two public dispensaries were moved to local government offices some 200 *li* or more from the capital. While shamans were forbidden from their independent religious activities, their role in public welfare such as invoking rain or healing disease was recognized to certain extents.

There are various records about queens and royal concubines seeking help from shamans in praying for peace in the royal household and health and longevity of their family members. When King Seongjong fell ill, his grandmother called in a shaman to perform rites to pray for his recovery, thereby inviting criticism from students of Seonggyungwan, the National Confucian Academy. In the intercalary fourth month of the 10th year of King Jungjong, a self-styled state shaman named Dolbi, who frequented the royal palace to pray for blessings, was awarded royal garb and treasures. The Office of the Inspector-General took issue of this and questioned her.

Another female shaman frequented the palace as a healer when Queen Insun fell ill in the eighth year of King Seonjo (r. 1567-1608). But she indulged in spell work and prayers, not using medicine, and was punished as she failed to cure the queen. According to records, she was the daughter of a nobleman and married a royal relative named Yogyeong. She was detained and tried at the request from the three advising and censoring court agencies, *Samsa*, which called for punishment of both the shaman and her husband. She was probably a very rare example of a shaman from nobility, whereas all shamans belonged to the lowest social class.

From time to time, shamans were involved in power struggle in the royal court at the instigation of queens or princesses. It is well known that, during the reign of King Sukjong (r. 1674-1720), his favorite concubine Lady Jang was executed with poison for installing a shamanic altar in the palace and cursing Queen Inhyeon. Toward the end of Joseon, a shaman named Jillyeonggun earned the favor of Queen Min after predicting when she could safely return to palace after fleeing to Janghowon in the wake of a military mutiny in 1882. The shaman became close to the royal family and wielded considerable power. Some shamans took up the role of political spies as they had access to confidential information through broad contacts with various people.

In the latter part of Joseon, the number of shamans increased so much that Jeong Yak-yong (1762-1836) wrote in his *Admonitions on Governing the People* (*Mongmin simseo*) that "every village with more than three households has a shaman." Particularly, the number of shamans residing in the capital rose notably. Under the norm of gender separation, female shamans with easier access to female clients had more chances to expand their influence. Male shamans gradually disappeared toward the end of the dynasty.

The government officially prohibited shaman activities in the capital. The proliferation of shamans despite the ban probably owed to the acceptance of shaman elements by most Koreans, including the Confucian-educated nobility and the royal family. The Joseon government collected taxes from shamans from its early years under King Sejong. The tax load on shamans increased steadily to an enormous amount, though shamans who showed outstanding ability in healing eventually were given tax benefits as incentives. Some members of the ruling elite questioned the taxation and occasionally there were voices calling for eradication of shaman activities. But the tax revenue helped quiet the misgivings.

Chapter 3

Diverse Aspects of the Life of Joseon Women

Selection of Queen Consorts

Marriages were arranged through matchmaking involving the parents or relatives of would-be couples during the Joseon Dynasty. But the spouses of royal family members were chosen through different procedures. Particularly, the consorts of kings and crown princes were selected unilaterally from among the young, unmarried daughters of aristocrats, who were denied any say if the palace knocked on their doors.

Selection of queen consorts and the wives of crown princes, called *wangbi* and *sejabin*, respectively, involved complicated procedures, called *gantaek*. Such formal procedures also were applied in selecting the king's other wives when he sired no heir from his queen consort to succeed the throne. Royal concubines thus picked were accorded the status of minor second rank (*jong ipum*) or higher. When a royal concubine had a son and her son was named crown prince, she was specially treated and granted a special title that would also be the name of her palace.

Before beginning the selection process for consorts of the king or the crown prince, the government issued a decree banning all marriages in noble households across the country. It indicated that all unmarried daughters of aristocrats, between some 13 and 17 years old, could be potential candidates. In case of the wife of a crown prince, those as young as nine years of age became targets, depending on the age of the crown prince. For a royal concubine the upper limit could be some 20. Following the decree, the Office of Royal Wedding (*Garye Dogam*) was temporarily installed in the palace to undertake all related tasks.

All young women who were from respectable aristocratic families and of beautiful appearance and virtuous character, including frugality, were considered potential candidates. The government gathered lists of unmarried daughters of noblemen from across the country for preliminary screening, from which three were selected through the second round of screening. The third round was conducted in the presence of the king and the queen dowager, who consulted with the three high state councillors before making their final decision. It means that political considerations were important in the selection of queen consorts or the wives of crown princes. Royal marriages were often regarded as useful for attaining higher plateau in power struggle.

Most queen consorts of the Joseon Dynasty looked elegant and beautiful because a good appearance was considered as important as a reputable family lineage and virtuous character. No matter how impressive their virtue or family background, those who were not beautiful were disqualified.

The final winner chosen after the third round of screening immediately moved into a detached palace and learned the lifestyle and etiquette of the royal household and received all necessary education as queen or consort to the crown prince. Royal weddings, basically similar to those of noble households, had six formal rites including those for sending gifts of silk and jewelry (*nappye*) and escorting the bride from her home (*chinyeong*). Then the ceremony for investiture of the queen or the consort to crown prince followed. The Office of Royal Wedding was closed after all the wedding rites and ceremonies were completed and those who served for them duly cited.

Following an investiture ceremony, the queen's family was bestowed various awards. Her parents were given the titles, *buwongun* for the father and *bubuin* for the mother, both of the major first rank (*jeong ilpum*), which was the highest official rank in Joseon. The queen's birthplace was promoted one level higher in the hierarchy of local administrative units. For example, a village was promoted to a prefecture, a prefecture to a county, or a county to a city. The father and grandfather of a queen or the consort to a crown prince were also appointed to appropriate public posts. These privileges were granted only to the families of the queen and the consort to crown prince, not other royal wives and concubines.

Joseon had a total of 41 formally invested queen consorts. Among them, 10 came from Kim clans, six were Yun and five were Han. More women from Kim families became queen consorts during the latter half of the dynasty while early Joseon kings married women from Han families most frequently. One unwritten rule was that no woman with the surname Yi, even from a clan outside the royal family, could ever be considered as a queen consort or a crown prince's wife. The ban was debated during the reigns of King Sejong and King Jungjong, suggesting the practice was established after years of discussions.

The title of *buwongun* had both bright and dark sides, however. Being the father of a queen consort could mean enjoying much power and privileges. But not many aristocrats actually wanted their daughters to marry the king. Therefore, not a few upper-class families hurriedly married off their young daughters when they anticipated a royal decree banning marriages. Queen consorts and their relatives were often embroiled in political turmoil and factional conflict. Being royal in-laws could be the cause of trouble.

One wise girl avoided a tragic fate by feigning insanity when King Injo (r. 1623-1649) was looking for the consort for his son, Crown Prince Sohyeon. A Gwon family in the capital was known to have a

Gyotaejeon This was the bedchamber of the Joseon queens in Gyeongbok Palace. (Gyeongbokgung Office)

beautiful and virtuous daughter. She indeed looked pretty and good-natured, but she puzzled those attending a court screening by grinning like an insane person and devouring food with her fingers. The king was displeased and the whole palace was dismayed. But it was learned later that the girl married another man and was living well. When he heard the news the king lamented saying, "So I was cleverly deceived." Later, Crown Prince Sohyeon died a mysterious death amid factional struggle. According to rumors, he was poisoned to death. His wife was given poison to end her life.

The royal family most preferred daughters of men with respectable lineages but not so powerful. Queen Munjeong (1501-1565), the third consort to King Jungjong, and Empress Myeongseong (1851-1895), consort to Emperor Gojong, were outstanding examples. What is noteworthy, however, is that both women intervened in state affairs more actively than any other queen consort throughout Joseon. They demonstrated prominent political ability by opening the road for many of their kinsmen to enter politics. Particularly, Empress Myeongseong had much conflict with her father-in-law, Regent Heungseon, due to her unusual political acumen.

Women's Faith in Buddhism and Shamanism

The Joseon Dynasty was under the predominant influence of Confucianism. But Confucianism was a system of practical thoughts focusing on moral obligations. It was far from a religious faith that soothed the inner distress of man or promising redemption in the netherworld. Harshly restricted by the tenets of Confucianism, Joseon women found an outlet in Buddhism and shamanism.

Buddhism was largely a women's religion during Joseon. The preceding Goryeo Dynasty worshipped Buddhism as the state religion and Buddhist monks actively participated in secular affairs. But Buddhism gradually lost its political and economic influence toward the end of Goryeo. As a result, it came to concentrate on teachings about afterlife and seeking blessings for happiness in this world. At the same time superstitious elements were strengthened to attract people from the commoner class and women became deeply attached to Buddhism.

The government tried, though in vain, to prohibit women from visiting Buddhist temples on the grounds that they would undermine public morals by mingling with male monks. But it was not easy to abruptly ban a religious faith that had been handed down over a thousand years. Buddhism could, in fact, complement the Confucian world view which was limited to the present life with little interest in life after death. Particularly, women and lowborns who were discriminated by the Confucian class theory needed a religion that could bring solace and hope to their soul. The Buddhist teachings on karma and reincarnation comforted their depressed souls. Therefore, the government kept one eye closed on women following Buddhism.

Another reason the Joseon government could not completely ban Buddhism was that many women in the royal family were devout Buddhists. Queen Dowager Insu (1437-1504), also known as Queen Sohye, who was the mother of King Seongjong, was a strong supporter of Buddhism. She issued orders that there would be disturbance among the public if Buddhism was suppressed and it should be duly considered that, though every Chinese family kept a Buddhist altar, China was successfully fending off barbarians. Later, while she was ruling as regent for her son, King Myeongjong, Queen Munjeong (1501-1565), the third consort to King Jungjong, made prominent efforts to revive Buddhism. She appointed Buddhist monk Bou to a government post, revived the monk registration system, and conducted state examinations for recruiting monks.

Though these measures were discontinued soon after her death, her pro-Buddhist policy had a great significance, particularly in that Great Masters Seosan and Samyeong, the valiant commanders of monk warriors during the Japanese invasions of 1592-1598, were both recruited through the state examinations.

When women visited Buddhist temples, they usually prayed for their families. They prayed for conception of sons, recovery of ailing family members, a peaceful respite in heavens for souls of the dead, health and longevity of their husbands and children, and their success in society. Women prayed and donated for temple projects on behalf of their families rather than themselves. Through praying for success of their husbands and children, women could have a sort of vicarious satisfaction and thereby overcome their painful reality.

Shamanism was also widely followed by women. During Joseon, shamanic customs were called *eumsa*, meaning "impure rites," as they were seen to worship improper objects. More specifically, all rites except Confucian rituals, such as those performed by shamans at their shrines or private homes or in the outdoors, were considered impure. Most rites held at shamanic shrines or in the outdoors were communal rites participated by the whole village, while rites at private homes were usually intended to pray for the host family.

Whether individual or communal, all shamanic rites included merrymaking participated by both men and women, and adults and children, enjoying singing and dancing over lots of food and drinks. For the majority of general populace, the rites were good occasions to relax from their tough daily routines and strengthen harmony and unity among neighbors. It was believed that all foods offered to gods should be consumed during the day. So invitations went to everyone and rites naturally turned into feasts for all.

The Joseon government, however, banned these rites on the grounds that they were improper activities harming public morals and wasting resources. *Grand Code for State Administration* (*Gyeongguk daejeon*), the main statute of Joseon, provided that anyone holding rites at a shamanic shrine or in the fields or mountains would be flogged 100 times. Shamans were not even allowed to live in the capital. Ordinary people were banned from staying at a shaman's house under the pretext of curing illness or holding ancestral rites.

Nevertheless, it was not easy to eliminate shamanism with its age-old traditions deeply rooted among the people. Like Buddhism, shamanism also had useful religious functions that Confucianism could not fulfill, such as dispelling bad luck, curing disease, guiding the souls of dead to heavens, and invoking blessings. Therefore, even the government depended on so-called state shamans when drought crippled the nation, or to pray for health and prosperity of the royal family. Indeed, many women in the royal household practiced shamanism, so they clashed from time to time with courtiers who banned shamanic rites. When King Seongjong (r. 1469-1494) fell ill, his grandmother Queen Dowager Jeonghui ordered shamans to hold a rite at a pavilion in the National Confucian Academy. Students at the academy threw stones at rice cake steamers, beat the shamans and kicked them out. The queen dowager was greatly enraged and ordered the apprehension of all the students.

Shamanism continued to be practiced in the royal household, whereas the shamanic tradition of village rites performed among the general population gradually disappeared under government control. Shamanism also remained largely as individual faith of women, while men distanced themselves from the "impure" customs in favor of Confucian rituals for ancestor worship. Through shamanic rites women prayed for health and happiness of their family and at the same time vented their suppressed frustration and sorrow while they mingled with other people.

Joseon women also held simple rites at home on their own to appease various deities or spirits governing different parts of their house. They believed there was not only one god but various gods resided in diverse parts of their house. They included *seongjusin* (tutelary god) dwelling in the main hall (*daecheong*), governing peace and prosperity of the family; *josangsin* (ancestral god) in the upper end of the inner room (*anbang*), governing longevity of the family members; *samsin* (birth goddess) in the lower end of the inner room, governing birth and child rearing; *jowangsin* (kitchen goddess) in cooking ranges, governing the life span of family members and their fortune; and *teojusin* (house site god) in the yard, governing safety and wealth of the family. There were more guardian deities like *eopsin* (snake god) in the barn, *cheollyungsin* (heavenly dragon god) in the terrace for sauce jars, *umasin* (cattle god) in the cow shed, and *sumunsin* (door god) in the gate.

Housewives held rites for all these gods in the tenth lunar month every year and for individual gods whenever deemed necessary. They prepared special foods, laid them out on a table, and prayed that the gods would bless their family with peace and happiness.

Introduction of Catholicism and Women's Conversion

Joseon society underwent various changes in the latter part of the dynasty. Among the most notable changes were the awakening of women to their position in society and family. Particularly, Catholicism had a great impact on women's life amid harsh persecution by the government. The Catholic teaching that all men and women are equal before God energized the awakening among Joseon women that they were human beings who deserved no less respect than men. Bible study offered access to knowledge for women who had been denied formal education. Evangelistic activity triggered social activity of women who had been alienated from society under the strict norms of gender separation.

Catholicism was first accepted among scholars of Practical Learning (*Sirhak*) of the Southerners faction, or Namin, largely out of their academic curiosity. But academic curiosity gradually developed into religious faith, which became much organized after Yi Seung-hun's baptism in Beijing in 1784. It spread from educated *yangban* of nobility and their families to the middle class and the number of believers reached some 10,000 after Father Zhou Wen-mo's arrival from China in 1795. Many women displayed zealous interest in Catholicism. Women accounted for two-thirds of all members of

Myeongdohoe, a missionary association founded by Zhou Wen-mo.

Among all early female converts, Kang Wan-suk certainly played the most prominent role in spreading Catholicism. When her husband kicked her out, blaming her faith, she came to Seoul with her son and helped Father Zhou with his missionary activity for six years. She actively propagated her faith among women of different classes from noble ladies to commoners and lowborns.

Many prominent Catholic figures and scholars frequented Kang's house as her place virtually served as the Catholic headquarters during the Joseon period. The well-known visitors included Hwang Sa-yeong, who wrote the famous "Silk Letter" accusing persecution of Catholics by the government, Hwang Sim and Jeong Yak-jong, elder brother of Jeong Yak-yong, a leading scholar of Practical Learning. Kang was a learned woman who didn't fall short in intellectual exchange with these men. She also had a virtuous character and was deeply interested in women's education. She invited many illiterate young girls to her home and taught them reading as well as Catholic doctrines.

Not a few female converts struggled to keep their virginity. For example, Yun Jeom-hye, the daughter of a provincial gentry family, was converted and decided to remain a virgin her whole life. Anticipating her family's opposition to her idea, she disguised herself as a man and hid at the house of her uncle, who had also converted. After her uncle was martyred and both her parents died, she stayed at the house of Kang Wan-suk. Feigning as a widow, she devoted herself to educating young girls there.

There also were virgin couples. Rejecting marriage itself was an unpardonable challenge to the Confucian social system of Joseon. The couples circumvented the institution by marrying but setting aside sexual relations by mutual consent to accomplish their religious convictions.

Two prominent virgin couples were Yu Yohan (John) and Yi Lugalda (Lutgarda), and Jo Bedro (Peter) and Gwon Deresa (Theresa).

Yi Lugalda was the daughter of Yi Yun-ha, a descendant of Yi Sugwang (1563-1628), who met Italian Jesuit priest Matteo Ricci in Beijing and brought back his book, *The True Meaning of the Lord of Heaven* (*Tianzhu shiyi*, or *Cheonju sireui* in Korean), to introduce the so-called Western Learning in Korea. She disclosed her determination to stay a virgin to Father Zhou, who introduced Yu Yohan, the eldest son of Yu Hang-geom, a rural nobleman who lived near Jeonju. They married but vowed to live like a brother and sister. Yi Lugalda was arrested during the persecution of 1801. In her letter written in prison to her mother, she wrote:

"When we realized together what I had longed for over so many years, he opened his heart and said to me that he also had the same wish even before our marriage. Our union was therefore a special blessing from God who proved our carrying out our plans and this is why we wanted to show our appreciation for the huge grace through giving our life for our faith in Jesus Christ. We promised that, when the day comes for us to take over the rights to manage the house and property of our family, we would divide the assets into three or four portions to give one portion to the poor and another, very large portion to our younger brothers so they would be able to take good care of our parents. And we also promised that if things get better, we would separate so each would live alone with the remaining assets. We promised that neither of us would ever break this agreement."

Thus they believed it was due to God's special grace that they were allowed to become a virgin couple. And in the inheritance of family property they made ethical as well as religious considerations. They also expressed concern about the underprivileged in society.

Gwon Deresa and Jo Bedro agreed to remain celibate on their wedding night. In their bridal chamber, the bride gave the groom a letter praising virginity and proposing they remain virgins. The groom was moved and accepted her proposal, and they promised to live like siblings.

These women defied the social institution as well as their human instinct to lead a pure and holy life in accordance with Catholic ideals. But their attitude was radical, or even revolutionary, from the viewpoint of Joseon society as they fundamentally denied the time-old custom of performing filial duties and continuing the family lineage. Though they had to face criticism and endure difficulties, female Catholic converts helped elevate women's social status by expanding the scope of their activity to outside their home. Thus they became the founding stones for women's movements in the modern era.

What is also worthy of note is that 29 out of 112 women sacrificed during the persecution of 1801 had occupations. Seventeen of them were servants, and the rest included court ladies, farm hands, merchants and seamstresses. In spite of their diverse social backgrounds, the majority of early female converts were poor and underprivileged. Naturally, they wished to pursue a better life in the world beyond death.

Fewer women were martyred considering that there were far more female than male believers at the time. It was probably because female believers were not easily found and the Joseon government was relatively lenient in punishing female criminals. But more men betrayed their faith when they faced martyrdom.

As Buddhist traditions in Korea were largely maintained by women over the centuries, so did Catholicism benefit from women's active role in the process of its propagation in Korea. The Catholic tenets of equality for everyone and redemption in heaven offered an escape for women from their frustrating reality and helped them experience the vitality of life — the realization of an ideal world.

Mothers' Zeal for Education

Korean mothers are zealous about children's education, as is well known not only in Korea but around overseas communities. Among the 55 ethnic minorities in China, the Korean Chinese are 11th in population size but rank at the top in education level. The Korean residents in Japan are also similarly well educated. The Korean communities in the United States do not have a long history but second-generation Korean Americans often make headlines with outstanding achievements in various areas. The Korean mothers' zeal for children's education was once dubbed the "skirt power," implying cynical scorn for its negative aspects. In reality, however, mothers' enthusiasm in giving a good education to their children has long been a driving force behind Korea's cultural advancement.

There are always great mothers behind great figures. Women of the Joseon period were denied any opportunity for formal schooling themselves but they nonetheless displayed an extraordinary zeal for education of their children. They did not hesitate to replace the master of their village school when his teaching was not satisfactory. When their children finished a textbook and advanced to the next level, mothers prepared special foods and threw a feast for the whole village. Thus they celebrated their children's achievement and at the same time

"Village School" (*Seodang*) by Kim Hong-do. The painting depicts a village school where boys studied under a master. (National Museum of Korea)

checked their progress in learning.

Giving a good education to children was essential for maintaining the reputation and prestige of a noble family. Joseon class society functioned around the *yangban* elites and joining the state bureaucracy by passing government examinations was regarded as the greatest success for men of noble class. In short, the civil service examination system was the only way to sustain the privileged status of a noble family.

In order to maintain social recognition, any upper class family had to have someone within the three generations of the father, grandfather and great-grandfather, and the maternal grandfather, serving in a public post at all time. Therefore, men of noble class had to consistently endeavor to attain academic knowledge and pass the recruitment examinations for public officials, called *gwageo*. And mothers were primarily responsible for encouraging their children to keep up their studies.

Joseon mothers supplemented their relentless support for their children's education with practical moral lessons on frugality, humility and diligence and the ability to handle crisis. Thus, despite their own lack of formal education, they imparted wisdom that enriched their children's lives.

As discussed earlier, manners and etiquette of married women constituted the major subject of most textbooks for women, such as *Instructions for Women* (*Naehun*), *Four Classics of Women* (*Yeosaseo*, or *Nusishu* in Chinese), *Uam's Book for Instructing a Daughter* (*Uam gyenyeoseo*) and *The Scholar's Seasonal Ways* (*Sasojeol*). These books taught women to sternly discipline their children. They instructed "to teach children only right things" and "not to reproach them with abusive language, cover their faults or boast of them before others, or take sides with them when they quarrel with others."

A lady's Handbook (*Gyujung yoram*) taught that women should only learn minimum knowledge such as "the names of ancient states and ancestors" through reading such basic classics as the *Book of History*, *Lesser Learning* and *Instructions for Women*. Still, many mothers defied the repressive social edicts and attained high levels of academic knowledge, and successfully educated their children, ultimately benefiting the nation. Among outstanding examples are the mothers of Confucian scholar Yi I (pen name Yulgok), scholar-official Yi Hangbok (Oseong), calligrapher Han Ho (Seokbong), novelist Kim Manjung (Seopo) and Admiral Yi Sun-sin (Lord of Chungmu).

Sin Saimdang (1504-1551) is widely known as a great woman. She successfully educated all of her seven children and fulfilled her filial duties for her parents-in-law as well as her own parents, while demonstrating prominent talents as a writer and painter. She encouraged her children to fully develop their potential abilities but carefully checked their progress in reading on a monthly basis. She also made tireless efforts to cultivate her skills for painting and writing poetry while devotedly looking after her ailing mother-in-law. Her third son, Yi I, attained fame as a distinguished scholar and statesman; her eldest daughter Maechang became a noted painter; and her fourth and youngest son U (pen name Oksan) was a famous calligrapher.

Han Ho (1543-1605), recognized as the greatest calligrapher in Joseon for his ingenious style, was raised by his mother alone after his father died when he was very young. His mother received no education but was a wise lady who taught her son to always guard himself against complacency. A rice cake vendor, she once had her son write in the dark while she was cutting her cake. When the light was turned on, her cake was cut impeccably but his writing fell far short of perfection. Thus she taught her son that he needed humility and diligence to perfect his skills.

Lady Choe, the mother of Yi Hang-bok (1556-1618), also raised her son by herself after her husband died and strictly disciplined her little son. As a young boy, Hang-bok was playful and mischievous, creating endless episodes along with his playmate Yi Deok-hyeong, who would remain his lifetime friend. His mother constantly pushed him to concentrate on his studies while she also taught him about moral cultivation as well as frugality and ability to cope with crisis.

One famous episode concerns the little boy littering the yard of his house with iron scraps he had gathered from a blacksmith's workshop. His mother scolded him, explaining how precious those small scraps could be when they were made into small tools like a gimlet or even bullets to use in battle for the country. From then on Hang-bok put all the iron scraps he brought home in a jar and in three years they filled three large jars. Then, one day he asked his mother if he might return the scrap iron to its owner who went bankrupt after indulging in drinking and gambling. Greatly pleased, his mother said she had been wondering how he would use the scraps. The blacksmith was deeply touched. He stopped drinking and worked hard.

When Yi was later sent into exile as a victim of political conspiracy, the blacksmith accompanied him and protected him on his journey. Yi found his mother's teachings and advice to be useful all the while he was serving in the government, especially in the top administrative post as the first state councillor during the seven-year war with Japanese invaders.

Women and Holidays

People put on new clothes and enjoyed special seasonal foods on holidays. They shared foods with neighbors to enhance communal harmony and unity, and also visited ancestors' tombs to hold rites, offering foods made from newly harvested crop. Ancestral rites were closely linked to the daily life of Koreans as Zhu Xi's *Family Rituals* (*Garye*, or *Jiali* in Chinese) became widely accepted as the basic guidebook under the Confucian-oriented government of Joseon.

Looking forward to holidays women were busier than usual making new clothes for their family members and preparing special foods. But holidays were also rare occasions for women to be freed, if briefly, from stifling daily routines within their homes. Among various seasonal holiday customs passed down from ancient times, three major holidays were chosen for nationwide celebration in the 13th year of King Jungjong (r. 1506-1544). They were the New Year's Day, Dano on the fifth day of the fifth lunar month, and Chuseok on the 15th day of the eighth lunar month.

On the New Year's Day, women of noble households sent their young female servants on a tour around their relatives' homes to convey New Year greetings on their behalf. The servants were well dressed to enliven the holiday atmosphere and delivered their lady's message in full courtesy.

Neol ttwigi, a popular game in which two people stood and jumped on a seesaw, was widely enjoyed among women on New Year's Day. An old saying goes that women thought up the game as they could peep at the outside world beyond the walls of their home when they jumped high enough. It was also said, "Fail to jump seesaw on New Year holidays and you will get a splinter in your feet." It probably indicates that the game might have been a health therapy for women who had few chances to exercise throughout the year.

Women spun cotton yarn for presents ahead of the 15th day of the first lunar month, called Daeboreum (Great Full Moon), as it was believed that wearing clothes made of newly woven cotton on the day would bring good luck. At dawn they broke open chestnuts, pine nuts and walnuts, sometimes in the numbers of their age and threw the first nut they broke through the gate of their house, shouting "*Bureom*!" It was a time-old custom for preventing maladies, especially boils, or *buseureom*, during the year. By eating nuts they also could have unsaturated fat in preparation for the approaching farming season.

Among women living in the capital there was a popular custom of enjoying three outings to the scenic valley near the North Gate before the year's first full moon day as it was believed the gate would chase away bad luck. The gate, also called Sukcheongmun (Gate of Solemn Rule), was kept shut throughout the year. It was said that if the gate was left open, it would bring in lewd winds to disturb women in the city. In fact the gate was kept shut for security of the royal palace located nearby.

People believed that the moon looked the largest on Daeboreum. They believed that treading a bridge, or *dari*, under the first full moon of the year, would keep their legs, also called *dari* in Korean, strong and free from illness throughout the year. Women were therefore allowed to come out of their house and walk across bridges under the

"Greeting the Moon" (Collection of Gertrud Krassen in Germany)

moon on this day. Hence the popular custom of *dapgyo nori*, or the "bridge treading play," developed. It was nonetheless forbidden in later years for fears of harming public morals as men and women mingled together under the moon.

Dano, or the Double Five, was a favorite holiday among women. It was a rare occasion for women to see the world outside their home. For the occasion, women washed their hair in water boiled with sweet flag leaves, giving their hair sweet aroma and luster, dressed up and came out to mingle with neighbors and enjoy swing (*geune*). The unforgiving rule of gender separation seemed to ease remarkably on this day.

The moon beams the brightest on Chuseok, the Autumn Moon Festival. Ancestral rites are held on Chuseok, offering foods made from the first crop to thank for rich harvests and invoke greater blessings for the coming year. In rural villages it is a nice break from hard work in the field during the summer, when farmers could rest to recharge themselves for the harvest period.

According to *History of the Three Kingdoms* (*Samguk sagi*), women of the six tribal villages in the early Silla Dynasty (57 B.C. - A.D. 935) were divided into two teams, each headed by a royal lady, for a weaving contest that continued for a month beginning on the 15th day of the seventh lunar month. The results were judged on the 15th day of the eighth lunar month. The losers entertained the winners with food and drinks, and they all enjoyed singing, dancing and playing games together. The feast was called *gawi*, or *gabae*, meaning the "middle." From this archaic word derived Hangawi, another name of Chuseok. *Han* means "great."

The popular circle dance of women, called *ganggang suwollae*, was mostly enjoyed on Chuseok nights. Scores of young women dressed up in new clothes gathered together in the evening of Chuseok and danced drawing circles, hand in hand. The best singer was chosen to sing the lead verses at the center while the dancers followed singing refrains. Dancing began slowly but quickened in varying tempos and continued as long as the lead singer sustained the upbeat mood and the dancers kept pace with her.

The dance is said to have originated from the strategic maneuvering of Admiral Yi Sun-sin during the Japanese invasions of 1592-1598. While he was heading the Jeolla provincial navy headquarters in Haenam, Yi mobilized women from nearby villages and had them disguised as men. The women danced around Mt. Ongmae and the Japanese, surprised to see so many "troops," retreated. The villagers in the region have since commemorated the victory by performing the circle dance.

Under the strict patriarchal family system of Joseon, married daughters were unable to visit their parents and neither could the

"**Woman on a Swing**" by Sin Yun-bok (National Museum of Korea)

parents visit their daughters, no matter how they missed or worried about one another. But around Chuseok, married daughters had a "half-day meeting," or *banbogi*, with their parents. Usually a messenger was sent to make an appointment to meet somewhere half way between their homes, or sometimes some lucky daughters could travel all the way to their parents' house. The reunions were always too brief. The daughter had to return in half a day.

Chapter 4

Women's Life and Role in War and Factional Struggle

Women in Royal Palace and Factional Conflict

War and Women

Women in Royal Palace and Factional Conflict

Partisan conflict during the Joseon period may be regarded as a positive form of politics from the Neo-Confucian viewpoint that defined politics as a means of proper guidance of people. From the Neo-Confucian perspective, it was appropriate for virtuous men of high moral standards to form factions or parties to advocate their principles, whereas political factions as interest groups of petty politicos were condemned as harmful to the country. This theory of political partisanship, propounded by Chinese Neo-Confucian scholars Zhu Xi (1130-1200) and Ouyang Xiu (1007-1072) of the Song Dynasty, was accepted by Joseon bureaucrats in the 16th century. Consequently, the latter part of Joseon saw the emergence of factions and parties confronting one another over many issues.

The literati bureaucrats of Joseon were first divided into the Easterners (Dongin) and Westerners (Seoin), and then in the latter part of the dynasty, the Easterners split into the Southerners (Namin) and Northerners (Bugin), and the Westerners into the Old Doctrine (Noron) and Young Doctrine (Soron). All these factions built connections with powerful members of the royal family, such as crown princes, queen dowagers, queen consorts or even royal concubines, in order to expand their influence. Women in the royal court were often victimized by political struggle, depending on the fate of their factions.

The three most well-known women who suffered due to factional struggle were Queen Inhyeon and Lady Jang during the reign of King Sukjong, and Lady Hong, or Princess Hyegyeong, during the reign of Yeongjo. Lady Jang (?-1701), a consort to King Sukjong, popularly known as Jang Huibin, in particular, lived during a politically turbulent period when severe factional conflicts led to a cycle of brutal retaliations. Lady Jang was connected to the Southerners faction and went through ups and downs in accordance with the fluctuating situation. So did Queen Inhyeon (1667-1701), the second consort to King Sukjong, whose family belonged to the Westerners faction.

Queen Inhyeon was a noble woman of a reputed background, the daughter of Min Yu-jung from the Yeoheung Min clan. In contrast, Lady Jang was born to a middle-class family from a long line of translators. It is not known exactly how she entered the palace, but she probably became a court lady through her family connections with the Southerners while they were in power during the early years of King Sukjong (r. 1674-1720). She succeeded in earning the king's favor and won his heart. She gave birth to Prince Gyun in 1688, while the king sired no heir from the queen. Sukjong named Gyun his legitimate son the next year and granted Lady Jang the title of *bin*, meaning a royal consort, the highest rank for women in court other than the queen. In the same year, he deposed Queen Inhyeon and banished her from the palace as a commoner. In 1690, Prince Gyun was invested as crown prince and Lady Jang as the queen consort.

Lady Jang's position was further fortified when the Southerners regained power after the execution of Song Si-yeol, a leader of the Old Doctrine faction, in 1689 for opposing the investiture of her son as crown prince. But the Southerners wielded power for only a few years and the Westerners ascended again. They campaigned for the reinstatement of Queen Inhyeon. She returned to the palace in 1694, while Lady Jang was demoted to her former position.

The disgraced Lady Jang ordered court ladies at her place to shoot arrows at a portrait of Queen Inhyeon three times a day. There is no way to confirm whether such a curse had any effect but the queen fell sick and never recovered. She died in 1701. It was only after her death that the king learned about Lady Jang's malicious secret rituals. The king ordered poison for her to put an end to her own life. Her relatives and accomplices were either executed or exiled. The courtiers who advised against giving poison to her on the grounds that her death would drive the crown prince into an insecure position were sent into exile.

Lady Jang's son ascended the throne in the wake of King Sukjong's death in 1720. He was King Gyeongjong, the 20th ruler of Joseon. But he was chronically ill and died without an heir four years later. His half brother and the 21st king, Yeongjo, accorded equal favor in official appointments to men of all factions in order to control factional strife. His policy was named *tangpyeongchaek*, quoting from the "Great Norm" chapter of the *Book of Documents* (*Shujing*, or *Seogyeong* in Korean), which said: "No sides and no parties, the kingship would be great and strong; No parties and no sides, the kingship would be easy and peaceful."

But the policy of impartiality failed to eradicate the root of factional strife. Instead, fresh conflict arose as the Old Doctrine faction tenaciously attacked the crown prince, who tilted toward the Young Doctrine faction. After he began administering state affairs as crown prince and regent in 1749, King Yeongjo's son clashed with his father over various matters. The conflict intensified following the death in 1757 of Queen Jeongseong, who had protected the crown prince. In 1762, Na Gyeong-eon of the Old Doctrine faction told the king that the crown prince was behaving like a deranged person, beating a court lady to death, bringing a Buddhist nun into the palace and secretly traveling to Pyongyang. On the 13th day of the intercalary fifth month that year, the crown prince was deposed and put in a grain chest and locked up. He died eight days later and was given the posthumous title of Crown Prince Sado. His wife, Lady Hyegyeong, was awarded the title Hyebin.

At age 10, Lady Hyegyeong (1735-1815) was selected as consort to the crown prince who was of the same age. Her life in court over the next 70 years — as consort to the crown prince and then the mother of King Jeongjo and grandmother of King Sunjo — was full of vicissitudes in the endless turmoil of severe factional conflicts. She had no opportunity to become active in state affairs, even from behind the bamboo screen. She might have been remembered simply as the wife of an ill-fated prince who died a tragic death by the hands of his own father amid extreme factional conflict, had she not recorded the events she had experienced in an autobiographical book. Through *The Memoirs of Lady Hyegyeong* (*Hanjungnok*), she successfully described herself as a remarkable woman who wisely coped with a chaotic sequence of bloody power struggles.

War and Women

Two major wars with Japan (1592-1598) and Qing China (1636-1637) caused great suffering of the Korean people during the Joseon period. Particularly, women had to struggle to sustain their lives and keep their chastity. Women of all classes, from the wives of high-ranking courtiers down to slaves, met with disasters.

According to *Revised Edition of Conduct of the Three Bonds in Korea* (*Dongguk sinsok samgang haengsil*), the government cited a total of 67 filial sons, 11 loyal subjects and 356 faithful wives in the wake of the seven-year Japanese invasions. All of the women commended died trying to keep their chastity from Japanese troops. Actually, even more women must have died while protecting their honor.

All that women could do was to resist at the cost of their lives or comply with the wanton desires of the invaders. Some threw themselves into rivers, some jumped off steep rocks, and some tried to defend themselves with wooden sticks or stones. Only a few killed the attackers while most others were brutally murdered. Many women sacrificed themselves to save their families as well. One woman known as Ha Sosa lured away the Japanese out of fear that they might attack her mother and sisters. After getting the enemy to chase her far enough, she jumped into a river carrying her baby on her back and drowned to death.

In his *Diary of a Refugee* (*Swaemirok*), Oh Hui-mun wrote that more than 100 women were able to escape from a Japanese camp as the Japanese troops went out to fight with Korean army. The Japanese detained hundreds of Korean women at each unit and brought them along on horsebacks when they moved. Those with good appearances were sent to Japan and some of them were carried away as far as to South Sea Islands, India and Europe. Most of these women were mostly from southern provinces. They never returned home.

While the traumatic memories from the war with Japan still remained vivid, the nation was driven into another nightmarish conflict with the Manchu invaders. This time many women in the northern provinces of Pyeongan and Hamgyeong suffered more. *The annals of the Joseon Dynasty* depict more than 10,000 women wailing toward King Injo and his retinue returning to the palace from Samjeondo where the king capitulated to the Manchu emperor in a humiliating ceremony ending his evacuation in the Namhan Mountain Fortress. Blocking the road, they cried, "Your Majesty! Your Majesty! Are you going to desert us?" Given that all these women were captured in the capital area alone, it can be easily imagined how many women were taken prisoner across the country.

After Joseon made peace with Qing, discussions on the repatriation of prisoners of war sparked tremendous controversy in Korean society. In the first place, Qing demanded a huge ransom. But even those women who could return had to face cold reception from their families as most of them had lost their chastity. Few were accepted by their in-laws in particular. A surge in divorce demands ensued, causing great social confusion. Taking precedence from similar incidents in the wake of the Japanese invasions, the government rejected the divorce requests, saying the repatriated women should not be regarded to have been dishonored. However, government decision could not mend broken ties between husbands and wives. Eventually, the word *hwanhyangnyeo*, meaning a "homecoming woman," evolved to *hwanyangnyeon*, a woman of loose morals.

Some women were martyred for the nation amid the raging winds of war. Nongae (?-1593), a *gisaeng* in Jinju, vowed avenge on the enemy who trampled upon her country and her family. When the Jinju fortress was conquered, she lured the commander of the Japanese forces to a party at a riverside pavilion. She held the drunken general in her arms and jumped into the river. Upon the death of their commander, the enemy forces were shattered and defeated.

Gyewolhyang (?-1592) was a gisaeng from Pyongyang. She was carried away by a deputy commander of General Konishi Yukinaga. She maneuvered with Kim Eung-seo, her lover and a famous general, to kill the Japanese deputy commander, also named Konishi. She died from deep wounds she incurred during the fight. Japanese forces were greatly discouraged when their brave commander was found as a headless body on a street in central Pyongyang. They finally withdrew from the city.

When the war ended, the government built memorial shrines for Nongae and Gyewolhyang in Jinju and Pyongyang, respectively.

Women also helped save the country as the mothers or the wives of great generals. Admiral Yi Sun-sin wrote in his *War Diary* (*Nanjung ilgi*) that his mother often wrote letters encouraging him to make honorable achievements for the country and the people. General Yu Geuk-ryang (?-1592) also had a very supportive mother. Lady Okho saved a trove of silver in preparation for war and expended it for buying military supplies to help her son make distinguished services. Lady Yi, the wife of militia commander Gwak Jae-u (1552-1617), raised bees and snakes and released them to attack the invading Japanese forces, clearing the way for her husband to lead his troops to advance.

Not only these famous women but numerous other nameless women also did not hesitate to sacrifice their lives in war to save their country.

Part II

Great Women in History

Chapter 5

Women of the Three Kingdoms Period

Yuhwa and Soseono Lead Nation Building

Queen U Marries Two Kings of Her Choice

Princess Pyeonggang Transcends Class Barriers

Domi's Wife Defies Royal Orders to Prove Her Fidelity

Manmyeong and Jiso Unsung Contributors to Unification

Queen Seondeok Paves the Road to Unification

Queen Jindeok Demonstrates Diplomatic Savvy

Queen Jinseong Tries to Sustain a Waning Dynasty

Yuhwa and Soseono Lead Nation Building

As far back as the first century B.C., two women of outstanding backgrounds and abilities helped build the kingdoms of Goguryeo and Baekje. Without Lady Yuhwa and Soseono the founding of these kingdoms would have been impossible.

According to *History of the Three Kingdoms* (*Samguk sagi*), Yuhwa was the daughter of Habaek, the god of water. While enjoying a picnic with her sisters by the river, she was lured by a man named Haemosu, claimed to be the son of heavenly emperor, to sleep with him. But Haemosu soon left, and her angry parents sent her to a place along the Ubalsu stream.

There, King Geumwa of Eastern Buyeo found Lady Yuhwa and confined her to a dark room. Before long she delivered a giant egg. The surprised king placed the egg before his dogs and pigs, but they would not eat it; he cast it on the road, but the cattle and horses would not tread on it; he took it to a field, but the birds would cover it with their feather. Then, Geumwa tried to crack the egg but to no avail. At last he gave it back to Yuhwa, who wrapped it in a warm cloth. Soon the shell cracked, and a lovely boy, who looked noble and gracious, came out.

By the time he was seven years old the boy was as strong and smart as a man. He was so excellent at archery that he was called Jumong, meaning a "good bowman," in accordance with the custom of the day.

King Geumwa had seven sons, but none of them was a match for Jumong in any art, civil or military. He was hated by the jealous princes and courtiers. When they were about to kill Jumong, Lady Yuhwa quickly detected the conspiracy and said to him, "Your life is in danger, my son. You have many heavenly gifts that I believe will ensure your success wherever you go. Leave here and do great work."

Lady Yuhwa selected the best horse for her son and gave him seeds of five grain that would be his economic base. Jumong fled immediately and went to Jolbon Buyeo, where he eventually married Soseono, a daughter of King Yeontabal. He later succeeded the throne and founded Goguryeo.

Without wholehearted support and encouragement from his wise mother, Jumong would not have been able to go through all the dangers and toils and finally build a great kingdom. With her boldness and farsighted vision for the future, Lady Yuhwa smartly resolved conflict in the royal court and opened a new era of coexistence instead of succumbing to the barriers of reality. In the kingdom of Goguryeo, she was worshiped in state rituals as the guardian spirit of prosperity and peace. Eastern Buyeo also revered her as its divine mother.

Soseono commanded overwhelming respect from the people of Baekje as their "great queen and founding ancestor," according to *Ancient History of Korea (Joseon sanggosa)*, written by journalist historian Sin Chae-ho (1880-1936, pen name Danjae). She was the second daughter of King Yeontabal of Jolbon Buyeo. A wealthy widow, she was instantly drawn to Jumong as soon as he took asylum in her country. *History of the Three Kingdoms* has two conflicting accounts about her: one is that she had two sons, Biryu and Onjo, with Jumong; the other is that her two sons were from her first marriage to Utae, an illegitimate grandson of King Haeburu of Northern Buyeo. In any case, her political background and economic ability laid a crucial foundation for Goguryeo.

But Jumong had another wife, Lady Ye, whom he had married while he was in Eastern Buyeo. When Lady Ye came with their son, Yuri, Jumong wanted to make him his successor. Upon learning his design, Soseono decided to leave with her two sons. They went south and founded Baekje. Again Soseono provided the financial resources needed to build a new kingdom and when she died, at 61, the court of Baekje was so shaken as to discuss moving its capital further to the south.

In the 17th year of King Onjo (r. 18 B.C.-A.D. 28), Baekje built a shrine for Soseono to worship her as its founding ancestor. She remained the goddess of protection for Baekje and its spiritual pillar at times of national crisis throughout its existence over the next six and a half centuries. That certainly was a reward she deserved for guiding her sons to avoid possible conflict surrounding the throne in Goguryeo and helping them realize their dreams in a new world. Thus she also secured strong political influence for herself, far surpassing most men of her time.

Goguryeo (37 B.C.-A.D. 668) and Baekje (18 B.C.-A.D. 660) could be founded and consolidate their power base, thanks to the two women who had tender hearts but strong minds. Lady Yuhwa and Soseono clearly understood the callings of their era and wisely harmonized the realistic problems they faced and the ideals they pursued. Thus these women left indelible legacies, beaming hope at the dawn of two kingdoms — Goguryeo of gallant warriors and Baekje of peace-loving people with warm smiles.

Queen U Marries Two Kings of Her Choice

Among all queen consorts distinguished for their political ability throughout Korean history, Queen U of the Goguryeo Dynasty stood out by formally marrying two kings — Gogukcheon (r. 179-197) and Sansang (r. 197-227) — in succession. What is noteworthy is that she married in accordance with her will, not under any pressure for strategic alliance or political maneuvering by others.

Queen U was the daughter of a nobleman named U So of Yeonna province. *History of the Three Kingdoms* (*Samguk sagi*) describes her as the powerful consort to Goguryeo's ninth ruler, King Gogukcheon, whose relatives possessed considerable power as well. When King Gogukcheon died without an heir to succeed him, she kept the king's demise secret in order to prevent possible conflict over royal succession and to protect herself from being driven into a helpless situation as a queen consort who failed to produce an heir to the throne. Meanwhile, she devised a strategy to find out what her two brothers-in-law were thinking.

She first called on the elder one, Balgi, and said to him, "As His Majesty has sired no heir, I believe Your Highness should succeed him." Without the faintest idea that the king had already passed away, Balgi said, "We must not discuss the matter imprudently because the

Ancient tombs of the Goguryeo Dynasty

mandate of heaven should know where to turn." Then he reproached her saying, "Furthermore, how can this be the manner of a decent lady as you have come to see your brother-in-law in the middle of night?" Embarrassed, the queen headed to the house of her younger brother-in-law, Yeonu.

Yeonu awakened, greeted the queen outside his gate and escorted her inside. While being entertained with drinks, she said to him, "His Majesty has passed away without an heir. I believed that His Highness Balgi should succeed the throne as he has become the eldest one. But he reproached me saying that I harbor treacherous intentions. He behaved rudely and arrogantly toward me, so I had to come to see you." Yeonu cut his finger while cutting meat for her and the queen bound his bleeding finger with a strap from her skirt. Upon leaving, she said, "I am afraid I might run into some unexpected occurrences on my way. Please escort me to the palace." Yeonu accepted her request. The queen returned to the palace, holding his hand.

The next morning, the queen told the courtiers that the deceased king had willed that Yeonu would be the king. Balgi became angry and surrounded the palace with troops. He roared, "As the king has died, I am undoubtedly the first in line to succeed him. It is high treason that you have usurped the throne ignoring the order of seniority." He tried to organize a rebellion but nobody supported him. He had no other choice but to flee to Liaodong.

Yeonu ascended the throne and married Queen U, but again they failed to produce an heir. So he prayed to the gods of mountains and rivers asking for a son and then one night, he heard heaven saying in his dream, "Don't worry as I will have your little consort bear you a son." Later, when the queen learned that the king was meeting a woman at Jutong Village to have a son, she became jealous and dispatched troops to kill her. But when she learned that the woman was already pregnant, she could not help but recognize the woman as the king's little consort. The woman delivered a son, who would become King Dongcheon, the 11th ruler of Goguryeo, following the death of his father, King Sansang, in 227.

King Dongcheon invested Queen U as queen dowager and accorded her utmost courtesy and respect. Preparing for death, the queen chose where to be buried herself. She said, "How can I face the deceased king in underworld when I have erred? If the courtiers cannot dare dump my body in a ditch, I hope they will kindly bury me with King Sansang." Her wishes were accepted and she was buried next to her second husband.

History of the Three Kingdoms has an interesting anecdote about her burial. When Queen U died, King Gogukcheon descended from heaven and said to a shaman, "I couldn't control my anger when I saw Lady U rejoining King Sansang in his grave yesterday. I fought with him, but thinking back, I am so ashamed that I cannot face my people. So, please convey my wish to the court so they would hide me with some objects." Therefore, seven layers of pine trees were planted before his tomb.

The unique political and social circumstances of early Goguryeo made Queen U's two marriages possible. First, the marriage custom in Goguryeo gave an advantage to the bride's family. The groom had to stay with the bride's family for a certain period before he could bring her to his home. Such a wedding custom must have been a factor behind Queen U's freedom to select her spouse.

Second, Goguryeo men often married the widows of their deceased elder brothers. A Chinese source, *Book of Liang* (*Liangshu*) said in its volume about Goguryeo (Volume 54) that marriage of younger brother to the wife of his deceased elder brother was as common in Goguryeo as in Xiongnu or Buyeo. As in the case of Queen U, seniority among the younger brothers was not considered important.

Third, Queen U had strong support from her aristocratic relatives of Yeonna province. But she herself was also a dynamic character with prominent political intuition. At a time when state power was gradually moving toward a strong patriarchal system, she displayed remarkable political acumen and exercised enormous power from a supreme position through three reigns. Debate on her ethical standard aside, Queen U deserves recognition as an independent-minded woman who led a successful life in accordance with her own design.

Princess Pyeonggang Transcends Class Barriers

In the sixth century, Goguryeo struggled against the Han Chinese and foreign tribes constantly invading its northern frontiers as well as the Baekje-Silla alliance to the south. King Pyeongwon (r. 559-590) opened diplomatic relations with Chinese dynasties of Chen, Shui, Northern Qi and Later Zhou, while moving the capital southward to Jangan, which is today's Pyongyang.

King Pyeongwon wanted his daughter, Pyeonggang, to marry the son of a nobleman named Go in Sang province when she became 16 years old. But she disobeyed, unlike most other girls at that time. She said she would marry Ondal, as she had always expected since she was a little child. Her father had joked, or threatened, that he would marry her off to Ondal the Fool to stop the little princess crying. She said the king's word should be kept, even toward a lowly man of humble class.

Defying the king's objection, the princess left the palace and went to Ondal's house. But the poor young man's mother was adamant that her son should not marry a princess. Ondal himself avoided her saying that she must be a "fox." It took a while before the princess persuaded them and realized her childhood dream. She not only lived happily thereafter but she successfully helped her husband transform into a great general fighting bravely for their country.

The famous episode of Princess Pyeonggang and Ondal offers useful lessons.

First, the princess was independent-minded and brave enough to plan her life on her own. She also displayed remarkable fidelity as a young woman.

Second, she deserved high recognition for her wisdom and persuasiveness. She succeeded in persuading the embarrassed young man and his mother with her good attitude. She was reasonable but realistic as well in assisting her husband and supported him with warm love until his death.

Third, she displayed excellent skills at improving the financial condition of her husband's family. She defied her father's wishes but she didn't blindly pursue romance. She carried her jewelry with her when she left the palace and smartly used it to change their fortunes. She believed that she could sew if she only had a piece of hemp cloth and that she could achieve affluence from scratch. In short, she was surprisingly well prepared to cope with harsh reality.

Fourth, her humanitarian spirit based on love and fidelity must be lauded. She delivered all her knowledge in the art of war and combat strategy to her husband, marvelously assisting his transformation from the "fool" heckled by villagers to a heroic general armed with bravery and loyalty to the nation. He made illustrious achievements in repelling the Han Chinese when they invaded the Liaodong region. He died fighting to recover the region north of Jungnyeong Pass occupied by Silla in the south. It is no exaggeration that all his abilities were nurtured by his wife's trust and recognition.

Fifth, the princess set a most praiseworthy example in transcending the fixed notions of morality and loyalty to serve her country at a critical time. She bravely stood up against her father saying that "even a king should not eat his words." She defied the ethical principles of a patrimonial society but eventually helped her father protect the territory of his kingdom from external invasions, thereby expanding his political base.

As a woman of rare courage and action, the princess also challenged the social order based on a class system. She married a man of humble status in accordance with her own decision, which was virtually unthinkable in her days. But her decision ultimately contributed to her country.

A fateful arrow killed General Ondal as he battled against Silla troops near a fortress on Mt. Acha by the Han River. Later, when it came time to lift his coffin and begin the journey to his funeral, nobody could budge it. Princess Pyeonggang came forward, caressed the coffin and said, "The question of life and death has already been decided. So, why don't we go back, my dear?" The coffin became unstuck and the funeral proceeded.

Princess Pyeonggang had tremendous foresight. With her outstanding wisdom and strength, she showed an example of how to explore the future for herself and for her country.

Domi's Wife Defies Royal Orders to Prove Her Fidelity

Domi was a poor farmer who lived in the countryside of Baekje. Though a man of humble status, he was faithful and trusted by everybody. He had a beautiful wife who looked so charming as to arouse interest of any man. As a young girl, she had been courted by numerous men, including those who possessed wealth and power. But she declined them all, saying that she regarded noble character more highly than social status or material wealth. And she chose to marry Domi.

Domi and his wife loved each other dearly and their story became widely known around the kingdom. From mouth to mouth it finally reached the royal palace. One day, King Gaero (r. 455-475) heard it and conspired to seduce the poor farmer's famously beautiful wife, who was also reputed to be chaste.

The king called Domi to the palace and said to him, "Chastity is undoubtedly the greatest virtue of women. But few could remain unmoved when they are lured with nice words in darkness with nobody around." Domi replied, "It is not easy to figure out other people's minds, but my wife will never change her mind." Then the king said he would test her. He confined Domi in the palace and had one of his close subjects disguised in the king's robe and gave him a horse and servants. A messenger was sent to Domi's wife to notify her that the king was coming to her house.

The man disguised as the king entered Domi's house and said, "I have heard about your beauty over so many years. Today I played chess with your husband, betting that if I lose, Domi will get a high government post, but if he loses, I will get you. Then I won. I will take you as my consort as was promised. From now your body is mine." And he attempted to assault her.

Domi's wife pleaded, "The king would never say unreasonable words. How could I ever dare to disobey you? I would like to ask you to get into my room first so I could change into new clothes and follow you." Then she dressed up a pretty female servant and let her serve the guest.

The king was furious when he learned that he was cheated. Charging Domi with treason, he ordered to pluck out both his eyes and sent him adrift aboard a tiny boat. Then he called his wife into the palace and tried to take her by force. She displayed her wit again.

She said to the king, "Now that I have lost my husband, how can I go on living alone? Moreover, how could I dare not obey when I am ordered to serve Your Majesty? But, unfortunately, this is my period and my body is not clean. So, I would like to come back another day, after taking a bath and dressing up." The king believed her and let her leave.

She fled immediately to the ferry, but there was no way for her to cross the river. All she could do was to look up to heaven and sob loudly. Suddenly she saw a boat sailing toward her. She boarded the boat and drifted along the river to reach Cheonseong Island, where she found her husband blinded and deserted.

They pulled themselves together eating grass roots and sailed on. When they landed in Goguryeo, people took pity on them and brought clothes and food. Though poor, the couple lived happily thereafter in a foreign land.

The episode of Domi and his wife has significant historical implications.

First, chastity of women was increasingly emphasized in the ancient kingdom where a patriarchal social system was taking firm root. Earlier, the eight-article code of Old Joseon noted that the wives in its territory were faithful and did not engage in loose sexual conduct. Buyeo had a legal provision that women who committed adultery should be killed. They were thrown away in the mountains to die alone and the law forbade recovery of their bodies before they rotted. All this clearly shows the social climate infusing women with an uncompromising principle of chastity.

Second, chastity, no matter how stern, was a moral value imposed on women only when their spouses were alive. Such a notion was widely accepted through the Goryeo period (918-1392), when there were no inhibitions against widows remarrying. Under the Joseon Dynasty, however, chastity became an unforgiving ideology that women had to uphold regardless of whether their husbands were alive or dead. Wives were required to prove their fidelity toward their dead husbands by all means. Society eulogized women who committed suicide to follow their husbands in death.

Third, the authoritarian power of kings was growing to the extent that they could even take the wives of other men if they desired. Confederations of tribal states had been dissolved and the monarchial authority was strengthening around royal families.

Domi's wife resisted the powerful king to keep her honor and remain faithful to her husband. She was not only brave but smart enough to use her wit in crisis.

Had Domi's wife yielded to the king's desire she might have enjoyed all privileges of a royal concubine. Instead she rejected the king's seduction and fulfilled her conjugal duties. Both she and her husband paid a life-changing price. But their love moved heaven and they were reunited to live together until death parted them. They were poor but happy.

Domi and his wife epitomized an ideal couple: he trusted his wife from the bottom of his heart; she proved her fidelity toward her husband by protecting her honor under threats from the king.

Manmyeong and Jiso
Unsung Contributors to Unification

History repeatedly shows that great men had great mothers. Kim Yu-sin (595-673), a general of Silla who led unification of the Three Kingdoms along with his friend Kim Chun-chu, who would later become known as Taejong the Great, had a great mother. His wife, Lady Jiso, also brought up their son, Won-sul, as a young hero on the battlefield.

Silla was once the weakest of the Three Kingdoms, lagging behind Goguryeo in the north and Baekje to the west. But it grew strong enough to conquer both its rivals in alliance with Tang China and achieved unity of the Korean nation in the late seventh century for the first time in history. Kim Yu-sin was a prominent politician and military leader who made the unification possible. He owed his accomplishments to his mother, Lady Manmyeong.

Lady Manmyeong was a niece of King Jinheung, the 24th ruler of Silla. She was attracted to Kim Seo-hyeon, who had an illustrious military record against Baekje. Kim himself had a remarkable family background as an 11th-generation descendant of King Suro, founder of the neighboring Gaya kingdom. However, Silla had a strict ranking system that divided its royalty into "hallowed bone" (*seonggol*) and "true bone" (*jingol*). Marriage across the bone ranks was considered taboo but Silla society was markedly lenient toward love and free marriage. It was obvious that Manmyeong would not be allowed to marry Kim Seo-hyeon. But she promised to marry him without her parents' approval and slept with him.

Manmyeong's father strongly opposed her engagement and confined her to a room with guards posted outside. Just when Manmyeong was plotting her escape, a sudden lightning bolt and clap of thunder shook open the doors of her room. Manmyeong fled amid the commotion and rejoined Kim Seo-hyeon. And they then went to Manno county.

One night soon after they arrived in Manno, Kim Seo-hyeon dreamt of embracing two falling stars. Manmyeong also saw in her dream a young boy in golden armor descending through clouds and entering her house. Soon she became pregnant and delivered a boy. He was Kim Yu-sin.

Lady Manmyeong also had two daughters, named Bo-hui and Mun-hui, and put her heart and soul into raising all her three children well. Particularly, Yu-sin became ever smarter as he grew up. Manmyeong disciplined him sternly. She believed he needed to be virtuous as well as smart and trained to endure difficulties if he was to become a prominent man serving the country. Among various episodes about her influence on her son, the following is the most well known:

Kim Yu-sin became *hwarang*, a member of the "flower youth" bands of elite warriors. A nice-looking young man with a congenial personality, he was popular and liked to frequent taverns and courtesan houses with his friends. Manmyeong was greatly disappointed when she learned her son was neglecting his studies and visiting courtesan houses. Blaming herself for failing to educate her son well, she said to him, "A man can't live twice. You must sacrifice yourself for your country and justice so your name will be remembered for a thousand years. Why don't you realize your duties?"

Yu-sin deeply repented and vowed that he would devote himself to studying and honing his military skills day and night. Then, one day as he was returning home from a picnic, sleepy from too much drinking, his horse drifted onto a familiar route, carrying its master to the home of his courtesan lover, Cheongwan. Yu-sin's senses reawakened when he heard Cheongwan happily greeting him from her door. At that moment he envisioned his mother scolding him bitterly and decapitated his beloved horse with one stroke of his sword. Then he ran home.

Yu-sin became a renowned politician and military strategist. His contribution to the unification of the Three Kingdoms left his name to posterity as his mother wished. Many years later, a Buddhist temple was established on the site of Cheongwan's house, marked with a "horse guillotine," the spot where Yu-sin killed his horse to remind himself of his obligations.

Lady Manmyeong educated her daughters well, too. Her younger daughter, Mun-hui, married Kim Chun-chu, who would later be known as Taejong the Great. He laid the groundwork for unification of the Three Kingdoms by forging military alliance with Tang China and conquering Baekje.

Kim Yu-sin also owed much of his illustrious service to his country to his wife, Lady Jiso. And Lady Jiso disciplined her son, Won-sul, as sternly as her mother-in-law did while bringing up her husband.

Also a hwarang warrior, Won-sul led campaigns against the forces of Tang China when they turned against Silla, their ally in defeating Baekje and Goguryeo. Despite being badly outnumbered, Won-sul ordered his army to advance against the Chinese invaders. His second in command, Damneung, argued, "We can either advance or retreat as needed in battle. But imprudent sacrifice is neither for our loyalty to the country nor for our filial duty." So they retreated. Kim Yu-sin reproached his son harshly and asked the king to order his execution under military law, but the king refused to accept the request.

Kim Yu-sin never faced his son until his death at 79 in 673. When he died, Won-sul begged his mother for the last chance to apologize to his father. But she refused. She said through a relative, “As a woman I am obliged to obey three men. I am now supposed to obey my son as I have become a widow. But how can I say I am his mother when he failed to fulfill his duties toward his father?”

As a result of self-cultivation and training over many years Won-sul was instrumental in repelling the Tang forces in 675. He returned home triumphantly but his mother had already passed away. He lamented having failed to be forgiven by his parents and finished his life as a plain man after turning down all offers for public service.

Manmyeong and Jiso were both wise women who successfully raised their children as capable persons to serve their country. And they were certainly luckier than most other women of their times in that they left their own names in history. Silla was obviously able to cultivate its national strength and unify the Three Kingdoms thanks to the hidden endeavors of its numerous nameless mothers.

Queen Seondeok Paves the Road to Unification

Korea had three female monarchs throughout its dynastic periods and all of them reigned in Silla. The unique bone rank system in Silla appears to have been a factor behind appointing female heirs to the throne. Silla also resorted to female leadership when it was in crisis.

Queen Seondeok (r. 632-647), the 27th ruler of Silla, was the first female sovereign in Korean history. She was the eldest daughter of King Jinpyeong. Her name was Kim Deok-man, and was appointed successor to her father as he had no son. She is said to have been broad-minded, compassionate and logical. She was widely revered as a wise ruler who greatly advanced culture and enhanced Silla's national prestige abroad to pave the road toward unification of the Three Kingdoms under Silla's initiative. Certainly, her successful rule assured the Silla court to have two more female sovereigns — Queen Jindeok (r. 647-654) and Queen Jinseong (r. 887-897).

During her reign Queen Seondeok made three remarkable prophesies attesting to her wisdom.

First, when Emperor Taizong of Tang China sent her a gift of three cupfuls of peony seeds and a picture of their flowers, the queen scrutinized the picture for a while and said, "The flowers will have no fragrance." The peonies were planted and when they blossomed, they indeed had no fragrance.

Second, a crowd of frogs gathered in Ongmunji, or the Jade Gate Pond, at Yeongmyosa Temple, in winter and croaked for several days. The people wondered at the unseasonal occurrence and asked the queen what its implications might be. She immediately commanded high minister Alcheon to take 2,000 crack troops to Yeogeungok, the Woman's Root Valley, on the western outskirts of the capital. She said they would find enemy troops hiding in the valley. The high minister set off with his troops and indeed found 500 soldiers of Baekje concealed in the valley forest. The Silla troops killed them all.

Third, one day while the queen was still in perfect health, she called her courtiers together and said, "I will die on a certain day of a certain year. When I die, bury me in the Tushita Heaven." As the courtiers did not know the place and asked for directions, the queen pointed to the south of Nangsan, Wolf Mountain. On the very day she predicted she died, and her ashes were interred on the site she had chosen. Some 10 years later, King Munmu had Sacheonwangsa, the Temple of Four Heavenly Kings, built beneath her tomb. All were amazed when they realized that Buddhist scriptures noted the Four Heavenly Kings resided on the lower slopes of Mount Meru, the lowest of the six deva worlds of the Tushita Heaven.

When courtiers asked the queen about her predictions, she replied: "The picture had flowers but no butterflies. It indicated that the peonies had no smell. The Tang emperor was teasing me because I had no husband. As for the frogs, angry frogs look like soldiers and a jade gate refers to a woman's genital. Female is *yin* and white is its symbolic color, which also stands for the west. So I could tell the invaders were coming from the west. A male organ will surely die when it enters a female organ, so I knew the enemy would be easily defeated." All the courtiers were deeply impressed by her wisdom.

With her outstanding judgment and insight, Queen Seondeok

accomplished one great project after another toward unification amid a severe contest of power among the Three Kingdoms. She clearly understood that the greatest task her country faced at the time was leading their unification and focused on rearing the necessary human resources. Kim Chun-chu, or Taejong the Great, and General Kim Yu-sin are the most well-known heroes who led Silla's unification of the Three Kingdoms. But Silla would not have been able to accomplish unity of the three rival states without the all-out support from Queen Seondeok. Particularly, she tied the two families through marriage so the two men could work together as leading players in the historic mission.

Queen Seondeok was astute in playing a diplomatic game amid a highly volatile power contest with Goguryeo and Baekje. For example, she forged an alliance with Goguryeo when Baekje invaded Silla, but when Goguryeo and Baekje jointly attacked Silla, she promoted friendly relations with Tang by dispatching royal emissaries and students. Her multilateral diplomacy helped Silla attain hegemony on the Korean peninsula. She took advantage of the Tang policy to expand its influence toward the east but skillfully maintained independence by keeping an appropriate distance when Tang intensified its interference. At the same time she retained her queenly dignity marvelously well under any circumstances.

The queen was also equipped with a broad heart to embrace the people of all stripes. Upon ascending the throne, she placed much emphasis on internal governance relieving poverty and improving welfare for those who could not stand on their own. She built Cheomseongdae, the star gazing observatory, to promote farming.

Many people adored the queen. Among her famous admirers was Jigwi. When he heard the queen was about to visit Yeongmyosa Temple, he waited for her under a pagoda on the temple ground. But he fell asleep while waiting and missed seeing the queen. When the queen

An architect's model of Hwangnyongsa The temple was founded in the sixth century Silla period. The nine-story wooden pagoda in front of the main hall was built in 643, during the reign of Queen Seondeok. (Gyeongju National Museum)

saw the man sleeping, she left her bracelet on his chest. Jigwi awoke to find the queen's bracelet and his heart was set ablaze with passion. So, legend has it that the flames from his heart burned the pagoda.

Buddhism was the state religion of Silla, serving as a spiritual pillar uniting the people toward the goal of unification. Queen Seondeok erected the state temples Bunhwangsa and Yeongmyosa, and sent monk Jajang to Tang to study the scriptures. She also set up the gigantic wooden pagoda of Hwangnyongsa representing Silla's national strength and stalwart will for defense. The nine-story pagoda was some 80 meters high. Each story was inscribed with the name of one of Silla's nine neighbors that it aspired to repel and subjugate. They were, from the first story upward, Japan, China, Wuyue (Owol), Tangna, Eungnyu, Mohe (Malgal), Danguk, Yeojeok and Yemaek.

Queen Jindeok Demonstrates Diplomatic Savvy

Queen Jindeok (r. 647-654), the 28th ruler of Silla, was a cousin of her predecessor, Queen Seondeok. She was the daughter of the Lord of Galmun, a younger brother of King Jinpyeong. Her name was Kim Seung-man. She is said to have looked beautiful and glamorous, as tall as seven feet and her arms reaching beyond her knees. With able assistance from Kim Chun-chu and Kim Yu-sin, she looked after state affairs in relative peace, though she pursued a pro-Tang foreign policy to lead the conflict with Baekje to victory.

Queen Jindeok reorganized the governing system and consolidated her royal power. She expanded *Pumju*, the tax-collecting agency, to *Jipsabu*, or the Chancellery Office, which functioned as a kind of executive council. She composed a five-character verse titled "Taepyeongsong," meaning the song of peaceful reign. She sent the poem, wrapped in a piece of silk brocade, to Emperor Gaozong of Tang through her envoy, Kim Beop-min, the son of Kim Chun-chu, who later became King Munmu. The poem read:

Great Tang created the powerful celestial dynasty,
The lofty royal achievements bloom high forever.
The monarch has ended war to give soldiers rest,

He esteems culture as a noble heir to hundred kings.
He presides over heavens to send down sweet rains,
He rules over all creation giving luster to every object.
His deep benevolence matches only the sun and moon,
His wheel of fortune heads to the era of Yao and Shun.
Brightly his banners flutter proudly covering the sky,
Loudly his gongs and drums ring reaching far and wide.
Barbarians that disobey the imperial orders
Will fall to his sword to be punished by heaven.
Virtuous winds gather dark or light from everywhere,
From far and near auspicious praise is offered.
The four seasons flow like burning candles,
The seven stars shine all over the universe.
From the high mountains his ministers descend,
The king entrusts his mandate to loyal vassals.
The virtues of five emperors and three kings in one,
The radiance illuminates our king of Tang.

Gaozong was greatly pleased and awarded her the title of the "King of Gyerim." The queen wove and embroidered the silk brocade she presented, according to historical records. Regardless of whether she wove the silk herself or not, her effort to improve ties with Tang and enlist its support at a time of national crisis deserves to be commended.

Queen Jindeok and Queen Seondeok deserve recognition for their endeavors in laying the groundwork for unification of the Three Kingdoms. The unity of the three ancient kingdoms had historic significance in that the Korean nation formed a single state for the first time. Silla achieved the momentous task largely through its diplomatic acumen rather than military superiority. A late bloomer in the trilateral power structure on the peninsula, Silla garnered the driving force toward unification by uniting its people under a single national goal.

A gold crown of the Silla Dynasty (Gyeongju National Museum)

The unification under Silla's initiative invited Chinese interference and curtailed the domain of the Korean state. But a prolonged division under the Three Kingdoms could have intensified their differences in all areas, eventually eroding the ethnic identity of the Korean people. Probably, the Korean nation as an independent political entity might have disappeared if the Three Kingdoms had not been unified at that time. Unity under a single dynasty multiplied the strength of the Korean nation to resist foreign interventions.

The two queens' contribution to the political and social advancement of Silla was recognized through generations to bring about the enthronement of a third female sovereign two centuries later. When the ailing King Jeonggang, the 50th ruler, had to appoint his successor, he said to the courtiers: "I am critically ill and will never recover. It is regretful that I have failed to sire an heir but, fortunately, my sister Man possesses a sagacious disposition and a strong physique like a man. Therefore, referring to the old examples of Seondeok and Jindeok, I want to ask you to have my sister succeed me." The king probably intended to have a female sovereign save the kingdom from a crisis following the precedents of his forebears.

Queen Jinseong Tries to Sustain a Waning Dynasty

All of the three female monarchs in Korean history came from Silla. They succeeded the throne under Silla's unique bone rank system but their accession would have been impossible without political demands of their eras. It must be admitted that their achievements as reigning queens were underestimated by Confucian-oriented historians of later years. Looking carefully into the accounts of their rule, they obviously made efforts to resolve problems of governance with their ingenious political insight.

Each of the three queens ruled when Silla faced a crisis. In the ninth century, 200 years after Queen Seondeok and her successor Queen Jindeok seized the initiative to unify the three kingdoms, another Silla princess was named the successor to her brother, King Jeonggang, the 50th ruler, who sired no heir. The king asked the court to approve her appointment, citing the precedents of the two previous queens. He probably wanted his sister, who had "a sagacious disposition and a strong physique like a man," to imbue the declining dynasty with a fresh vitality.

Queen Jinseong (r. 887-897) is widely known as an incapable and debauched ruler who accelerated Silla's demise. This derogatory view, however, obviously reflects the Confucian-oriented perception of female inferiority among historians of later years, such as Kim Bu-sik, who wrote *History of the Three Kingdoms* (*Samguk sagi*) in the 12th century Goryeo period. She was blamed for calling in a few fine-looking young men to the inner palace and appointing them to important positions after her confidant and high courtier Wihong died in the second year of her reign. But the handsome men were most likely *hwarang*, young noble warriors. She apparently tried to stabilize her power with their support.

Her close association with the hwarang may be explained through her family lineage. Her father, King Gyeongmun (r. 861-875), the 48th ruler, had been a hwarang. He married the daughter of King Heonan, the 47th ruler, who had no son. When he fell critically ill, King Heonan appointed his son-in-law his heir, asserting that he should not test the old saying that "the house will fall into ruin when the hen crows."

King Heonan might have hoped that his son-in-law could consolidate the throne with help from the hwarang warriors in the face of strong challenge from anti-royal forces. King Gyeongmun's three children ascended the throne one after another — King Heongang (r. 875-886), King Jeonggang (r. 886-887) and Queen Jinseong.

Queen Jinseong abdicated in favor of the illegitimate son of King Heongang, her elder brother, when he was old enough. He was King Hyogong (r. 897-912), the 52nd ruler. The throne was then succeeded solely by members of King Heongang's direct lineage until Silla fell under King Gyeongsun (r. 927-935), the 56th and last ruler. In the meantime, the rival forces of King Gyeongmun persistently challenged the royal authority. As part of her measures to control resistance of these "true bone" (*jingol*) lineages, Queen Jinseong appointed Choe Chi-won as *achan*, an official post of sixth rank, and accepted his reform proposal.

During the reign of Queen Jinseong there were far more Buddhist events than before, which was probably due to the wishes of the royal household to elicit assistance from Buddhism in turning around the national fortune. Also, the queen committed the monk Daegu Hwasang and the high courtier Wihong to compile an anthology of *hyangga*, the folk songs of Silla, under the title *Samdaemok* (*Collection of hyangga from the three periods of Silla*). The project shows her insight as a ruler of the long-lived dynasty during its waning period.

Despite the queen's efforts, Silla never recovered its old splendor. Peasant rebellions and insurgent military forces of local gentries, such as Gyeonhwon, Yanggil and Gungye, constantly challenged and pressured the central government. But it certainly is unfair to blame the queen entirely for all the chaos.

Court intrigues and conflicts had already been aggravating since King Seondeok murdered King Hyegong to usurp the throne a century earlier. The ruling class was divided over political interests and state affairs were drifting in confusion. The royal authority alone was not sufficient but a solid military support was necessary for handling the situation.

Those who were victimized or defeated in power struggle joined the insurgent forces that grew increasingly out of control. The central government was incapable of suppressing them. Queen Jinseong was enthroned at a critical time with the heavy burden of salvaging the kingdom from its apocalyptic problems. It was not her personal agony but of the entire kingdom, a dilemma of ancient Korean society in transition. The queen made all possible efforts but when it seemed impossible, she abdicated to pursue peace in the royal household. She was ultimately a responsible leader.

Chapter 6
Women of the Goryeo Period

Queen Janghwa Assists Cementing Royal Power

Queen Janghwa, also known as Lady Oh, was the second consort to King Taejo, the founding monarch of the Goryeo Dynasty (918-1392), and one of his 29 wives. Taejo's numerous marriages were part of a grand strategy to forge alliances with landed gentries while territories were being unified. His marriages may be divided into three periods: Those of the early period when he served as a commander for Gungye, the king of Later Goguryeo, in his hometown Songak, which would later be renamed Gaegyeong (present-day Gaeseong) as the capital of Goryeo; the middle period after he founded Goryeo; and the last period when he was engaged in completing the unification of Later Three Kingdoms.

Queen Sinhye, or Lady Yu, was the first wife of King Taejo, whose name was Wang Geon. She was born in Jeongju, near Gaeseong, as the daughter of local gentry Cheongung. According to legend, Wang as a commander for Gungye was passing by Jeongju one day and met a young girl with a virtuous appearance by a stream — the daughter of the village leader. Wang stayed at her house that night. His troops were lavishly entertained and Wang was served by the young girl under orders from her father. She became a nun when she did not hear from Wang for a long time after that night. But she eventually became his first wife.

Queen Janghwa came from Naju, now in South Jeolla Province. She was the daughter of the Lord of Daryeon, a rich nobleman. Sometime after she dreamt of a dragon entering her belly, Wang advanced to Naju as a navy commander. When he had his ship anchored at Mokpo, he saw five-colored clouds and followed them until he found a girl doing laundry beside a well. Wang called on her and slept with her. She became pregnant and had a son, who later became King Hyejong, the second ruler of Goryeo.

According to an anecdote in *History of Goryeo* (*Goryeosa*), Wang was reluctant to have a child by Lady Oh because her family was rich but not powerful enough. So he ejaculated on the mat but Lady Oh quickly took in his semen and became pregnant. Her son, who later became King Hyejong, had many wrinkles on his face, so people called him the "Wrinkle King." They said he got his wrinkles from the mat.

Wang's storied waterside encounters with women suggested that they had a maritime background. Their families accumulated wealth through sea trade, mostly on the West or the South Seas. They came from regions where he actively staged military campaigns. By marrying these daughters of wealthy and powerful local gentries, Wang effectively took control of their native places, Jeongju and Naju, and greatly benefited from their economic support.

After he ascended the throne, King Taejo continued to marry the daughters of powerful local gentries from various regions to secure as much support powers as possible amid unceasing political confusion. Actually, chaos lasted over six months after he proclaimed the founding of a new dynasty. He married 25 out of all his 29 wives during this period. They came from all over the peninsula, including Hwanghae, Gyeonggi, Gyeongsang, Chungcheong, Gangwon and Jeolla provinces. Thus he could stabilize his royal power, paving the road toward unifying Later Three Kingdoms.

Three out of his 29 wives were referred to as the "queen consort" (*wanghu*), three others as the "queen dowager" (*taehu*), and the remaining 23 as the "lady" (*buin*). All the three queen consorts were probably the official wives. There seems to have been little difference in their status.

King Taejo is officially recognized to have had 25 sons and nine daughters. Of his 25 sons, seven became kings or monks and 11 of the remaining 18 sons called themselves "crown prince" (*taeja*) and the rest "prince" (*gun*). In other words, all of the 11 princes considered themselves successor to their father. It indicates they all had powerful family backgrounds on their mothers' sides. Also, there was yet no clear distinction between legitimate and illegitimate children at the time.

King Taejo appointed Lady Oh's son, Mu, his successor. Mu was Taejo's only son when he founded a new kingdom and he had a virtuous personality required for a royal heir. Upon ascending the throne, King Taejo wanted to name seven-year-old Mu as his successor but hesitated because of Lady Oh's insignificant background. Her family was of a relatively humble means compared to those of his other wives and had no realistic ability to mobilize troops. Therefore, Taejo clandestinely instructed his powerful army commander, Bak Sulhui, who had made meritorious contributions to the establishment of Goryeo, so he would propose the young prince's investiture as heir to the throne. In 921, the fourth year of King Taejo, Prince Mu at age 10 was formally appointed *jeongyun*, the first in line to the throne, or the crown prince.

Queen Janghwa was alongside King Taejo through all the volatile years while he founded a new kingdom, unified the divided territories and consolidated his power. Taejo had to move from one battle ground to another year after year. All this time he had to stay alert against insurgency by local gentries. His conciliatory gesture of marrying their daughters and the sons they produced threatened Queen Janghwa and her son. But she coped with the precarious situation most wisely and devoted herself to supporting the king and educating the crown prince. Thus she successfully assisted her son in succeeding to the throne and strengthened her position as well. In the process her maiden family and the residents of her native place, Naju, rendered unsparing support and cooperation.

Yeom Gyeong-ae Stands Out as a Model Housewife

During the Goryeo period, a man named Choe Ru-baek was listed as a filial son in the "Biographies" volume of *History of Goryeo* (*Goryeosa*). When his wife, Yeom Geyong-ae, died, he wrote an inscription for her tomb plate in deep grief, expressing his love and respect for her great deeds as a wife and mother. His soul-touching expression was a rarity: few other husbands in his days wrote inscriptions for their wives' tomb plates. Besides, the tomb plate of Yeom Gyeong-ae is the oldest extant one for a woman in the country.

The beautifully named Yeom Gyeong-ae was born to a reputed family. Her mother, Lady Sim, was the daughter of a high-ranking official of the Royal Secretariat (*Chumirwon*). She was smart and diligent, drawing praise from her early childhood. She became an impeccable wife and mother, educating all of her four sons and two daughters very well. Gyeong-ae was her elder daughter and grew up as a wise and virtuous young lady in a Confucian family environment.

At 25 she married Choe, a man of outstanding filial devotion whose ancestors served as local functionaries in Suwon. After a tiger fatally mauled his father, the 15-year-old Choe went into the mountains, defying everyone's objections, and beat the tiger to death. He opened the beast's belly to collect his father's remains and buried them. Then he built a grass hut beside his father's grave and mourned for three years, after which he prepared for the civil service examinations while supporting his mother. Choe passed the examinations but only gained a low-ranking government post with a meager salary. Consequently, his wife struggled to make ends meet while bringing up their six children.

Although Choe eventually became a senior royal advisor with the title *jwajeongeon*, he had to remind his elated wife that his salary would not yet be high because a royal advisor was expected to be of high repute. She replied: "My heart will rejoice if you can ever stand only once on stairs to the throne hall and face the king to discuss right and wrong. I will never mind living in poverty until the day I die, wearing hemp clothes and a thorn bush hairpin, and carrying a basket on my head."

Her remarks immensely touched her husband, ever deepening his trust and respect toward her. He realized once again that his wife was no ordinary woman. Ironically, she died a year later when their financial condition had finally improved substantially. She was 47. The following is the last part of the inscription written by her grief-stricken husband:

> Our confidence and vows unforsaken,
> Grieved that we failed to die together.
> Our sons and daughters flying like geese,
> Surely to prosper through generations
> As you so wished.

Through the inscription Choe extolled his wife for fulfilling her filial duties toward her parents-in-law and successfully educating their children while devotedly assisting him. She supported his mother with all her heart and held memorial rites for his father the best she could, regretting that she had not been able to serve him while he was alive.

She carefully prepared foods and clothes to offer at the rites. Also, when her husband was leaving for battle, she made him a purple coat to be worn over his armor. Sometimes, she sent food to the frontline in spite of her dire circumstances.

Choe also rhapsodized about his wife's extensive knowledge and insight, her unerring words and actions stemming from her righteous mind, and her prominent judgment. She tried to manage all the household needs in order to help her husband devote himself to his public career and her children to their studies. She ceaselessly worked, weaving and doing all kinds of exchange work with her neighbors. But she always worried about one thing: "My ability as manager of family economy is limited so there are things I fail to do as I wish even though I do my best regarding my family's clothes and food. I am afraid that, when my children get high salaries and find things go smoothly as they wish, they may think I was incapable and forget all the hardships I had to make ends meet."

Here she pointed out that her children could lack abilities as public officials when they fail to realize the difficulties and value of home management. She was indeed thoughtful. Her husband recalled later that the higher salaries he earned after her death did not lead to a family life that was better than the old days when she struggled to manage their household.

Finally, Choe's inscription expressed his amazement at his wife's marvelous insight and chivalrous spirit that few men matched. He complimented her for wisely and justly coping with all situations. Indeed, she greatly encouraged her husband when he was appointed a royal advisor by imbuing him with a sense of mission and pride in his work regardless of his income.

A handful of queens and queen mothers represent the elite women of the Goryeo period who are known today. There are fewer Goryeo women recognized for their intellectual ability than those from the subsequent Joseon period. In this regard, the inscription on Yeom Gyeong-ae's tomb plate, admiring her as a woman of intellect, is worthy of special note. Living at a time when women had no opportunity to advance to public posts or engage in social activities, she was the driving force that inspired her husband and children to serve their country and society. There is little doubt that if she had been born today, she would demonstrate far greater ability than most men in society.

Chapter 7

Women of the Joseon Period

Queen Jeonghui Rules behind the Bamboo Screen

Queen Munjeong Also a Powerful Regent

Lady Saimdang's Life and Artistic Achievements

Heo Nanseolheon a Short-Lived Literary Genius

Lady Jang Fulfills the Spirit of Practical Learning

Queen Jeonghui Rules behind the Bamboo Screen

The first female regent of the Joseon Dynasty was Queen Jeonghui (1418-1483), consort to King Sejo. Through her regency she effectively prevented possible conspiracies to usurp the throne from young monarchs and protected them from being alienated from state affairs by powerful courtiers. She thereby cemented the foundation of the dynasty and paved the road for her grandson, King Seongjong, to accomplish many useful projects to consolidate the royal power.

Queen Jeonghui ruled from behind the bamboo screen from the reign of her son, King Yejong (r. 1468-1469), to early years of her grandson, King Seongjong (r. 1469-1494). "Ruling from behind the bamboo screen," or *suryeom cheongjeong*, was needed when the king was too young to oversee state affairs when he succeeded to the throne. The regency role fell to the most senior member of the royal family, the queen dowager or the queen grandmother. The "bamboo screen" denoted the Confucian norm of gender separation that forbade face-to-face encounters between the queen and male courtiers.

Queen Jeonghui was the daughter of Yun Beon (1384-1448), who served as first state councillor, or *yeongeuijeong*, under King Sejong. She was from the Papyeong Yun clan which had been producing numerous high-ranking courtiers since the Goryeo period. She married

Prince Suyang, the second son of King Sejong, in 1428, and was invested as Her Royal Highness of Nangnang (*Nangnangbu daebuin*).

There are various episodes attesting to the queen's daring personality. One of them was on the day when a lady-in-waiting from the royal palace visited Yun Beon's house on a leg of her tour to meet potential consort to Prince Suyang. Yun Beon's wife brought her elder daughter to show her to the lady-in-waiting. Then her younger daughter, a short-haired little girl wearing a short skirt, trailed peeping out from behind them. Her mother harshly scolded her and pushed her back into a room. However, the lady-in-waiting said, "I would like to see that child, too. She looks so uncommon, far too different from ordinary people." She was very impressed by Yun Beon's younger daughter and reported on her with strong recommendation.

Prince Suyang conspired to usurp his nephew, King Danjong, who had ascended the throne at 12 years of age in 1452. On the day he planned to eliminate elder statesman Kim Jong-seo and other loyal supporters of the boy king, the prince hesitated as he recalled his aides' advice to reconsider his plot. But his wife urged him to proceed and helped him don his armor. The prince assaulted Kim's house outside the West Gate and killed him and his other political opponents. The so-called Gyeyu Incident led to the overthrow of King Danjong with Prince Suyang mounting the throne. Lady Yun became the queen consort.

Queen Jeonghui had three children — Prince Euigyeong (posthumously titled King Deokjong), King Yejong and Princess Euisuk. Prince Euigyeong was named crown prince as soon as his father ascended the throne but died two years later at 20. He had married a daughter of second state minister Han Hwak and had two sons — Prince Wolsan and Prince Jasan, who was later known as King Seongjong. Yejong married a daughter of Han Myeong-hoe and had a son, but both his wife and son died prematurely. He remarried a daughter of Han Baek-ryun with a powerful family background and had two sons and two daughters from her. Princess Euisuk was married off to the family of the meritorious and powerful courtier Jeong Hyeon-jo.

King Sejo died 13 years after he took over the throne. He was 52 years old. His second son, Gwang, succeeded him at the age of 19, to be later known as King Yejong. With her young son's ascension, Queen Jeonghui became actively involved in politics. She had already been taking part in handling state affairs while King Sejo was ailing and her smart and accurate judgment had attained his approval. The king even said he was pleased to have someone as able as the queen to look after things after his death.

However, King Yejong died 14 months after he ascended the throne. When Sin Suk-ju and other senior ministers appealed to the queen to appoint the heir to the throne, she said: "Ah, heaven has no mercy to inflict disasters upon our dynasty so Sejo the Great passed away at a premature age. The succeeding king fell ill grieving over his father's death and succumbed suddenly. Misfortunes came one after another. How can I find words to describe these extremely sad events? I think the throne must not be left unoccupied even for a short while, but the succeeding king's son is yet wrapped in swaddling cloths, ailing from the start.

"Now, the two sons of Crown Prince Euigyeong are the only legitimate grandsons of Sejo. But Prince Wolsan has been sick too often since he was a child. His younger brother by the same mother, Prince Jasan, is talented and smart for his age, so Sejo praised his unusual disposition and broad mind, even comparing him to our Taejo. Though he is still young, his knowledge will increase as he grows up so he may be entrusted with great tasks. In this regard, I would like to discuss this matter with you so you will all agree among yourselves to say with one voice that everyone hopes to have Yi Hyeol succeed the throne. With the future (of the kingdom) at stake, I can hardly feel at ease. All of you, courtiers of all ranks, are asked to support from left and right with all your might as I wish. Ah, it is sad."

Queen Jeonghui thus put the second son of her deceased elder son, Crown Prince Euigyeong, or posthumous King Deokjong, on the throne. He was 13-year-old Prince Jasan, who would later be known as King Seongjong.

The succession of Seongjong was possible through political collusion between Queen Jeonghui and high courtier Han Myeong-hoe. Han was the prince's father-in-law and from the queen's position, she must have thought that with the young prince on the throne she would be able to rule as regent for a relatively long time to place the dynasty on a solid foundation. Therefore, they chose Prince Jasan.

There were other eligible candidates besides Prince Jasan. Prince Jean, the son of King Yejong, was alive at the time though he was only four years old. There also was Prince Wolsan, the elder brother of Prince Jasan. The 16-year-old Prince Wolsan was the eldest grandson of King Sejo, so he evidently was closer to the throne. He was said to be in poor health but there was little clear evidence. Following the coronation of King Seongjong, Queen Jeonghui, who was now the queen grandmother and regent, promoted both Jean and Wolsan to "great prince," or *daegun*. Particularly, Prince Wolsan was cited as a meritorious subject of second grade.

At this time, political power was concentrated on those who were close to the regent queen grandmother and *wonsang*, the senior ministers temporarily appointed to supervise state affairs to support the child king. The two parties formed mutually interdependent power groups. The emergency system of senior ministers was first adopted during the years of King Sejo when he became ill. This allowed the elderly and experienced courtiers to fill the power vaccuum. They administered state affairs in four shifts along with the crown prince. It became a permanent executive board during the short reign of King Yejong, with Sin Suk-ju, Han Myeong-hoe and Gu Chi-gwan, all powerful courtiers who had special relationships with King Sejo, serving as regular members.

Most of these powerful ruling elites were commended as "meritorious subjects" in the second year of King Seongjong. The king declared in a special statement that the titles were rewards to Queen Jeonghui and those courtiers who contributed to stabilizing governance. Since the advent of the dynasty, Joseon kings bestowed the titles of meritorious subjects on power elites who assisted the throne in consolidating royal authority for national security. The titles accompanied political, economic and social compensation for their service. Those cited by King Seongjong obviously fell short of exhibiting meritorious service during a national crisis, but the total number recognized was 75, nearly twice as many as those cited under all previous Joseon kings.

Another notable fact is that among those commended at this time were not only those courtiers who actually served the throne but their family members and close relatives as well. For example, Sin Suk-ju was awarded along with his two sons and so was Jeong In-ji. Han Myeong-hoe also earned the title along with his son. In other words, a small number of power elites monopolized the privileges of meritorious subjects. Eventually, those who were excluded from power complained and the senior minister system itself was abolished when the queen grandmother announced the cessation of her regency in the seventh year of King Seongjong on the grounds that the king was old enough to rule.

Major events under the regency of Queen Jeonghui included the promulgation of *Grand Code for State Administration* (*Gyeongguk daejeon*), the basic statutes of the dynasty; and the abolition of the identification tags (*hopae*) law, which helped appease the public by reducing government surveillance on the population. Also, Joseon reinforced its anti-Buddhist policy in favor of Confucianism, prohibiting cremation and shutting down Buddhist chapels in the capital. Monks were banned from entering the capital and women of the literati class were not allowed to become nuns. Marriage between man and woman with the same family name was prohibited and *Conduct of the Three Bonds* (*Samgang haengsil*) was adopted for mandatory reading of students throughout the country in order to promote Confucian moral education. Queen Sohye, widow of Crown Prince Euigyeong, the eldest son of King Sejo, wrote *Instructions for Women* (*Naehun*) in the sixth year of King Seongjong.

As efforts at improving public welfare, the number of local branches for the Office of Royal Estate (*Naesusa*) was reduced to 235 and silkworm cultivation was encouraged as a sideline for farming households. The royal family saved goods to set an example of frugality.

Surely, none of these steps could be taken arbitrarily by Queen Jeonghui. Instead she pursued them smoothly by soliciting cooperation from senior ministers in appropriate ways and guarding against excessive interference by her relatives. Therefore, there was no serious dispute or the need to reorganize the power structure. She flexibly coped with the political environment, thereby extending her power base. Thus she could lay the groundwork for King Seongjong to employ officials from the broad classes of Neo-Confucian literati, contributing to his political base and further to the balance of power throughout his reign. All in all, Queen Jeonghui's maneuvering stabilized the throne and cemented the foundation of the dynasty.

It is also worthy of note that the queen dowager showed a strong attachment to Buddhism throughout the period of her regency in spite of the official policy to promote Confucianism. The courtiers repeatedly opposed her attempts to import Buddhist scriptures from China. They also argued against her visit to the palace temple. Court annals quote them as saying: "Why should we seek more Buddhist scriptures from China when we cannot but say the Sutra Publishing Institute (*Gangyeong Dogam*) already keeps too many of them? In your early days on the throne, Your Majesty ordered to remove the temple on the palace grounds and ban the people from becoming monks and nuns. Therefore, we as Your Majesty's subjects believe the unnecessary sutra publication projects should also be put to an end. We wonder when the projects for securing and publishing Buddhist scriptures would be suspended."

The king replied, "The Great Dowager Queen is seeking the sutras for King Sejo." He also said, "I hope to collect a complete set of Buddhist scriptures during my lifetime. What would be the harm of buying more of them now?" He is again quoted as saying, "How could I say anything when the Great Dowager Queen is seeking sutras for King Sejo? But I also think what you are saying is right, so I will again discuss this matter with courtiers." These records show Queen Dowager Jeonghui's commitment to Buddhist projects and response from officials at the three major royal advisory bodies, or *Samsa*.

The queen dowager also held rites to pray for peace of the soul of King Sejo and longevity of King Seongjong at Byeoksongjeong pavilion on the grounds of Seonggyungwan, the National Confucian Academy, provoking attacks from its students. She probably attempted to elicit spiritual assistance from Buddhism as the realistic Confucian thought denied life after death, thus shunning prayers to seek blessings for the living or redemption of the dead. Women of the Joseon royal family believed that their duties from one generation to the next included praying for the health and longevity of kings and crown princes and peace in the royal household. Particularly, Queen Jeonghui must have felt deep anxiety as well as moral responsibility since her husband usurped the throne from his nephew through bloodbaths.

Queen Jeonghui left a great lesson by demonstrating outstanding political ability to rule through harmony and flexibility rather than division and conflict. Instead of asserting dogmatic views, she embraced a wide spectrum of forces to gain a broad perspective to see the whole political structure. She also acted boldly when necessary.

Queen Munjeong
Also a Powerful Regent

Joseon's second most renowned female regent was Queen Munjeong (1501-1565) who ruled on behalf of her son, King Myeongjong. She was the daughter of Yun Ji-im, minister for royal family affairs. She became the third consort to King Jungjong in 1517, after his second consort, Queen Janggyeong, died seven days after delivering a son who later had a brief reign as King Injong.

The death of Queen Janggyeong provoked a dispute in court over how to choose her successor. Some insisted that the king's deposed first wife, Queen Dangyeong, should be reinstated; some advocated investing royal concubine Lady Gyeongbin who was the mother of Prince Bokseong, as the queen consort; and others insisted on looking for a new queen. The last opinion prevailed and Queen Dowager Jeonghyeon selected Yun Ji-im's daughter.

Queen Munjeong was strongly supported by Yun Im, elder brother of Queen Janggyeong. She was a smart and thoughtful girl. From the age of 11, since her mother passed away, she had to look after her younger siblings. When she entered the palace, the Joseon court was torn by conflict among the king's many concubines, in-laws and meritorious courtiers. Though she was still young, Queen Munjeong did not waste her time looking up to the king in the conflict-ridden palace. Instead she honed her political skill reading history books such as Sima Qian's *Historical Records* (*Shiji*, or *Sagi* in Korean).

She earnestly wished to have a son of her own though the king had a son by Queen Janggyeong, who was already named heir presumptive. In 1534 she finally delivered a son, Prince Gyeongwon. When King Injong ascended the throne following the death of King Jungjong in 1544, Queen Munjeong called him to her place and lamented, "Now I am afraid I can't even protect my lonely son. I can see our road ahead is pitch black as the relatives of your deceased mother will certainly rise to power. I think I had better move into a temple and devote myself to praying for the soul of the deceased king."

The tender-hearted Injong was shocked. He knelt down before her pavilion apologizing for his impiety. Exhausted from funeral rites for the late king, he fell ill and died the next year at 31.

Anticipating his death, King Injong said to his subjects: "I am very ill and I don't think I will ever get well. I have no son, and I and Prince Gyeongwon are the late king's only legitimate sons. Prince Gyeongwon, at his young age, is bright and mature enough to be entrusted with events following my death. Therefore, I want you all to assist him to be enthroned as next king." But King Injong's orders on his half brother's succession effectively meant the demise of his uncle, Yun Im, and the rise of Prince Gyeongwon's uncle, Yun Won-hyeong. King Injong was never free from the influence of powerful courtiers during his eight-month reign. His death signaled an instant shift of power from the so-called "Big Yun" faction to "Small Yun" faction, which led to the purge of 1545, known as *eulsa sahwa*.

When her son, Prince Gyeongwon, ascended the throne at the age of 12 in 1545, Queen Munjeong embarked on her "rule from behind the bamboo screen" and wielded enormous power throughout her regency over eight years. Her younger brother Yun Won-hyeong eliminated his political opponents through the purge of 1545, in which many

Neo-Confucian literati were killed. It was different from the three previous purges, however. This time round, the Neo-Confucian literati were sacrificed in a bloody power struggle among relatives of two queens rather than their confrontation with the powerful mainstream faction of meritorious officials.

Yun Won-hyeong and his in-law group led government with stalwart support from the queen dowager. At first Yun and his minions allied with the mainstream meritorious courtiers. Once they took control of the government, however, they eliminated the mainstream courtiers to build a powerful ruling system of their own. They caused many problems by monopolizing the rights to personnel appointment and wealth and ruthlessly persecuting opponents. They eventually fell victim to attacks from the Neo-Confucian literati, who demanded broader political participation. Particularly, the policies accepting the separation of the two Buddhist sects emphasizing scriptural study (Gyojong) and Zen meditation (Seonjong) respectively, and use of the official seal of the Office of Royal Estate (*Naesusa*) drew strong criticism. They were perceived as tools to pursue the personal interests of royal in-laws. Thus the power base of Queen Munjeong and her relatives gradually eroded.

Queen Munjeong's pro-Buddhist policy provoked widespread resistance. The anti-Buddhist policy initiated during the final years of the Goryeo Dynasty and inherited by founders of the Joseon Dynasty was not a sheer ideological or academic movement. It rather represented the governing policy to stabilize the state finance by seizing the enormous property of Buddhist temples that had been secularized as a political force. Buddhism appeared to regain some strength under a few early Joseon kings but in fact it barely avoided total extinction.

The anti-Buddhist policy of Joseon consisted of restructuring temples and confiscating of temple estates; implementing and abolishing the licensed monk system and the state examinations for recruiting monks; integrating different sects regardless of their doctrinal characteristics; and prohibiting cremation and other Buddhist customs. In particular, the abolition of monk licenses and the state examinations for monks signified a complete withdrawal of government interest and support for Buddhism. The social status of monks further deteriorated and, in the 16th century, after the licensing system ended under King Seongjong, illegal monks caused various social problems. But the majority of these monks were peasants alienated from land ownership due to the ever expanding land holdings by the meritorious elite.

The pro-Buddhist policy of the queen dowager and her powerful relatives could have stemmed from their personal faith. At the same time, though, they were also under pressure to resolve social problems derived from the rising number of monks exempted from military duties and corvee labor. But it seemed obvious that the queen dowager and her supporters were unable to resolve the problems on their own. So they looked for a capable leader of the Buddhist world. The queen dowager and the monk Bou met under these circumstances.

Bou could realize his dreams of revitalizing Buddhism under absolute support of Queen Munjeong. In 1551, despite strong objection from Confucian courtiers, he separated the two major sects, Seonjong and Gyojong, naming Bongeunsa and Bongseonsa as their respective head temples. The state examinations for monks were revived in 1552, to recruit such prominent monks as Hyujeong (Great Master Seosan) and Yujeong (Great Master Samyeong). These measures were initiated as part of efforts to resolve social problems caused by illegal monks dodging their duties to the state. But the predominantly Confucian court suspected the measures were a means to promote Buddhism. The queen dowager went further to appoint Bou as the minister of military affairs. Students at Seonggyungwan, the National Confucian Academy, walked out of classes in protest.

It may be assumed that, as an ambitious woman with no political or educational background, Queen Munjeong had no other choice but to solicit support from her blood kin. Riding the waves of political turmoil, she might also have found considerable peace in her heart by holding Buddhist rites to pray for her only son, King Myeongjong, and prosperity of the royal family. Nonetheless, her explicitly pro-Buddhist policy was seen to disrupt the ideological platform of the Confucian-oriented Joseon court. The rampant corruption and irregularities committed by her relatives seriously undermined her political base as well.

Regency by a queen dowager was intended to protect the throne with official political participation of the king's mother. But the impact on state governance differed depending on the circumstances not to mention the individual position of each regent. Queen Jeonghui governed rather smoothly and efficiently to pave the road for her grandson, King Seongjeong, to elicit broad support from varied political forces to improve the governing system and stabilize the dynasty. Queen Munjeong also was smart and had charismatic leadership qualities. But her outright support to Buddhism impeded the governing principles of the Confucian dynasty. She invited biting criticism for her arbitrary rule, excessive pressure on the king, overdependence on her relatives, and exclusive control of personnel and financial administration.

In both cases, however, the queen dowagers' regency protected the throne and thereby contributed to sustaining the dynasty for over five centuries by entrusting the most senior member of the royal household with state affairs before the boy kings grew old enough to rule.

Lady Saimdang's Life and Artistic Achievements

More than a few women of the Joseon Dynasty overcame the confinements of a Confucian-oriented patriarchal society to make notable achievements in cultural fields. Sin Saimdang (1504-1551) is most widely recognized for her literary and artistic talents among these remarkable women.

Lady Saimdang almost perfectly carried out her filial duties to her parents as well as to her parents-in-law and her roles as a faithful wife and a wise and virtuous mother. Thus she achieved utmost harmony within her family, but she was not content with her roles as a woman. She overcame the social restrictions of her time by demonstrating wisdom and individuality through the arts, ultimately contributing greatly to the cultural development of Joseon. Moreover, her unceasing efforts to exploit her literary and artistic talents in leading an independent life in her own way, laid out a path for Korean women to follow even today.

Saimdang was the second of five daughters of a relatively well-to-do nobleman. Her childhood name was In-seon, and she earned her pen name Saimdang. Her father, Sin Myeong-hwa, a literary licentiate (*jinsa*), had passed a lower level civil service examination. Unlike other men of his time, he apparently believed in gender equality. While

A folding screen with embroidered design of grass and insects, supposedly made by Sin Saimdang (Dong-a University Museum)

most young girls of her days were not given an education, Saimdang's father taught her how to read and write. His instructions after his death included an equal division of his property among his five daughters. Later, Saimdang also divided her family property among all her seven children.

Saimdang was known as a "prodigy" at an early age. She taught herself how to paint and began to elicit praise for her works when she was only seven years old. Later, she also exhibited prominent skills in writing poetry, calligraphy and embroidery.

When she was 19, Saimdang married Yi Won-su. The couple lived with her family in Gangneung along the east cost and then moved to Seoul after a three-year mourning period for Saimdang's father. Saimdang supported her mother with great devotion during the mourning period and even after moving to Seoul, she traveled quite frequently between Seoul and Gangneung to visit her mother. Saimdang is known to have been a wise spouse for her weak-hearted husband, carefully assisting him so he could maintain his reputation as a scholar with an upright mind. She successfully educated all her seven children. Three of them earned fame as scholars and artists. Her third

son is Yi I, one of the most revered scholars in Korean history, better known by his pen name Yulgok. Her eldest daughter Maechang was a famous embroiderer, and her fourth son U was a noted writer and calligrapher.

Saimdang took her motifs — landscapes, flowers, fruits, insects and birds — from nature around her and depicted their subtle beauty to extreme details. In his *Miscellany from a Storyteller* (*Paegwan japgi*), famous scholar Eo Suk-gwon wrote: "Lady Sin (Saimdang) learned painting from an early age. Her grapevines and landscapes were so exquisite that critics said she came next only to An Gyeon. So how can we take lightly of her paintings simply because they were done by a woman? Also, how can we say it (painting) is not an appropriate job for women?"

There are various interesting episodes attesting to her ingenious talent. One episode goes that her style was so realistic that when she painted cucumbers or eggplants, rats would try to bite them. In a more famous story, Saimdang instantly saved a neighboring woman from embarrassment when her skirt was stained while helping prepare a feast at her home. When the woman seemed at a loss over a stain on her new skirt, Saimdang promptly brought her brush and painted gorgeous grapevines on her skirt, amazing everyone around.

Also of particular note is that most of her poems handed down until today are about her love for her mother. The following are among the most widely known pieces:

Leaving white-haired Mother in Gangneung,
With my forlorn heart I head to Seoul.
Turning back awhile to the village in north, I see
White clouds drift over green mountains in sunset.

— From "Beholding Home from Daegwallyeong Pass"

Every night I pray to the moon
Longing to see her while alive.

— From "Missing My Mother"

Heo Nanseolheon
a Short-Lived Literary Genius

Heo Nanseolheon was born in 1563 in the eastern coastal city of Gangneung as the youngest daughter of Heo Yeop, a renowned man of letters and leader of the Easterners (Dongin) faction. Her native place, Chodang-ri, became widely known for the Chodang bean curd, which was developed by her father while he was serving as magistrate of Gangneung.

Heo Yeop had three sons and three daughters. All of his three sons — Seong, Bong and Gyun — had great literary talent and so did Nanseolheon, whose childhood name was Cho-hui. She grew up in an affluent environment.

Her family moved to Seoul when Nanseolheon was five years old. At first she studied reading by herself overhearing the lessons given to her brothers. As she displayed extraordinary talent, however, her elder brother Bong arranged poetry lessons for her and her younger brother Gyun under Yi Dal, the most famous lyricist and Daoist scholar at the time.

Her father had studied under Seo Gyeong-deok, a renowned Confucian scholar well versed in Daoist philosophy, and all her siblings read extensively about Daoism. In such a family environment the young Nanseolheon wrote scores of poems on Daoist themes.

In my dream last night I climbed Mt. Bongnae,
I rode on a dragon back rolled in waves.
The immortals with blue bead sticks
received me warmly from the lotus peak.
Far away under my feet, the East Sea
seemed as tiny as a wine cup.
On a flower petal a phoenix was blowing a flute,
Silently the moonlight beamed on a golden water jar.

— From "Encounter" (*Gamu*), a poem by Heo Nanseolheon

At seven, Nanseolheon wrote a ceremonial invocation on raising the main ridge beam for the White Jade Pavilion (Baegongnu) at the imaginary Palace of the Moon (Gwanghanjeon), where Daoist fairies are believed to reside. Her poem drew admiration as it showed an incredible scope of knowledge and poetic imagery for a young girl.

Sunshades made of assorted jewels flutter in the air,
Like clouds curtains are draped in gorgeous colors,
In the sun the silver attics shine,
Columns of twilight have eluded the worldly maze.
A palace of bead tiles has been created because
the voice of immortals cannot revive the energies.
Already a mystic blue dragon has spouted out haze
and built a palace of cinnamon wood.

At such a young age, Nanseolheon could already depict the imaginary world of Daoist immortals so vividly and splendidly. She often discussed poetry with her younger brother Gyun and coached him on poetry writing when he was about to take the state examinations for civil service. She demonstrated her rich imagination in the following poem:

Blue as jade was the clear autumn lake,
Amid the lush lotus I tied a peony boat.
Across the water meeting my lover,
I plucked a lotus flower and threw it to him.
Fretting if anyone might have seen,
Much of the day I blushed.

She was as much romantic as intellectual. But happiness eluded her. Her married life was miserable. Her husband, Kim Seong-rip, a boy from the powerful Andong Kim clan, was a womanizer and her mother-in-law treated her coldly. Her two children died prematurely and the third died unborn to inflict even deeper wounds on her heart.

A strongly self-conscious woman, Nanseolheon grew skeptical about society and her husband. First of all, she questioned why she was born in Joseon of all countries in the whole world. Second, why was she born as a woman only to experience the sorrow of being childless? Third, why, at 14, did she become the wife of Kim Seong-rip among all the countless men in the world? Her agony continued to deepen as she resisted the various ethical restraints confining women, such as the male superiority over women, the Three Obediences and Seven Evils. She vented her inner conflict through her great poems.

Nanseolheon grew up reading many books about Daoism. She believed there was the utopian world of immortals in heaven. In some of her poems she depicted the difficulties she faced in her life in this world, such as her loneliness caused by her unfaithful husband, her sadness over losing her children, and her worries about her brother in exile. In a greater number of other poems, however, she expressed her unworldly yearnings for the Daoist fairyland or her wishes to become an immortal.

She freely dealt with a great diversity of themes. She wrote about her candid thought about love and the fleeting power of aristocrats. She even described the exhausting life of poor women in remarkable detail to show the painful reality of the masses. She internalized the sufferings of the underprivileged classes, particularly those of women, critically scrutinizing the unreasonable norms and class discrimination in a feudalistic society.

With an appearance as good as anyone,
I also have fine skills for sewing and weaving.
As I was born and grew up in a poor family,
No matchmaking granny would notice me.

— "Elegy of a Poor Woman"

On the day a noble family thrives
with power raging like wild flames,
Music resounds around lofty pavilions
while poor people in rags starve,
with their hungry stomachs empty,
their homes reduced to ruins.
Only when their family declines in a day
would noblemen be envious of the people.
The cycle of rise and fall turns with time
who would dare disobey the law of heaven?

— "Encounter"

Nanseolheon had deep sympathy toward poor people. She clearly expressed her humanistic and socialist ideals as an intellectual member of society, while writing about love and nature as well.

On her deathbed, however, she made a will that "all my poems would be burned so that no other women might become unhappy writing poetry like me." She died at 27, after burning all of her books and her poems that filled her place.

Her younger brother, Heo Gyun, salvaged some of her works from the flames and had them published in Ming China some years later. Her poetry collection became famous in China and was later published in Japan as well. She posthumously earned international fame as a poet representing the 16th century Joseon.

Nanseolheon realized that women's social position had to be improved if their ability and role were to be duly recognized by society. Therefore, she tried to overthrow the Confucian social order based on gender discrimination. In spite of her struggle as an intellectual who thought ahead of time, she eventually failed to overcome the institutional barriers. But she did not completely run aground. Instead, she sublimated her inner conflict and frustration through her poetry.

Her pioneering spirit remains palpable as a valuable legacy of her era, conveying a powerful message of courage and hope to women through succeeding generations.

Lady Jang Fulfills the Spirit of Practical Learning

Born to a noble family of reputed scholarly tradition in Andong, Lady Jang authored the oldest known cookbook in Korean language. *Gourmet Recipes* (*Eumsik dimibang*), written in the classical palace style of Korean script, Hangeul, appeared around 1670. An important historical source on ancient Korean living culture, the book contains recipes for various dishes, alcoholic drinks and other beverages, and fermented foods, mostly handed down in the Gyeongsang region or devised by the author. The title literally means the "ways to discern tastes of food."

Lady Jang's handwritten copy has two titles — *Eumsik dimibang* in Korean and *Gyugon sieuibang* in Chinese. The Chinese title, meaning a "lady's guidebook," was probably added by her husband or some descendants who might have thought that the book needed a Chinese title to have the proper authority or formality. *Gyugon* means a lady's room in the inner quarters of an aristocratic residence.

Jang's work is significant in that she recorded native Korean recipes, unlike earlier cookbooks or food guides such as *Assorted Recipes for Fine Food (Suun japbang)*, written in Chinese characters by a male scholar quoting frequently from Chinese sources. She probably intended her work in the vernacular script to teach traditional Korean

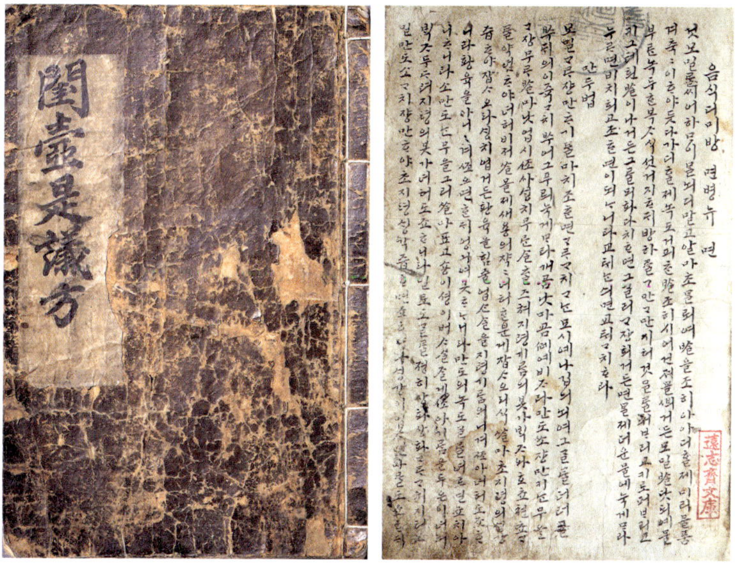

Gourmet Recipes (*Eumsik dimibang*) (Kyungpook National University Central Library)

cuisine to posterity.

Gourmet Recipes consists of two parts: Part One introduces recipes for a total of 93 kinds of food and Part Two has recipes for 51 kinds of alcoholic beverages and vinegars. Part One explains cooking methods for 11 kinds of main dishes including noodles and dumplings; 55 kinds of side dishes including soups, broiled dishes, stews, stuffed dishes, fresh or parboiled vegetables, stir-fried, pan-fried or deep-fried dishes, grilled dishes, raw meat or fish, and salted seafoods; and 25 kinds of deserts and beverages, including rice cakes, fried and honeyed cookies and pastries. The recipes, regarding highly of taste and nutrition, were mostly used in local upper-class families of Gyeongsang Province around the 17th century.

Among notable points is that red pepper was yet to be used in the southeastern region whereas it was introduced in *Topical Discourses of Jibong* (*Jibong yuseol*) written in 1614 by Yi Su-gwang. Black pepper, mustard, scallion and ginger were instead used for spicy condiments. Ginger was more profusely used than garlic for many dishes.

It also is worthy of note that dog meat was widely eaten along with wild boar and pheasant meat. Particularly, pheasant meat was used for making kimchi and no less interesting is that bear's paw dishes are discussed here and there. Given that storing food was not an easy task without refrigeration means, the book explains sun drying, smoking and salting methods in considerable detail.

Lady Jang was not only a food expert but an able home manager equipped with academic and literary talents. Her tomb stele has an inscription reading, "In retrospect, Madame was peerless in the level of her academic knowledge and virtuous deeds." She practiced the spirit of Neo-Confucianism and Practical Learning (*Sirhak*) in her everyday life.

Jang was born in 1598 as the only child of Jang Heung-hyo (pen name Gyeongdang). Her father was a prominent scholar who inherited the academic lineage of Yi Hwang, a Confucian sage who is widely known by his pen name Toegye. Her parents educated her with love and discipline and she displayed outstanding academic talent from her early childhood. At 19, she was married to Yi Si-myeong (pen name Seokgye), a student of her father, and lived in Inyang-ri, Yeonghae-myeon, some 200 *li* away from her maiden home.

Yi Si-myeong already had a son and a daughter from his deceased first wife, Lady Kim. Jang devoted herself to educating her stepson, Sang-il, as if he was her own son. She escorted the boy to and from his teacher's house, which was quite far from their home, for five years when he was young. She had six sons and two daughters of her own during her 60-year-long married life and successfully educated all of them. Her three sons — second son Hwi-il, third son Hyeon-il and fourth son Sung-il — became prominent scholars. Particularly, Hyeon-il firmly established the academic tradition of the Toegye school as a regional leader of Neo-Confucian studies. He also served as minister of personnel administration.

Jang taught her children that "she would not consider highly of compliments for their outstanding academic performance but would be truly pleased and remember if her children were praised for a single good deed." It indicates that she asked them to devote themselves to deepening their knowledge and putting academic theories into practice instead of preparations for the state examinations to seek public posts and material wealth. When her father passed away leaving behind his four young children born through his second wife, Lady Jang had them move near her house and looked after them until they all grew up and married. She administered all important events and rituals like ancestral rites and wedding ceremonies of both families — the Andong Jang family of her own and the Jaeryeong Yi family of her husband. She thus made enormous contributions to consolidating the scholarly and moral traditions of both families so they would grow into leaders of the regional academic school.

From modern perspective, Lady Jang's role is highly considered for several reasons.

First, her humanitarian spirit deserves recognition. In her self-realization process, she displayed humane wisdom to look around herself and get along with others in her family and neighborhood.

Second, she had a rational mind to smartly resolve her realistic problems in ways not to depart from the Confucian moral precepts. As the only child of her parents, she smoothly harmonized her duties toward her husband's family and her own, pursuing the continued prosperity of both families, in the patriarchal family and social system regarding married daughters as outsiders.

Third, she had pragmatic values rooted in the reality. Amid poverty in the wake of war, she recorded in detail the cooking materials and methods chosen in consideration of the seasonal and regional characteristics and nutritional value in the vernacular script. Probably she wanted her book to help others find the wisdom of frugality.

Fourth, she pursued harmony and unity in her family structure and human relations. A short poem entitled "Elegy" (*Sosoeum*), written when she was still young, implies the meaning of human existence that can be realized through harmony with nature.

The sound of rain drizzling out of the window,
Gently, gently, it must be the sound of nature.
As I am listening to the sound of nature,
My heart feels like nature as well.

Lady Jang almost perfectly carried out her filial obligations toward her parents and parents-in-law, assisted her husband as a faithful and virtuous wife, and reared her children as a wise and benevolent mother. The Yi family keeps holding memorial rites for her as an ancestor deserving eternal worship.

Fifth, she made an outstanding contribution to the cultural advancement of Joseon. Her academic knowledge and writings were recognized among her contemporaries to be superior to most men of her time and are highly evaluated until today. She has left various writings in Chinese characters, including those written in adroit cursive style, but her *Gourmet Recipes* written in Korean greatly contributed to the development of the vernacular script. The academic community recognizes her as a female heir to the lineage of the Toegye school.

No less significant is that she provided momentum to rediscover other prominent women of Joseon from behind the biased veils of history. She served as a kind of cornerstone for outstanding female scholars and writers of the ensuing centuries to form a proud pedigree of intellectual women. The Ministry of Culture and Tourism named her the "Cultural Figure of the Month" in November 1999. She was the second woman given the title next to Sin Saimdang.

Chapter 8

Women of the Modern Period

Empress Myeongseong Displays Excellent Political Acumen

Yun Hui-sun the First Women's Militia Leader

Founders of the First Modern Women's Association

Park Esther the First Modern Woman Doctor

Hah Ran-sa the First Woman to Attain B.A. in Literature

Yu Gwan-sun a Young Martyr for Independence

Choe Eun-hui the First Woman Journalist

Rha Hye-suk the First Female Western Painter

Park Gyeong-won a Pioneer Woman Aviator

Choe Seung-hui a Legendary Modern Dance Diva

Jeong Chan-yeong a Master of Fine Brush Painting

Jeong Jeong-hwa the Mistress of Provisional Government

Helen Kim the First Female Ph.D. and University President

Han Do-sin the Helpful Wife of an Independence Fighter

Empress Myeongseong Displays Excellent Political Acumen

As for her political intuition and ability, Empress Myeongseong bows to no one among all the queen consorts of the Joseon Dynasty. But historical evaluation of her role has been distorted as much as her life was full of highs and lows. One reason was that women's political participation was not favorably seen from the Confucian historical perspective. Also, her staunch anti-Japanese stance has incited hostile assessments from Japanese academic circles in their attempts to justify Japan's assassination of her from their colonial standpoint.

Empress Myeongseong, or Queen Min (1851-1895), lived during a most tumultuous period in Korean history domestically as well as internationally. The popular forces resisting the institutions of Joseon society were swelling internally, while the Western imperial powers were accelerating their aggressive designs on the Korean peninsula. The nation was under the double burden of undertaking modernization and forestalling foreign invasion.

Queen Min came from the Yeoheung Min clan though her family was in a destitute condition. She was a sixth-generation descendant of Min Yu-jung, the father of Queen Inhyeon, the second consort of King Sukjong. She was born in Yeoju, Gyeonggi Province, as Min Ja-yeong, the only child of Min Chi-rok and his wife, Lady Yi. She lost both her parents at the age of eight and was reared by a relative in Seoul.

Almost an orphan from an impoverished noble family, she reached the position of a queen consort under the political design of her ambitious father-in-law. Regent Heungseon, the father of King Gojong, popularly known as Daewongun, wanted the Mins who had been in the in-law relations with his family for two generations to help expand his political base. Both his mother and his wife were from the same clan. So he hoped that they would assist him in legitimizing his rule while checking the powerful Andong Kim clan, which had wielded enormous power by forming the so-called "in-law governments." He believed that by choosing a queen from a family with insignificant background, he could prevent his in-laws from seizing power.

In 1866, the 16-year-old Min Ja-yeong was picked to be consort to King Gojong, who was a year younger than her. Upon entering the palace, she quickly earned praise from everyone for properly venerating the regent and his wife and behaving nicely toward all other senior members of the royal family and court ladies. But she failed to win the king's love. Reading avidly, the downhearted Ja-yeong bid her time until she could be in a stronger position as queen. She broadly read Chinese classics and history books such as *Notes of Jwa on the Spring and Autumn Annals* (*Chunchu jwassijeon*, or *Chunqiu zuoshizhuan* in Chinese).

But her desperation deepened as Lady Yi, a court lady favored by the king, had a son in 1868. Her sense of crisis grew further as the king and the regent were greatly fond of the boy, Prince Wanhwa, and there were even moves in and outside the palace to formally invest him as crown prince. She found her position seriously threatened. Worse still, her long-awaited first son died five days after birth in 1871.

The queen came to hate the regent even more as she believed her baby son was poisoned by the wild ginseng given to her by the regent.

A portrait of Empress Myeongseong by Gwon O-chang (Memorial Hall of Empress Myeongseong)

She began to approach the king not as a mere woman coveting his love but as a possible political partner because she knew that he now wanted to rule on his own. She started revolting against her father-in-law by taking sides with her husband to instigate the conflict brewing between the father and son.

Daewongun's dogmatic governing system began to weaken in the 1870s, creating a favorable condition for Queen Min's political leap. Opposition forces began to surface as the public opinion grew critical about the regent's mismanagement of major state affairs.

King Gojong lacked an independent political base. Therefore, he probably believed he could use the queen's relatives as his political background to realize direct rule. He also could indirectly attack the regent through the queen when direct assault on his father was condemnable under the Confucian moral principle of filial piety. On the other hand, the regent must have found it difficult to challenge his son face-to-face in view of the Confucian principle of loyalty to the king. Under such circumstances, King Gojong could initially succeed in breaking the political barriers created by his father through Queen Min. In the 1870s, amid the division of national opinion regarding whether to adopt an open-door policy or keep the country shut, he could tackle the pending political questions with support from the queen and her relatives, who were allied with the enlightenment forces.

Queen Min continued to exert tremendous influence on King Gojong's decision making on state affairs. She emphasized introducing modern Western technologies and culture to build a strong nation. Foreigners' records of the Joseon court at this period unanimously say that Queen Min was considerate, smart and more capable than Gojong. English traveller Isabella B. Bishop, the author of *Korea and Her Neighbors*, wrote in her accounts of the last of her four meetings with the Korean queen: "On each occasion I was impressed with the grace and charming manner of the Queen, her thoughtful kindness, her singular intelligence and force, and her remarkable conversational power, even through an interpreter. I could not but be surprised at her extraordinary political influence and her coordinating means on the King and many other problems."

Amid the severe contest of power between Qing and Japan, Queen Min checked them through a foreign policy seeking balance of power. She adopted an even stronger pro-Russian and anti-Japanese policy as Japan tightened its control over internal political matters in the wake of its victory in the Sino-Japanese War in 1894. Consequently, Japan came to consider the queen as the greatest obstacle in its annexation of Korea. Under a carefully wrought scheme, Japanese troops and assassins invaded the royal palace to seize power on an early morning in October 1895, nominally empowering Daewongun. Queen Min was brutally murdered and her body was burned on the palace grounds. She was 45.

Queen Min played an important role in preventing direct clashes between King Gojong and his regent father amid the extreme political turmoil of the late 19th century. She used her political base to assist the king to strengthen his power. Cleverly handling external relations with her shrewd intelligence, she also succeeded remarkably in keeping Japan's imperial aggression at bay.

Queen Min was an ambitious and capable woman. But her active political participation may rather be seen as the outcome of her efforts to cope with the peculiar circumstances in the royal household surrounding the conflict between the king and his father. She probably tried to be a buffer to support her tender-hearted husband, who could not realize his wishes for direct rule due to his overly ambitious father.

Queen Min's political role clearly differed from those of the royal in-laws of the Andong Kim clan or Regent Heungseon himself in that she never attempted to override the king and garner absolute power for herself. She instead assisted the king, assuming the role of his political

Seal of Empress Myeongseong (National Museum of Korea)

base. In other words, she created a new political force uniting the king with her relatives to fortify his power.

As a central figure of the political scene, Queen Min exerted great influence on King Gojong's decision making on state affairs but no conflict surfaced between the king and the queen in the process. They trusted each other and had same opinions. After the military mutiny of 1882, or *imo gullan*, in particular, King Gojong increasingly tended to rely on Queen Min and her political role grew even more active.

Unlike the regent, who clung to a conservative position, Queen Min pursued reforms in alliance with her relatives. She properly understood the historical stream and adopted an open-door policy, asserting that the nation should learn new technologies from abroad and positively accommodate modern Western culture for self-fortification. She thoroughly kept the Japanese in check. Her foreign policy deserves positive evaluation in that she struggled to retain independence by balancing the interests of foreign powers against each other. Japan was more eager than others to infiltrate Korean politics, economy and society in general with its tenacious territorial ambition over the Korean peninsula.

Nevertheless, there were clear limitations to Queen Min's political role. Regardless of the justification of her political participation, she had to waste considerable energy to overcome negative public opinion and resistance toward her public role in the male-centered Confucian monarchy. Queen Min's brilliant intelligence and political insight could have contributed more efficiently to the modernization of Korea if King Gojong was able to demonstrate his political ability more boldly.

In the wake of her assassination, the Korean peninsular turned into an arena of heated contest for privileged concessions among foreign powers. Ten years later, Japan succeeded in making Korea its protectorate. These events have crucial implications for estimating the political position of Queen Min, whose tragic end foretold the fate of her country.

Yun Hui-sun the First Women's Militia Leader

An ordinary housewife, Yun Hui-sun (1860-1935) organized a women's militia group to save the nation from an emergency state after Japanese assassins killed Queen Min. She urged other housewives to stand up and fight. She trained them in military skills and led fund-raising campaigns to support *euibyeong*, or the "righteous armies."

Yun was born as the daughter of Yun Ik-sang in Seoul. She was brilliant and high-spirited, and filial toward her parents from an early age. At 16 she was married to Yu Jae-won (pen name Hangjae), of Gajeong-ri, Chuncheon, Gangwon Province. He was the son of Yu Hong-seok (pen name Oedang), a local militia commander.

Yu Hong-seok was a reputed scholar who had studied under Yi Hang-ro. His worries about the growing confusion engulfing the nation prompted him to organize a militia. Yun was deeply devoted to her father-in-law and faithfully carried out her obligations toward her husband's relatives and ancestors, while treating her inferiors with affection. She properly handled all household affairs, contributing to harmony in the family and drawing praise from her father-in-law.

When the government issued an order to cut topknots in the wake of Queen Min's assassination in 1895, the public reacted with vehement opposition. Yu Hong-seok set out to engage in a militia-led war with his second cousin, Yu In-seok. Yun beseeched her father-in-law to take her with them, but he adamantly refused. After he left, Yun made an altar in a mountain behind her house and prayed everyday at 3 a.m. for his victory. She offered her prayers before a clean bowl of fresh water after taking a bath.

She also sent letters declaring war to Japanese army commanders and warnings to Korean troops serving the Japanese as their agents. She composed battle songs to encourage other women to help Korean militia, of which nine pieces remain today. They include "Song of Women Militia" (*Ansaram euibyeong ga*), "A Soldier's Song" (*Byeongjeong norae*), "A Battle Song of Militia" (*Euibyeong gunga*) and "A Song of My Tough Life" (*Sinse taryeong*). She also wrote essays like "Look, Japanese Commander!" and "I Warn to Barbarians!" The lyric of the "Song of Women Militia" goes:

However strong and prosperous
the Japanese may be,
If united, we can defeat them easily.
Let the world say we are mere women,
But how can we not know love for the country
Without a country, any use for man or woman?
Let us march out to join the righteous army,
Let us help our militia troops.
If they are seized by beasts,
Would the Japanese ever save them?
Let us help our militia troops.
Success for us, hurrah for our nation!
Ten thousand hurrahs for women!

Militia troops resisted fiercely across the country when the Protectorate Treaty was forcibly signed in 1905 and the Korean army

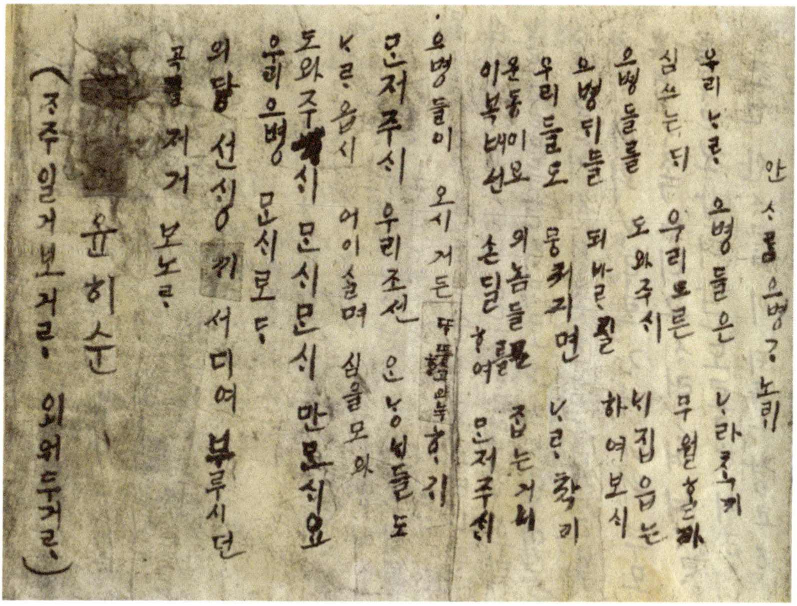

The lyric of "The Song of Women Militia" written by Yun Hui-sun (Independence Hall of Korea)

was disbanded following the forced abdication of King Gojong in 1907. Yu Hong-seok gathered his comrades again to raise militia troops. Some 600 young men had military training in Yeounae village, along with other villagers including women, children and old men, before engaging in a battle at Jugil-ri, Gapyeong.

At this time Yun organized a women's militia band. Some 30 women, including the wife of Yu In-seok, volunteered for military training in the inner valley of their village. They joined in battle and undertook supportive duties such as cooking and producing gunpowder. They also collected donations from other women to raise funds for militia campaign.

Yu Hong-seok was injured during the battle at Jugil-ri. And Korea was annexed by Japan while he was trying to put together remnants of the defeated troops for another round of resistance after treating his wounds at a relative's house at Jecheon. Deeply frustrated, he decided to commit suicide. But he was persuaded to move to Liaodong in southern Manchuria to prepare for further resistance against Japan. His family was to follow him after disposing of their property, but on the day after her father-in-law left, Japanese troops raided their home and captured Yun and her son, Yu Don-sang.

They threatened her to force her to disclose where her father-in-law was, but she glared at them and shouted, "I can't reveal to my enemy even if I knew the whereabouts of my father-in-law who is struggling for the liberation of our nation." As the Japanese beat her son, threatening to kill him, she bellowed, "It's no use if you kill my little son. How do you expect me to trade my son for such a great independence fighter like my father-in-law?" The Japanese troops retreated as they were impressed by her valor. Her family immediately left for Liaodong.

Her father-in-law passed away in December 1913, two years after their arrival in Manchuria. Yu In-seok also passed away in 1915. On October 2 of the same year, her husband died as well, after Japanese police had severely tortured him. Nonetheless, Yun was unflinching. While holding funerals for her father-in-law and her husband, she continued to support the militiamen and led the women troops training for military skills and attacking Japanese camps. She encouraged them to form family units to train harder and make greater contributions to independence campaign.

Yun was determined to devote herself to independence movement along with her son to avenge her family and her country. While helping the independence army, she saved Korean troops captured by the Japanese and hid them in a secret cave. She fed them while she was starving.

In 1935 her son was captured by the Japanese in Fushun and martyred in July of the same year. Overcome with grief, Yun died 11 days later, leaving instructions for her descendants in an essay, "A Record of My life" (*Ilsaengnok*).

The women's militia organized by Yun Hui-sun was the first female military force in Korea. Their mantle and spirit passed on to women's anti-Japanese organizations forming part of the armed resistance during the colonial period. Yun's "Song of Women Militia" was the first militia song written in Korean and the first song written by a female militia. Though it lacked form and style, the lyric conveys an honest and familiar feeling. It consists mostly of Korean words appropriate for rallying and awaking the masses.

Yun may seem to have been moved by her conservative views to participate in nationalist movement. But her militia activities should be seen to have embodied modern feminist values that may well be inherited by contemporary women for the following reasons.

First, she had a humanitarian spirit. Her selfless support for militia was derived from her love for her family and neighbors and her love for her country and nation. She gave away everything she possessed to others, showing a beautiful example of self-sacrifice needed for building a humanitarian society.

Second, she had a rational spirit. With her conviction that gender distinction should not bar women from fighting for national independence, she urged women to assume an active role in nationalist struggle and thereby awakened them to the meaning of their existence. Through division of role and cooperation, she could help bolster resistence against Japanese colonial rule.

Third, she had a nationalist spirit. She resisted the Japanese scheme to occupy Korea with all her might. She sacrificed herself for independence movement with her noble spirit of protecting the national identity of the Korean people.

Fourth, she had a feminist spirit. With her belief that women can become leading players of history, she presented positive and active images of women breaking gender barriers.

In recognition of her contribution to independence campaign, the Ministry of Patriots and Veterans Affairs awarded her the Patriotism Medal of the Order of Merit for National Foundation in 1991. Her remains were repatriated to be buried in Gwancheon-ri, Nam-myeon, Chuncheon County, Gangwon Province, in 1994.

Founders of the First Modern Women's Association

Korea's first modern women's organization was launched in December 1898. Chanyanghoe, literally the "association for support and nurture," was founded in Seoul by women with enlightened thoughts from various social backgrounds. Their primary objective was to establish a school for women. The association thrived, though briefly. Records indicate that it had some 400 members and each meeting drew as many as 100 observers. Its staff included Yi Yangseongdang, Kim Yanghyeondang and Go Jeonggildang.

Yi Yangseongdang, president of the association, was a woman from a noble family in Bukchon, the upper-class residential area in northern Seoul. She is known to have been well educated. She was an excellent public speaker. Kim Yanghyeondang, vice president, was a gentle and well-mannered woman who originally came from Pyongyang. She had no children and lived alone after her husband died. She had academic talent and well versed in modern thoughts. She had many friends among aristocratic women in Bukchon. Go Jeonggildang, a clerk, was born to a Korean family that became naturalized citizens of Russia after emigrating from Hamgyeong Province. Tongnip Sinmun (The Independent) described her as "an extraordinary woman speaking Russian and Chinese fluently." She was mainly responsible for organization of the association.

As such, Chanyanghoe was led mostly by intellectual women from an aristocratic residential area in Seoul, who either had lived abroad or had contacts with modern culture. Among its members were graduates of schools founded by foreign missionaries, commoners and *gisaeng*, the traditional artist entertainers.

One reason that the association was able to recruit so many members was that the number of women who received modern education had increased since the opening of Ewha Haktang, the first modern school for women, in 1886, and other missionary schools thereafter. Secondly, the mass media, including the Tongnip Sinmun, urged women to awaken and cultivate themselves so they could play proper roles in society and improve their social position. Thirdly, an enlightening atmosphere was spreading among the noble classes with conservative backgrounds to increase realization that the nation needed to educate women to achieve modernization.

"Circular on Women's Rights" (*Yeokwon tongmun*) published by two newspapers, the Hwangseong Sinmun on September 8, 1898 and the Tongnip Sinmun on the next day, was the first declaration of women's rights in Korea and the start of women's movement to secure educational rights. Chanyanghoe had its first official meeting on September 25, 1898 at the house of Hong Sosa in Seung-dong. Some 150 members and observers gathered at the meeting, where the declaration was read.

The circular was not simply aimed at establishing a school for women. It also intended to achieve gender equality based on the Western concept of human rights endowed by God on every person. It asserted that women had an equal place in the national march toward enlightened politics and civilization; women had an equal right to have an occupation and to work; and women should be able to cultivate themselves with equal access to education.

Unlike similar declarations in other countries, the Korean women's first proclamation of their rights singularly emphasized women's educational rights to destroy the traditional perception that men should study but it would be better for women to remain uneducated. Therefore, it even became known as a "circular on establishing a women's school." It called for modern academic education for women to nurture them as modern citizens with an independent personality.

Chanyanghoe actively campaigned for the establishment of a public school for women on the grounds that the government should bear the responsibility to educate women as dutiful citizens loyal to their king and their country. On October 13, 1898, some 100 members presented a written appeal for creating a public school for women to Emperor Gojong from the gate of Deoksu Palace. Emperor Gojong immediately replied that he would instruct the Ministry of Education to take appropriate measures. He was also interested in women's education and had encouraged educational projects of missionaries by conferring the name of Ewha Haktang.

The emperor's response, however, was not sufficient by itself to build a school. The proposal required cabinet discussion. The Chanyanghoe members were not aware of the procedure and wrote again to the minister of education a week later, pushing him to put the emperor's response into practice. But there were no signs that the government would open a school until the end of that year.

Chanyanghoe recruited students, expecting that a public school would be established by the end of February 1899. Frustrated by the government's lukewarm attitude, however, they opened Sunseong Women's School in Eoeui-dong (or Neuritgol) in Seoul on February 26, 1899, with some 30 students enrolled. They planned to run the school "until a public school is formally founded." It was the first school for Korean women established by Koreans, especially by Korean women.

The school offered an elementary curriculum for students aged 7 to 13. It used textbooks designated by the Ministry of Education, but because of its abrupt opening, it initially lacked enough teachers and class preparation was inadequate. According to its "academic regulations," the school was to offer elementary and secondary curriculums. The elementary course included ethics, reading, calligraphy, arithmetic and sewing; and the secondary course would have ethics, reading, calligraphy, arithmetic, composition, sewing, geography, history, science and Korean.

Chanyanghoe appointed Kim Yanghyeondang as head mistress. Go Jeonggildang was the only full-time teacher, and some foreign wives, mostly missionaries who were proficient in Korean and Chinese characters, volunteered as teachers. Go Jeonggildang taught *Thousand Character Classic* (*Cheonjamun*), *Lesser Learning* (*Sohak*) and *The Nineteenth Century*: *A History* (*Taeseo sinsa*, or *Taixi xinshi* in Chinese, translated from the original written by British missionary Robert Mackenzie), as well as the popular Korean primer *Children's Reader* (*Dongmong seonseup*). Sewing was taught with a sewing machine for the first time.

Financial difficulty was the greatest problem they faced in running the school. Due to its waning activity, Chanyanghoe discontinued its financial support to the school in the latter half of 1899. Kim Yanghyeondang eventually ran the school, meeting its expenses out of her own pocket and teaching classes. She made all-out efforts to keep the school open, while appealing to the Ministry of Education to turn it into a public school as soon as possible. She once took her students to the ministry and had them demonstrate their reading ability before the minister.

Before her death in March 1903, Kim said: "As a woman, I have prayed day and night to the gods of heaven and earth so as to give a civilized education to women of my country like those in other countries. Unfortunately, however, I am not destined to live long and am soon going to the nine heavens. I am worried who will educate these students after my death."

Sunseong Women's School failed to provide a good education amid financial hardship, though it contributed greatly to the social campaign to establish schools for women. While its founders fell short of achieving their initial goal of opening a public school, they awakened the government and society from their indifference to women's education and increased public awareness to the issue.

Park Esther the First Modern Woman Doctor

The first female practitioner of Western medicine in Korea was Park Esther (1876-1910). She was born Kim Jeom-dong, the fourth daughter of Kim Hong-taek, of a Gwangsan Kim clan. Her mother was from a Yeonan Yi clan. She was Christened Esther and later adopted her husband's family name Park after marriage.

Park was one of early students of Ewha Haktang, the first school for young women in Korea founded by American Methodist missionary Mary F. Scranton in May 1886. Park entered the school in November of the same year under influence of her father, who worked for another American missionary, the Rev. Henry G. Appenzeller. In that year she was baptized at Jeongdong Church, the predecessor of today's Jeongdong (Chungdong) Methodist Church, which was founded by Appenzeller. She was very talented and particularly good at English. So she was picked as interpreter for Rosetta Sherwood Hall, a teacher at Ewha Haktang and physician at Bogu Yeogwan, a women's hospital opened in 1887 by the Ewha founder's son William B. Scranton, a medical missionary dispatched by the American Methodist Episcopal Mission. The hospital was on the Ehwa campus and only treated women and children. Empress Myeongseong, or Queen Min, bestowed its name. It was the forerunner of today's Ewha Womans University

Medical Center.

Mrs. Hall brought about a major turning point to Park Esther's life. She deplored how Korean women could not be properly treated because they were so deeply inculcated with Confucian moral teachings that they didn't want to show their bodies to male physicians under any circumstances. She realized female doctors were urgently needed and wanted Park Esther to study medical science. Park thus began to work as a medical assistant at Bogu Yeogwan, filling prescriptions and looking after patients.

Park accompanied Mrs. Hall and her husband on their mission to open Gwanghyewon, the first modern hospital in Pyongyang. The hospital was opened in May 1894, and they all devotedly treated the numerous casualties of the Sino-Japanese War that broke out soon. Around this time Park earned a U.S. scholarship arranged by Mrs. Hall. Since her parents refused to allow their daughter to go alone to such a faraway land, she got married and left for the United States with her husband, Park Yu-san, in 1894.

In February 1895 Park entered a public school in Liberty, New York. She studied Latin, physics and mathematics, among other subjects, while working for a children's hospital to earn living expenses. In October 1896 she enrolled at Women's Medical College of Baltimore and graduated in June 1900 with outstanding academic records. Thus she became Korea's first female doctor in modern medicine. But her husband died of tuberculosis while supporting her studies by working as a farm hand.

Upon returning to Korea in November 1900, Park began her medical service at Bogu Yeogwan with formal assignment from the Women's Foreign Missionary Society of Methodist Episcopal Church in America. Her service was truly successful as most Korean women at the time avoided male doctors. When cholera raged in 1903, she toured remote villages in the northern provinces of Pyeongan and Hamgyeong

Bogu Yeogwan This building on the grounds of Ewha Hakdang housed a hospital for women and children. (Ewha Archives)

to provide free medical service, putting her life at the risk. She also gave many lectures to educate the people in sanitary matters and improve public health.

In 1903 Park moved to Gwanghyewon in Pyongyang, where Mrs. Hall was serving. She left legendary episodes about her activity there. She is said to have treated over 3,000 patients in 10 months and her surgical skill was so excellent that people whispered that she performed magic. Earning fame as a doctor, she also served as a teacher at the school for the deaf and dumb founded by Mrs. Hall. At the same time, she led the founding of a nursing school along with Mrs. Hall to train female medical personnel who would lead the next generation of medical service in Korea.

Apart from her active medical service and social work, Park strived to educate women and advance their social position. While she proved her prominent ability as the nation's first practicing woman doctor, she continued to lecture on the importance of women's education as the most urgent task to bring about a better future to Korea. She also engaged in evangelical work to spread Christianity.

On April 28, 1909, a huge party was thrown at Gyeonghui Palace to celebrate the achievements of Park Esther and two other pioneer women who had studied abroad — Hah Ran-sa, the first Korean woman who attained a bachelor's degree in literature from an American university, and Yun Jeong-won who had studied music at Meiji Women's School in Japan. The party was organized under the initiative of American missionaries Appenzeller and Underwood and Korean celebrities such as Yun Chi-ho and Kim Pil-sun. It drew some 7,800 guests, including leaders of Korean society and representatives of women's and religious organizations. The three women received citations jointly given by the Women's Education Association and the Women's Planning Association.

In April 1910, Park died of tuberculosis at the age of 34. A successful medical doctor and a trailblazer in her profession, she was probably too busy to take care of her own health. Her life was short but inspirational.

Hah Ran-sa the First Woman to Attain B.A. in Literature

Her real name is unknown but her English name was Nancy and she was from a Kim family hailing from Gimhae. Hah Ran-sa (1875-1919) was born in Pyongyang and supposedly worked as a *gisaeng* (artist entertainer) before she married Hah Sang-gi, a customs official in Incheon who had a son and three daughters from his first wife, and hefty wages to provide an affluent life.

Hah Ran-sa could not find contentment from her comfortable daily life. Instead she fervently wished to explore her future, to keep pace with the changing times. She was stimulated by foreign women missionaries in her neighborhood, who were working on their own as proud individuals. Under their influence she grew ever more enthusiastic about studying modern sciences. She believed that by advancing her knowledge she could overcome the social discrimination she had to endure as a second wife and even free herself from the conventional restrictions imposed on all Korean women.

In the early 1890s, Hah repeatedly knocked on the door of Ewha Haktang, the nation's first institution for higher education for women. But every time she was rejected for the sole reason that she was married. Actually, Ewha's first student was a Kim, a concubine of a government official who wanted her to learn English so she could interpret for Queen Min and help him grab power. A few more married women were admitted thereafter but none of them continued to study. Therefore, in the 1890s, Ewha made it a rule to accept only unmarried women.

Hah Ran-sa (Ewha Archives)

After being turned away three times, Hah visited Ewha one night with a servant. She asked for a meeting with the then head teacher, Lulu E. Frey, and as she watched, blew out the lamp her servant was holding and said, "You see, Ma'am, it is pitch black. We, Korean women, are in darkness like this. Please open the door for us to a bright world of learning." Impressed by her strong will and courage, Frey accepted her. She saw the making of a pioneer in the brave young woman.

Hah successfully completed her studies with outstanding performance, despite giving birth to a daughter while doing her coursework. Her husband paid her school expenses and supported her studies wholeheartedly, an extremely rare act for a Korean husband at the time. She was truly a chosen woman in this regard. Upon her graduation in 1896, Hah continued her studies abroad with consent from her husband. Leaving her infant daughter under care of a nanny, she studied in Japan for a year and then went to the United States, where she graduated from Ohio Wesleyan University as an English literature major in 1900. Her bachelor of arts degree was the first awarded to a Korean woman.

After returning to Seoul, Hah lived at the Dalseong Detached Palace with the founder of Ewha Haktang, Mary F. Scranton, assisting her in the opening of the Sangdong Church. The church became the hub of a nationalist movement opposing the 1905 Protectorate Treaty with Japan and ensuing anti-Japanese campaigns. It established the Sangdong Youth Institute to educate young people for independence movement and Hah opened an English class at the church.

In 1906, Hah became a teacher at Ewha Haktang and the first supervisor of its dormitory. With her fluent English she conveyed the opinions of other teachers and students to the foreign missionary staff and actively participated in school administration. She was soon appointed head teacher to oversee the entire school operations. She strictly disciplined students; it was said not a single Ewha student graduated without getting a scolding from her. On the other hand, she took care of needy and outstanding students as warmly as their parents, hence her nickname "Tiger Mother."

Whether in school or in society, Hah worked passionately with her deep love for the country. As a pioneer for women's education and liberation movement during the last years of the Joseon Dynasty, Hah stressed the importance of welfare work for orphans and educating women through her lectures for feminist groups such as the Jahye Women's Association and the Jinmyeong Women's Association. She led various campaigns for enlightening women and promoting public education as well as repaying state debts as vice president of the Jinmyeong Women's Association, the first feminist organization run by Korean women. She also served as general secretary for the United Association of Public and Private Women's Schools, which was launched in June 1909 to advance school education for women. Her work with church and school led her to visit the United States several times, during which she introduced Korea through lectures and raised funds for Korean women's education. She once gathered considerable donations from Korean communities in Chicago and Los Angeles.

Hah also promoted evangelism. After returning from her studies in

America, she opened a women's Bible school near Ewha Haktang along with an American missionary to spread the Christian faith among Korean women. She attended in turns the Sunday services at nine churches on the suburbs of Seoul and made a total of 1,426 home visits to gain some 250 new converts by 1911. She also opened a "mothers' class" at each church in the name of "normal school affiliated with Ewha." She visited each of these classes once a week to lecture on childcare and advanced foreign culture. Through these lectures she is also known to have encouraged nationalism and an independent spirit.

As her prominent activities drew broad attention from society, King Gojong and his wife, Queen Eom, sought her advice. On April 28, 1909, Hah and two other women who had returned from overseas studies were welcomed in a huge party at Gyeonghui Palace, which was organized by leaders of Korean society and American missionaries under royal instructions. The two other women were Park Esther, Korea's first female doctor of modern medicine, and Yun Jeong-won who studied music in Japan.

Hah actively participated in independence movement after Korea was colonized by Japan in 1910. She attended the 1916 World Conference of the United Methodist Church, held in Saratoga Springs, New York, along with Sin Heung-u. After the month-long conference was over, she stayed on alone to give lectures to promote independent spirit among the Korean Americans. She insisted that Korea was forcibly annexed by Japan and therefore should be liberated as soon as possible. Back in Korea, she assumed responsibility for secret communication between independence fighters at home and abroad.

After World War I, U.S. President Woodrow Wilson's proclamation of the self-determination of nations encouraged small nations around the world to rise to cry for freedom and independence. The anti-Japanese resistance by the Korean people also was greatly invigorated. Particularly, the deposed King Gojong planned to dispatch his son,

Prince Euichin, to the Paris Peace Conference to appeal for Korea's independence. King Gojong wanted Hah Ran-sa to accompany the prince and carry the original copies of treaties Japan forced his government to sign to colonize Korea as well as his personal letter of petition addressed to delegates from other countries. The king's messengers intended to meet President Wilson and other foreign leaders. Gojong planned to give palace jewelry to Hah Ran-sa so that she and Prince Euichin could support overseas independence movement. However, Gojong died abruptly on January 21, 1919, and his plan was aborted.

Shortly after King Gojong's death, Hah feared she was under Japanese police surveillance and in order to keep fighting for independence, she headed to Beijing, where she was given a warm welcome by the local Korean community. But she was sickened by food eaten at a party thrown for her by a Chinese Korean. Rumors circulated that Bae Jeong-ja, a Korean agent for Japan, had followed her to Beijing and poisoned her. Hah never recovered and died soon. She was 45.

Yu Gwan-sun a Young Martyr for Independence

Well past 2 p.m. on March 1, 1919, the cries for independence were heard much closer as demonstrators milled through the alley near Ewha Haktang. The young students tried to join the crowd but they were stopped by Principal Frey. The school gate was firmly locked under her instruction.

In the evening of March 4, word spread through the Ewha dormitory that demonstrators would gather again at 8 o'clock the next morning before the Namdaemun (South Gate) Station to rally for independence. Around 5 a.m. Yu Gwan-sun and some of her close friends — Guk Hyeon-suk, Seo Myeong-hak, Kim Hui-ja, Seong Chang-ho, Sin Teuk-sil and No Ye-dal — slipped out of their school over the collapsing dormitory fence and ran toward the South Gate, where many people already had gathered, shouting "*manse*," or "long live," for Korea. Many students had a red band around their heads, and some were waving their headbands. Gwan-sun and her friends participated in the demonstration and safely returned to their school in the evening.

Yu Gwan-sun (1904-1920), widely known as "a flower of the March First Movement" or "a symbol of Korean independence campaign," was born in a small village of some 50 households in Cheonan County, South Chungcheong Province. She was the only daughter among the four children of Yu Jung-gwon and Yi So-je. Her father founded Heungho School and a church in his village by disposing of his land. As churches were then hotbeds of Korean nationalism and democratic spirit, Gwan-sun naturally became familiar with these ideals at young age. She was known as a bright and faithful girl around her home village.

In the spring of 1917, when Gwan-sun was 14 years old, an American missionary woman in Gongju heard about her and offered to send her to Ewha Haktang in Seoul at her expenses. Thus Gwan-sun was enrolled in the third year of Ewha's normal school course. She was diligent and warm-hearted. She did laundry and ironing for other students. She even paid meal fees for her needy friends, delaying her own payment. Her good physique went well with her strong and persistent character.

On March 8, 1919, Ewha Haktang was temporarily closed like all other schools under orders of the Japanese government-general. Gwan-sun returned to her home and on March 9, after Sunday church service, she and her cousin, Yu Ae-der, explained the situation in Seoul to a group of some 20 local young men. They immediately agreed to discuss how to put on an independence campaign in their region.

The young men picked the first day of the third lunar month as the D-day and decided to start a rally at noon. It was the market day at Byeongcheon. They agreed to set up the headquarters at Jiryeong-ri, where Gwan-sun lived, and local communication centers at six villages including Jangmyeong-ri, Baekjeon-ri and Mokcheon. They also planned to persuade the representatives of local Confucian scholars' circles and the heads of large clans, which had hundreds of households in each village. Those districts that had completed preparations would send a delegate to the church in Jiryeong-ri and on the night of the last day of lunar February, the first signal fire would be raised on Maebong Peak in Jiryeong-ri. They agreed that the headquarters and the six local communication centers would raise the money needed for making national flags to be distributed to ralliers on the D-day and that women from Jiryeong-ri and nearby villages would be mobilized for the task.

On the next day, Gwan-sun embarked on her daily tours from one village to another. Wearing comfortable straw shoes, she walked some 80 *li*, approximately 32 kilometers, everyday with her cousin, Ae-der. The first person she visited to ask for cooperation was Kim Gu-eung, a teacher at Cheongsan School in Jangmyeong-ri. Kim enthusiastically responded to her request saying, "I will be responsible for a communication center and organizing a rally in Jangmyeong-ri, and then we will dispatch our delegates to Baekjeon-ri and adjacent villages to form a strong organization. So don't worry about us." He also offered that his mother and his wife would mobilize women from around their district.

Kim Sang-hun, leader of the local Confucian scholars' group, carefully listened to Gwan-sun's explanation and readily assured her of his support. He said, "You won't need to worry about us since we are going to do everything as you have planned." She met many people in Cheongju as well, explaining the plan and asking for their cooperation. She visited from village to village on her way back to Yeongi and talked to many villagers. Some handed her small amounts of money to be spent for the campaign.

On the last night of February, Gwan-sun climbed the mountain in darkness to Maebong Peak with her brother, Gwan-bok, and her nephew, Je-han, carrying several torches. As soon as they lit up the first beacon, seven signal fires rose one after another on the top of distant mountains. And before long the number of torches increased to 24 in all directions around the six local centers including Cheonan, Anseong, Jincheon, Yeongi and Mokcheon.

Gwan-sun left her home early the next morning. She first met her friends who would distribute national flag door to door and then headed to the marketplace. Around noon some 3,000 people were headed to the marketplace. As soon as a rally was announced, they took out the Korean national flag from under their coats and skirts and began shouting manse and marched toward the Byeongcheon station of the Japanese military police. With thunderous cries for independence, they marched forming endless rows of Taegeukgi, the Korean national flag.

Japanese military police initially remained quiet. Then they opened fire on the crowd and drew their swords. When some 20 support troops arrived, they began indiscriminately shooting at the demonstrators. Gwan-sun's parents were among the first casualties. She cried looking at her dying parents, but other demonstrators helped her run away. She returned home that night only to be arrested by Japanese military police.

Gwan-sun kept shouting manse as she was carried to the military police station, where she refused to disclose any name despite all kinds of harsh tortures. She was initially sentenced to three years of imprisonment but her time was extended to seven years on an additional charge of contempt of court. During her trial, she shouted to the judge, "As invaders of my country, what rights in the world do you have to punish me?" Gwan-sun even threw a chair toward the judge.

Most other demonstrators were given less than a year in prison or released with their sentence suspended. But Gwan-sun was transferred to the Seodaemun Prison in Seoul. Though a minor aged 16, she was classified as a felon and wore prison uniform. On October 12, 1920, Gwan-sun's elder brother was notified of her death. No cause was given. It was assumed that she had been extremely tortured.

The young student's body was released to Ewha Haktang and placed in a coffin covered with a Korean national flag. Following a funeral at Chungdong Church, she was buried in a cemetery at Itaewon. Principal A. Jeannette Walter, Kim Hwal-ran (Helen Kim) and a few other teachers and some friends of Gwan-sun attended her burial.

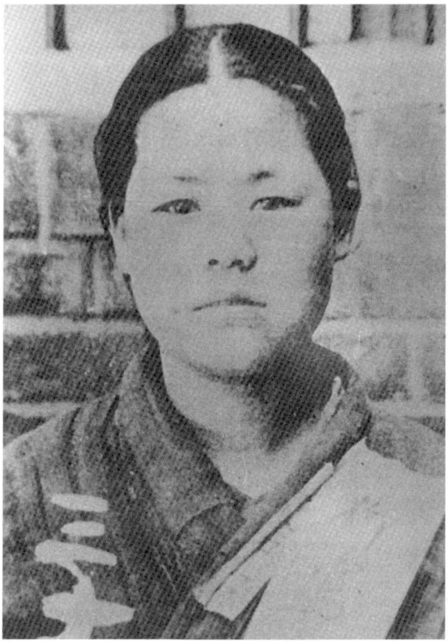

Yu Gwan-sun (Ewha Archives)

It is not known what happened to Gwan-sun's tomb thereafter and the Japanese government-general destroyed her family register. For a long time, a memorial shrine in Cheonan, where her portrait was kept, was the only legacy from her short but meaningful life. Then, in 1960, a biographical novel entitled, "A Burning Star," was written by Park Hwa-seong at the request of Sin Bong-jo, then principal of Ewha Girls' Middle and High School. Later her statue was erected in front of the South Gate by her supporters. A memorial hall bearing her name was dedicated on the grounds of Ewha Girls' Middle and High School in 1974.

Choe Eun-hui the First Woman Journalist

In the wake of the March First Movement of 1919, Japan changed its colonial policy in Korea, though cosmetically, from military oppression to what it called "cultural rule." Japan's so-called *munhwa tongchi* was aimed at controlling the minds of Koreans by means of "philosophy, religion, education and culture." As part of this new strategy, Koreans were granted limited freedom of press, publication and assembly. Eventually, the Japanese government-general permitted Koreans to publish newspapers in Korean. Hence the Chosun Ilbo, Dong-a Ilbo and Sisa Sinbo were founded, among other dailies.

The Chosun Ilbo was founded on March 5, 1920 as an organ of the Daejeong Industrial Fraternity Association, a pro-Japanese organization of Koreans. But it sought an independent editorial policy after Yi Sang-jae and Sin Seok-u were inaugurated as its publisher and deputy publisher, respectively, in September 1924. They decided to recruit a "lady reporter" (*buin gija*) as part of plans to reform the newspaper. It was an epoch-making decision when most Korean women had to stay at home with no opportunities to receive formal education. They had to cover their face with a skirt-like veil when they went out and speaking to men other than their family members was considered improper.

Choe Eun-hui (1904-1984) was the lucky woman who was picked

out to work as a reporter for the Chosun Ilbo. A student of Japan Women's University in Tokyo, she was then in Seoul during summer vacation and the chance came as a kind of coincidence after her visit with novelist Yi Gwang-su at his home. During her visit, she happened to hear that Yi's obstetrician wife, Heo Yeong-suk, had failed to collect her fees from a wealthy family. Heo said that she delivered a baby for a very rich family and carefully looked after the mother for five days with assistance from a nurse. But when she gave them a bill, the rich man dragged his feet for months claiming that she was overcharging for her service. Choe volunteered to help and went to the rich man's house. After persuading him tenaciously from 9 a.m. to 7 p.m., she succeeded in collecting 85 *won* and 10 *jeon*, the exact amount requested.

Considering her commendable, Yi strongly recommended her to executives of the Chosun Ilbo. He told them about how she pressed a stingy millionaire to pay overdue doctor's fees. He spared no praise saying, "Don't you think she has enough ability and guts?" She was thus employed as the first woman reporter not only for the Chosun Ilbo but in all Korea.

Choe was born on November 21, 1904 by the lunar calendar, in Baekcheon (or Baecheon), Yeonbaek County, Hwanghae Province. She went to school under influence of her affluent and well-educated parents. But she obviously displayed special talents at young age, when considering that her elder sister, who was just three years older than her, only learned Chinese and Korean at home because "a young lady as big as 10 years old should not gad about outside home."

After finishing a local elementary school, Choe advanced to Euijeong Girls' School in Haeju. The school had secret circles where students cultivated social awareness. She graduated the school as top student, receiving the governor's award as well as a missionary society's scholarship for studies in Tokyo. As a preparatory course for admissions to a Japanese university, she had to attend Gyeongseong Girls' High School, the predecessor of the current Kyunggi Girls' High School, in Seoul. In her third year at Gyeongseong, she took part in the March First Movement.

March 1, 1919 was a Saturday. The students were instructed to stay inside the school after copies of the declaration of independence were found in bundles on the school grounds early in the morning. But the students broke the dormitory door with knives, stones and axe and slipped out of the school while the faculty was having a meeting. All of the school's some 300 students demonstrated on the streets all day. Choe was arrested in the evening and sentenced to detention for 24 days.

Choe went back to Baecheon on March 27 and learning that there had been no rallies for independence in her hometown, she organized a demonstration with her brother-in-law, Song Heung-guk. Choe and her family printed all the necessary leaflets and made national flags to distribute to demonstrators. She was again detained at the Haeju prison and sentenced to six months of imprisonment suspended for two years. She was released but still had to give up going to Tokyo because she couldn't get her passport during the suspension period. She took a teaching job at Samil Girls' School in Suwon and Yusin Girls' School in Anju. The Japanese police kept a watch on her. She was arrested for giving lectures on women's enlightenment, which the Japanese considered agitating. But she was granted a special amnesty before long and enrolled at the Department of Social Work Studies of Japan Women's University.

She joined the Chosun Ilbo on October 5, 1924, while she was in the third year of university. Her first published article was a report on a group study tour of women sponsored by the Chosun Ilbo. She joined the tour and wrote a fine piece, which received favorable response and virtually earned her a certificate as a reporter. She once received a cash award for an investigative story she covered in disguise. During her eight years as a journalist, she worked for the political desk, city desk, and the culture and arts desk, and finally as culture and arts editor. She grew more famous as the first reporter who covered the test flight of an airplane in the air and the first journalist MC of a radio program.

Through the 1920s, Choe was known as a member of the famous "Pheasant Trio." The other two "pheasants" were Yu Yeong-jun and Hwang Sin-deok, who both had studied in Tokyo and shared their ideals about feminist movement with her. They believed they could ably lead the women's world as a trio just like a tripod giving stability to a round object. They all used similar pen names — Yu Yeong-jun was Chuseong (Autumn Star), Hwang Sin-deok was Chucheon (Autumn Stream), Heo Yeong-suk was Chungye (Spring Valley), and Choe Eun-hui was Chugye (Autumn Valley). Later Hwang also wanted to be called Chugye, hence there were two Chugye — one Hwang Chugye and the other Choe Chugye. Their similar pen names represented their camaraderie. Yi Gwang-su made pen names for most of

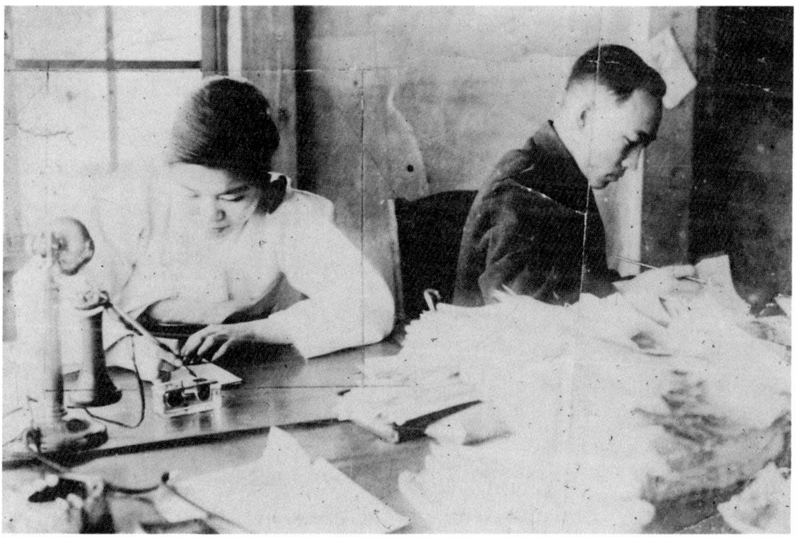

Choe Eun-hui at the Chosun Ilbo newsroom

these "new women."

After returning from Tokyo, these women formed a fraternity group to maintain exchange among themselves. When Singanhoe was launched as a single united group of nationalist and communist forces in 1927, they were inspired to organize a united association of women from broader backgrounds. Geunuhoe was thus kicked off soon. Choe played a vital role as a member of the preparation committee for its foundation and the executive committee. She served for the finance division along with Kim Seon, Bang Sin-yeong and U Bong-un. Their activity continued until Geunuhoe became a nominal organization in 1931.

In July 1930, Choe married Yi Seok-yeong, a court official, who was seven years older than her. He graduated from the Law Department of Nihon University. In 1932 she resigned from the newspaper due to pleurisy and spent the next 14 years until national liberation as a housewife devoting all her time to her family. After her husband died of illness in 1942, she took responsibility for her family's livelihood sewing or running a small store selling stamps and other miscellaneous goods. She educated her children well. All of her one son and two daughters attained doctorate degrees.

In September 1945, shortly after national liberation, Choe formed a women's rights campaign club and led a movement to have "women principals for women's schools." The movement led to the appointment of women principals for several schools, such as Go Hwang-gyeong of Kyunggi Girls' High School, Cha Sa-baek of Muhak Girls' High School and Son Jeong-gyu of Gyeongseong Women's Normal School. From 1946 she served as vice president of the Seoul Women's Health Association and from December 1952 as a key member of the Korean Women's National Party, led by Yim Yong-sin (Louise Yim), and its Seoul chapter head. She also served as a founding member of the Women's National Defense Association, a subsidiary body of the party, as well as its chief inspector. In the wake of the May 16 coup d'etat of 1961, she served as a member of the Central Committee for National Rehabilitation, a woman representative to the National Federation for Protection of Fatherland, and a founding member of the Yongsin Academy.

Choe wrote a history of modern Korean women based on her extensive experience and her historical and social views. It was a live history containing her firsthand experience as a journalist, an independence fighter and a feminist campaigner, as well as her conversations with various people.

In 1983, from the Seoul Red Cross Hospital where she was hospitalized, Choe entrusted 50 million won with the Chosun Ilbo as a fund for an award for women journalists. Accordingly, the Chosun Ilbo founded the annual Choe Eun-hui Award for Women Journalists in 1984. Looking ahead to her death, the nation's first woman journalist who had to struggle through harsh years of colonialism and war, sowed a seed for an institution to nurture other women who would come after her for a tough but rewarding career in journalism.

Rha Hye-suk the First Female Western Painter

To many Koreans she may be better known as an advocate of free love who cared little about society casting scornful eyes at her sensational love affairs and divorce. However, Rha Hye-suk (1896-1948: pen name Jeongwol) deserves greater recognition for her other strengths. She was a pioneer who championed the early movement to improve women's social status while leaving significant footsteps in the history of modern Korean fine art, literature and culture in general.

Rha was born to a noble family in Suwon. Her great-grandfather served as assistant minister of taxation and her father as a county magistrate under the Joseon Dynasty. She was the second daughter among her parents' five children. Her father, Rha Gi-jeong, came in contact with enlightened thoughts and provided a modern education to all of his children. Hye-suk attended Samil Girls' School in Suwon and graduated from Jinmyeong Girls' School in Seoul in 1913. She was bright and talented displaying an unsual gift in painting at an early age. At the urging of her elder brother, who was studying in Tokyo, she entered Private Women's School of Fine Art in Tokyo to study Western painting in 1913. Her Tokyo sojourn created a great sensation back home. No other Korean woman had studied Western oil painting before.

"Dancers" by Rha Hye-suk (National Museum of Contemporary Art, Korea)

Rha completed her studies and returned to Seoul in 1918. She joined the faculty at Yeongsaeng Middle School in Hamheung and then Jeongsin Girls' School in Seoul. When the March First Movement of 1919 erupted, she held secret meetings with other women teachers such as Kim Maria, Kim Hwal-ran (Helen Kim) and Park In-deok in the basement of Ewha Haktang to organize demonstrations by intellectual women and girl students. But that led to her arrest and a prison term.

In 1921, Rha held an oil painting exhibition at Naecheonggak hall in the Gyeongseong Daily News building in Seoul. Through the two-day exhibition, held on March 17-18, she made a gorgeous debut as queen of the cultural world. It was the first Western painting exhibition ever held in Korea and the artist's personal aura also contributed to its huge success. According to newspaper reports, endless crowds rushed to see her paintings. Her fame continued to grow thereafter as she captured top awards at the Joseon Fine Art Exhibition, sponsored by the colonial government, year after year. Her paintings grew even more appealing after she adopted pure expressionist techniques under Fauvist influence during her studies in Paris.

At the same time, Rha drew attention as a writer by frequently contributing to various newspapers and magazines, including *Sin Yeoja* (New Women). Among her notable contributions of feminist themes was an article entitled, "Problems in Improving Women's Clothes." She was also a founding member of *Pyeheo* (Ruins), a short-lived coterie magazine of active writers who pursued decadent romanticism.

Rha tried to put into practice her ideal image of the liberated woman challenging the feudalistic conventions and chauvinistic values, and such endeavors also led to a series of unusual love affairs and divorce. Episodes from her conjugal life became sources of extreme criticism from society in later years.

While in Tokyo, Rha fell in love with a Korean student, Choe Seung-gu, but he died of illness in 1917. Choe was a poet who participated in the publication of *Hakjigwang* (Light of Study), a coterie magazine of Korean students in Tokyo. He wrote poems showing a transitional tendency from bourgeois enlightenment to aestheticism. As he was both a lover and artistic partner, Rha was deeply shocked and wounded by his death. By taking a teaching job in the faraway place, Hamheung, upon returning from Tokyo, she is said to have been able to avoid her father's forcible demand that she marry.

A popular artist adored by numerous men, Rha met famous novelist Yi Gwang-su and an affair ensued. It was a hot topic for gossipers, particularly since Yi had a wife.

In 1920 Rha married lawyer Kim U-yeong. A widower 10 years older than her, Kim had graduated from the Law Department of Kyoto Imperial University. They met while he was serving as defense counsel for those accused of participating in the March First Movement in 1919. Her family adamantly opposed the marriage and tried to persuade her to find another man through matchmaking but to no avail. Again a barrage of public rebuke was heaped on her.

The stir did not end there. After their wedding, Rha and her husband took a detour on their honeymoon trip to the grave of her former fiancé, Choe Seung-gu, and set up a tomb stele for him. As most of the Korean society was still under the predominant influence of Confucian morality, their behavior was seen as nothing less than radical. The unusual love affair was widely talked about for a long time and in 1923, author Yeom Sang-seop actually based the theme of his novel, "Sunflower," on Rha and her lawyer husband.

From the very beginning, Rha's conjugal life appeared to be of a kind that drew envy from other women but sneers from men. She made a candid confession about her married life in an essay written in the style of "a dialogue between husband and wife," contributed to *Sin Yeoseong* (New Women) magazine in 1923. The essay convinced the readers that her ideals for women's liberation were becoming a reality in her personal life.

In 1927, Rha embarked on a two-year tour of Europe with her diplomat husband. She contributed a series of her travel accounts to *Samcheolli* magazine for a year. Under the title "Record of Travel to Europe" (*Gumi yugi*), Rha wrote about her visits to museums, art galleries and tourist facilities as well as her firsthand observation of women's rights and status that she had read much about. Compared to Yu Gil-jun's more famous book, *Observations on a Journey to the West* (*Seoyu gyeonmun*), her stories are characterized by a soft

Rha Hye-suk and her husband before leaving for a trip to Europe
(Association of Commemorative Services for Rha Hye-suk)

feminine style. They are an important source of knowledge about Europe in the early 20th century.

After returning from her trip in 1929, Rha gave a solo exhibition and resumed her writing activity as well to enhance women's rights. But she grew increasingly lonely amid indifference from society that entailed her scandalous love affairs, unhappy family life and divorce. In 1934, she surprised Korean society once again by contributing an open letter to her ex-husband, entitled "Confession on Divorce," to *Samcheolli* magazine. She acidly denounced the male-dominated social structure in the article by saying, "Korean men have a strange mentality. While they have no notion of chastity themselves, they demand chastity of their wives and other women, and even attempt to snatch other people's chastity." In 1935, she held another exhibition with hopes to recover her reputation but it ended in a devastating failure. Her artistic as well as social activities were virtually over.

As she wrote in the introduction to her "Record of Travel to Europe," Rha constantly felt insecure due to the four haunting questions: first, what is the proper way to live?; second, how can a man and woman live peacefully together?; third, what is the woman's right position?; and fourth, what is the point of her painting? She strived to find answers but had to pay a price for her unbridled indulgence. She failed to overcome the common fate of Korean women of her time by wisely reconciling her ideals to the reality surrounding her. Contrary to her brilliant activities and reputation that once was a bright light for many women, she died a lonely death after years of hiding and solitary wandering.

Park Gyeong-won
a Pioneer Woman Aviator

Women aviators form a special breed of professionals even in this space age. But there were already a few amazing Korean women who flew aircraft in the 1920s. They included Kwon Gi-ok and Park Gyeong-won, both born in 1901 to an affluent family, each with one son and four daughters.

Park Gyeong-won was the youngest daughter of a rich, enlightened farmer in Daegu. She attended Simsang Girls' Primary School and at 14 entered Sinmyeong Girls' High School. Thanks to her parents, who were eager to give her a good education, she enrolled at the Kasahara Crafts Institute in Yokohama, Japan. After returning home, she completed a midwife and nursing course at Jahye Hospital. She was particularly adept in mathematics and adventurous as well. With her unusual experience in studying in Japan and traveling to the United States, she dreamed of becoming the nation's first woman to fly an airplane. The homecoming flight of An Chang-nam, Korea's first male pilot, in 1922 made her even more determined to realize her dream.

Defying her parents' objection, she returned to Japan in 1924 and entered an automobile school in Tokyo to learn driving as a preparatory course for flying instruction. Thus she became the first Korean woman to get a driving license. In 1925 she enrolled at Tachikawa Aviation

School. She was the only Korean in her class, which had 33 students, including six women. Japanese newspapers gave special coverage to her enrollment. When asked why she wanted to become a pilot, she stunned reporters by replying, "Most people seem to think an airplane is something that would fall and kill you, not a flying machine. I will surely become a successful pilot."

Park lived near the Tachikawa Airport, earning her tuition fees from odd jobs like driving. Nobody knew she was a poor student supporting herself; she was stylish and attractive, and often the talk of the town around Tokyo. She had numerous admirers though she insisted on being single.

Her strength and pride were not to be taken lightly. Standing 165cm, Park was strong enough to beat most men and brave enough to slap anyone who uttered "Josenjin" (the derogatory Japanese term meaning "Korean") no matter where or when. Although the Japanese colonial government's policy required Koreans to adopt Japanese surnames, she kept her Korean family name and never hesitated to introduce herself saying, "I am Park."

Still, Park got along with her Japanese classmates. She made tasty Korean dishes improving on the salty and spicy diet of her native Gyeongsang province and served them to her classmates to introduce Korea among them. During vacation she brought them to Seoul and told them about Korea's long history. Sometimes she had fun making them cry eating cold noodles with red pepper powder.

Park achieved a third class pilot certificate in 1926, and two years later in July 1928, became the first Korean woman to attain a second class pilot certificate. She won high prizes in various flying races and graduated the three-year aviation school as top student. It is said that her male classmates at back seats made noises ripping their diplomas when she received top student awards at the commencement ceremony. She taught at her alma mater and welcomed visiting foreign women aviators on behalf of Japan. She continued to practice flying, setting up plans to fly to Korea, Manchuria, America and Europe.

At 10 a.m. on August 7, 1933, a large crowd gathered at Tokyo's Haneda Airport to congratulate Park Gyeong-won on her takeoff for a homecoming flight. On the same day, there was also a crowd gathered at Yeouido preparing for a gala welcome for her. Among them was Korean pilot Seo Ung-seong who had arrived 10 days earlier. In front of her beloved "Blue Swallow" (Cheong Yeon), a Salmson 2A2 biplane, the latest model at the time, Park looked radiant in her khaki pilot uniform. Wearing a neat pilot cap and sunglasses, she was all smiles waving toward figures representing Japanese aviation community, her alumni, friends and fans. She boarded her plane and took off to fly into the blue sky.

Past Hakone some 50 minutes after takeoff, she lost sight of her route in dense fog and crashed into Mount Gengaku in Shizuoka Prefecture. Without a level indicator or any other gauge, aircraft flying depended entirely on human vision at the time. Park's dreams as a pioneer female pilot were buried in Mount Gengaku along with her flight time of 200 hours, including 11 hours of flying solo. Her remains were carried home by her younger brother, a medical doctor in Daegu. Her watch had stopped at 11:25:30 a.m., August 7, 1933. Her death was covered by many newspapers, including the Dong-a Ilbo which had supported her. In July 1934, a memorial stele was erected in Mount Gengaku, on the spot some 800m above sea level where her plane fell, in the name of then Japanese minister of transportation.

Another Korean woman, Yi Jeong-hui, graduated from Tachikawa Aviation School one year after Park. She was born to a reputable family at Nusang-dong, Seoul, and attended Sukmyeong Girls' High School before going to Tokyo to realize her dream to become an aircraft pilot. As her family was not affluent enough to meet her expenses, she received support from Seo Ung-seong, a Korean pilot, for her tuition at Kamada Aviation School. She attained a third class pilot certificate in 1927 and a second class pilot certificate in 1928. But her flying certificates were of no help in finding a job. She returned to Seoul in the winter of 1928, bought a taxi to start Asia Taxi Co. and married a doctor, but her husband died soon.

Yi joined the ROK Air Force as soon as it was founded in 1948. In February 1949 she was appointed a first lieutenant and the founding commander of the Women's Air Force Corps. She was later promoted to a captain but carried away to North Korea soon after the Korean War broke out. Kim Gyeong-o, who became an Air Force pilot after Yi, had a long, successful career as a pioneer airwoman.

These early women aviators nurtured a pioneering spirit from early age and realized their dreams of flying to explore a new world even few men dared to enter. They successfully overcame varied limitations imposed on women, opening new horizons for other women.

Choe Seung-hui a Legendary Modern Dance Diva

Korea's first modern theater, Wongaksa, opened in central Seoul in 1908 to present dramas, concerts and dance shows. But Korean dance, at this time, had yet to evolve to artistic dancing from the traditional banquet dancing performed largely for events in royal palaces or aristocratic mansions by *gisaeng*, the female artist entertainers. Choe Seung-hui made monumental achievements as a pioneer in modern creative dance incorporating traditional Korean dances with Western techniques.

Choe was born in 1911 as the youngest among the two sons and two daughters of a nobleman in Seoul. Her father, Choe Jun-hyeon, who enjoyed an affluent heritage, had passed the state examination for literary licentiate (*jinsa*). He was enthusiastic about his children's education. The young Seung-hui was bright and talented. She skipped for early graduation from primary school and entered Sukmyeong Girls' School at 12. She was not only excellent in academics but sang so well that everybody believed she would become a great vocalist. Upon graduation in 1925 she wanted to advance to a music school in Tokyo but was denied admission on the grounds that she was too young. She applied for a normal school to become a teacher only to get a notice that she had to wait a year to reach the legal age.

Choe was saved from despair by her elder brother, Choe Seung-il, who was participating in a new theater movement after returning from his studies in Japan. He perceived outstanding artistic talent in his little sister and strongly recommended that she study dance. On March 21, 1926, he took her to a performance of Baku Ishii, a famous Japanese modern dancer, at the public hall in Janggokcheon-jeong, the present-day Sogong-dong. She was so much impressed by Ishii's performance that she instantly decided to study dance instead of music. She went to the backstage to meet Ishii and pleaded with him to take her as his student. Her appeal was accepted and several days later she followed Ishii to Tokyo. Her parents strongly opposed because dancers at the time were generally seen as lowly entertainers pleasing drinkers. Still, they could not change her mind. Choe began her study at Ishii's studio located at Musashisakai on the outskirts of Tokyo. She stood out quickly with her inborn talent and painstaking efforts.

In October 1926, six months after she became a student of Ishii, Choe debuted with "Goldfish," drawing favorable reviews from critics. After another six months, she successfully debuted at home with a solo piece, "Serenade," when Ishii's company gave its second performance in Seoul. Thus, after just three years of dancing, she emerged as the most promising new dancer in both Korea and Japan. In 1929 she parted with Ishii and opened her own dance studio at Jeokseon-dong, Seoul to develop dance drama as a new artistic genre and systematically educate young dancers. Her brother Seung-il assisted her as studio manager so she could teach some 10 students.

After strenuous training, Choe and her students gave their first performance at the public hall of Janggokcheon-jeong on February 1, 1930, under the sponsorship of the Gyeongseong Daily News. The entire repertoire consisted of creative pieces choreographed by Choe, including "Yeongsanmu," a modern version of traditional Korean dance of Buddhist theme. Her works earned critical acclaim for their high

Choe Seung-hui performing "Shaman Dance"
(Ha Jung-woong's Collection, Gwangju Museum of Art)

artistic standard and she came to turn her eyes to Korean dance traditions as a breakthrough to outgrow Ishii's influence. That was why she sought teaching from Han Seong-jun, a master of traditional Korean dance, and her dance remarkably changed. Traditional Korean dance formed the basis of all her creation thereafter.

In 1931, Choe met another man, after Baku Ishii and Han Seong-jun, who would lead her to bloom as a dancer: An Mak (real name An Pil-seung), a 22-year-old Russian literature major at Waseda University, actively writing about literary theories as a member of KAPF (Korean Proletarian Artists Federation). They met through her brother and married in May 1931. In the autumn of the same year, An was jailed along with Im Hwa and Kim Nam-cheon on charges of implication with an independence movement. While her husband was in prison, Choe did not despair but continued touring provincial areas to give performances mostly full of anti-Japanese sentiment.

In June 1932, with her husband released from prison, Choe closed her studio in a financial strap and went back to Japan with him. As a student of Ishii she made a successful comeback and in 1936, she published an autobiography and played the lead role in the dance movie, "A Dancer of Peninsula," based on her life story. The movie was a smashing success running for four years in Tokyo alone. Her popularity soared beyond Japan. An able agent as well as a prominent theorist, her husband was always by her side assisting her to advance to the world stage. In December 1937, she went to New York and performed at the Metropolitan Opera. She was the third Asian to perform at the theater but unfortunately her contract was canceled midway. She persisted for a year in New York modeling for a famous painter before leaving for Paris in 1939.

Her performance at a theater on the Champs-Elysees on January 31, 1939 was a great success. Particularly, she clearly identified herself as "a Korean dancer" on her pamphlet. The program consisted mainly of her creative pieces based on Korean native dance, such as "Let's Play" (*Ehera noara*), "Sword Dance" (*Geommu*), "A Country Boy with Grass Hat" (*Choripdong*), "Hourglass Drum Dance" (*Janggochum*), "Farmers' Dance" (*Nongakmu*), "Fan Dance" (*Buchaechum*), "Guardian General" (*Cheonha daejanggun*) and "Bodhisattva Dance" (*Bosalchum*). They were rich in pastoral atmosphere, Korean folk style and national spirit. Modern reinterpretations of native Korean dances, they represented the artistic culmination of Korean dance traditions. Through her dance Choe introduced Korean culture to the world, encouraging her compatriots to take pride in their national legacy and resist the cultural aggression by the Japanese imperialists.

Choe went on to perform in Cannes, Marseille, Milan, Florence, Rome, Geneva, Lausanne, Belgium and the Netherlands. She lorded it over the European art world as each of her performances turned out a raging success with full house audience. The media called her a genius dancer and even big name artists such as Pablo Picasso and Romain Rolland did not spare compliments. Toward the end of the year she had to suspend performing due to the outbreak of World War II. A timely invitation from the Metropolitan Opera brought her back to New York, where she performed at the Carnegie Hall as well. From there she proceeded to perform in Central and South American countries including Brazil, Uruguay, Argentina, Peru, Colombia and Mexico.

Every performance drew enthusiastic response. Wherever she went, the media and the artists praised in unison her attractive dance world ingeniously harmonizing the Eastern and Western traditions.

The Japanese imperialists, however, needed her service when they started the Pacific War in 1941. She returned to Tokyo upon finishing her South American tour and engaged in pro-Japanese activities performing for the Japanese troops in China, Korea and Japan, and donating the proceeds for military use. From 1944 she traveled around China to perform for Japanese troops and stayed on in Beijing in the wake of national liberation in August 1945. She returned to Seoul in June 1946, but her husband went to North Korea. Upon her arrival she announced her plans to found Korean ballet and operate a dance institute. But public opinion was cynical as she was now seen to be taking up Western ballet after dancing in Japanese style when the nation was under the Japanese rule. She also had to face rightwing criticism as the wife of a leftist who had chosen to go to the North. She too eventually went to the North with her family sometime around July 1946.

Choe settled down in North Korea and devoted herself to producing dance dramas of revolutionary themes, including "The Song of Liberation" (*Haebang-eui norae*), "The Story of Chunhyang" (*Chunhyang jeon*) and "Midnight Moon Elegy" (*Banya wolsonggok*). She also was politically active running in general elections for the Central People's Committee. In 1955 she was named a People's Actress, the highest honor for artists in North Korea. In 1959, however, her husband who had served as president of a music university and minister of culture and propaganda, was classified as an anti-revolutionary dissident and purged. In 1967, Choe was also purged on charges of not accepting the ideology of *juche* (self-reliance) arts. She is said to have died in anonymity and disgrace in August 1969. *Korean Children's Dance Basics* (*Joseon adong muyong gibon*), written in 1964, remains probably among her last works.

Jeong Chan-yeong a Master of Fine Brush Painting

A young Korean girl quietly gazing at a distant spot, depicted with a fine brush with an obvious feminine touch, drew attention at the 14th Joseon (Korean) Fine Art Exhibition in 1935. Wearing a pigtail and a Korean native costume, a crimson skirt and a white jacket with a collar and a ribbon tie in matching crimson, the girl was sitting alone with a bamboo basket and nameless wild flowers behind her. She was probably on break between gathering herbs on a spring day.

What was she gazing at? What was she thinking of? The girl attracted warm glances from many Koreans and melted their hearts, a rare solace while they were suffering under the increasingly oppressive rule during the final years of Japanese colonial occupation. Though faintly, she seemed to beam a ray of hope to the future of the Korean people.

"Girl" (*Sonyeo*) stood out not only because it calmly asserted Korean local color but it also won the top prize in the nationwide fine art contest that year. The prize-winning artist was a woman named Jeong Chan-yeong (1906-1988).

To date very little has been known about Jeong, who displayed remarkable talent in the traditional genre of colorful fine brush painting. Fortunately, one of her few surviving paintings was put on permanent exhibition at the National Museum of Contemporary Art in

"Girl"
by Jeong Chan-yeong

Gwacheon. It also has been revealed that the Korean Art Museum in Pyongyang keeps her work. Some research papers and a catalogue of her paintings were recently published to bring light to her outstanding contributions to the Korean art world.

Since Rha Hye-suk gave her first solo exhibition in 1921 after returning from her studies in Japan, the small community of Korean women artists was steadily growing. Rha and another female Western painter, Baik Nam-sun, who also had studied abroad, were most active through the 1920s, but Jeong and other homegrown Oriental painters distinguished themselves during the 1930s. Then the 1940s saw the emergence of overseas educated Oriental painters such as Park Rae-hyeon and Cheon Gyeong-ja. They led the art world into the 1950s.

In view of the general trends in Korean art under colonial rule, Jeong painted in a rare style applying brilliant colors. She demonstrated her artistic ability mostly through the government-sponsored annual art exhibitions. She was accepted six times for the exhibition and captured special awards and then finally the top award, dubbed the "Changdeok Palace Prize." Many newspaper and magazine articles about her painting as well as her activity as a professional woman from those years are the evidence of remarkable social attention she enjoyed. She obviously occupied an important position in the Korean art community beyond gender barriers.

Jeong was born in Pyongyang as the youngest among the five children, three sons and two daughters, of businessman Jeong Gi-hwan. Her name, Chan-yeong, meaning a "splendid flower," was given by Gil Seon-ju, then a famous revivalist pastor.

Though in a stern family environment, the young Chan-yeong earned recognition for her artistic disposition in her early childhood by expressing a keen interest in observing even extremely trivial phenomena occurring in nature around her and sensitively responding to them. She became a teacher at Sunghyeon Women's School after graduating from Seomun Girls' High School in Pyongyang and planned to go to Tokyo to study painting. But her parents did not allow her to go abroad alone. Her only option was to sneak away to Seoul. Two Hwang sisters, Sin-deok and Ae-deok, both hometown neighbors of her grandmother, secretly helped her leave.

Jeong entered Gyeongseong (Seoul) College of Fine Art in 1925. But the school shut down soon and she received private instruction from Yi Yeong-il, an Oriental painter highly reputed for his fine brush work in rich colors.

She was accepted for the 8th Joseon Fine Art Exhibition, held in 1929, for the first time for a colored brush painting entitled "Water Lily" (*Suryeon*). In 1930 she married Do Bong-seop, a professor at

"Peacock"
by Jeong Chan-yeong
(National Museum of Contemporary Art, Korea)

Gyeongseong College of Pharmacy, on condition that he would fully support her future painting activity. She was again accepted for the 9th Joseon Fine Art Exhibition, held in 1930, for "Cranes in Snow" (*Seoljung baengno*), and received a special prize for "Beautiful Light" (*Yeogwang*) in the 10th exhibition in 1931. She applied again for the 12th exhibition with "Falling Flowers and Water Fowl" (*Nakhwa yugeum*) and "Folding Screen" (*Byeongpung*), the 14th exhibition with "Girl" (*Sonyeo*), and the 16th exhibition with "Peacock" (*Gongjak*). She also submitted her works for the annual exhibitions of the Calligraphy and Painting Association for three consecutive years beginning in 1929. In the 10th exhibition in 1930, she won a special award for "Peonies" (*Moran*).

Jeong shared special awards at the 10th Joseon Fine Art Exhibition with Rha Hye-suk. Her prize-winning work, "Beautiful Light," earned her a reputation as a genius painter from the media. It was the first time that the exhibition gave a special award to a woman in the category of ink painting with color.

Throughout the colonial period, few other women painters had such a brilliant career winning various important awards. Yun Seong-sang, a female journalist reputed for her gorgeous writing style, wrote in her "Essay on Jeong Chan-yeong": "If anyone asks me who I think is the No. 1 woman painter in Korea at this moment, I would not hesitate a bit to name Jeong Chan-yeong. I must not be the only person to do so. Anyone who is interested in art should remember her name. I never intend to limit her reputation to the domain of female artists. Instead, as a woman myself, I am rather trying to excuse myself for expressing my pride and respect for this great painter who happens to be a woman also. Yes, she deserves much more than recognition as a woman painter. By all standards she is one of Korea's greatest painters."

"Peacock," shown at the 16th Joseon Fine Art Exhibition in 1937, was created with great devotion to commemorate the birth of her first son. It has a nice composition featuring a blue peacock spreading its wings to the full, the splendid feathers depicted in fine details with an impressive brushwork. It is said that Jeong visited Changgyeongwon Palace Zoo at noon everyday for a month to sketch the peacocks while they stretched their colorful wings in elegant postures. At the time, she was not aware that it would be her last piece to remain to this date.

Jeong's ingenious colorful style imbued a unique flavor and vitality to Korean art during the gloomy years of the 1930s. While professional women suffered in the early stages of women's social participation, Jeong devoted herself to painting quietly and consistently and built her own art world successfully. Thus she slowly destroyed the lofty social barriers against women. However, Jeong's painting career was cut short. After her husband was carried away to the North during the Korean War, she discontinued painting to support her family with her earnings as an art teacher. Instead of pursuing her career as a successful painter, she decided to dedicate herself to rearing her children. She could have made more illustrious achievements as a painter if she had continued her creative activity. The Korean art world should regret having lost a resourceful painter. Meanwhile, Jeong made a humane choice to fulfill her obligations as a wife and mother, a familiar path of life for Korean women in a turbulent period of history.

Jeong Jeong-hwa the Mistress of Provisional Government

August 15 is a double anniversary of national liberation and the birth of the Republic of Korea. Korea was freed from Japan's 35-year-long colonial rule on August 15, 1945 and three years later to the day, the nation founded an independent government, though divided into the South and North. These events would not have been possible without the selfless struggle of patriots. Not every patriot fought with guns and swords — and they all were not men.

Jeong Jeong-hwa (1900-1991) devoted herself to supplying independence campaign funds and assisting leaders of the Korean Provisional Government in Shanghai, where she spent most of her time in exile from 1920 to 1946. All the famous leaders of the government in exile, including Kim Gu (pen name Baekbeom), Yi Dong-nyeong (Seogo) and Yi Si-yeong (Seongjae), ate meals from her kitchen, and she shared their pain and joy. In recognition of her distinguished service, the Ministry of Patriots and Veterans Affairs has honored her as an independence fighter. Humbly recalling her years in China, Jeong said:

"It was purely due to my personal wishes that I could participate in the Korean Provisional Government to share destiny with anti-Japanese resistance warriors. The Provisional Government that represented the Korean nation assigned me jobs and I just carried out my duties. I simply lacked the talent for ignoring the duties given to me. Therefore, the reason those who have known me speak highly of me is because they regard highly of my lacking such a talent.

"Whenever dusty winds stormed across the vast continent, where even mail correspondence was unavailable, or the rain poured down as if in a punishment from heavens to tear my heart into pieces, and so I felt lonely and sorrowful, my mind always drifted in one and the only direction toward my country, my motherland. My homeland always remained vivid and alive in my heart. Like a little child who would think of her mother waiting for her at home, I always thought of my homeland, my lost homeland."

— From "On the Eve of Homecoming," a chapter of *Mung Bean Flowers* (*Nokdukkot*), a memoirs of Jeong Jeong-hwa

Jeong was born in Seoul in August 1900. Her parents, Jeong Ju-yeong and Yi In-hwa, had two sons and four daughters, and she was their third daughter. Her father was a major land owner in Yesan, South Chungcheong Province and once served as magistrate of Suwon. Although she grew up in a loving and well-off environment, her father would not allow her to go to school. She picked up bits of knowledge at home but knew Chinese characters well enough to read newspapers without much difficulty.

In 1910, when she was 11 years old, Jeong married Kim Eui-han, who was of the same age. The groom was the third son of Kim Ga-jin, who had served the Joseon Dynasty in high government positions. After marrying she began to open her eyes to the world under the influence of her husband, who grew up in an enlightened family.

Kim Eui-han entered Maedong Primary School in 1914 and

advanced to Jungdong Middle School in 1917. He often told his wife that there might be chances for Korea to regain independence as many other nations were liberated with the end of World War I. Thus he informed her of world affairs and stirred her national awareness. Particularly, her father-in-law became president of Daedongdan, a secret alliance of Korean nationalists, which was organized in the wake of the March First Movement in 1919. As both her father-in-law and her husband left soon to seek refuge in Shanghai, Jeong was determined to engage in the independence movement herself. She decided to leave for Shanghai.

After traveling more than 10 days, changing trains in Euiju, Fengtian, Tianjin and Nanjing, Jeong arrived in Shanghai in mid-January 1920. But she was soon dispatched back to Seoul with a mission to raise funds for independence campaign. From then to 1931 she sneaked into Korea six times to supply funds to the Provisional Government. During these missions she was arrested by the Japanese police and went through a hard time.

After returning to Shanghai in 1931 upon completion of her sixth clandestine mission in Korea, she served as the virtual mistress of the Korean Provisional Government until her homecoming in 1946. Particularly, she looked over its frequent move following the Japanese invasion of China and worked hard to protect its leaders and their family members. She also joined the Korean National Party and the Korean Independence Party, both overseas organizations for independence movement, as part of her efforts to support the Provisional Government.

A national unification front was formed around the Provisional Government following its relocation to Zhongqing in September 1940, in order to rally all nationalist forces for anti-Japanese resistance. In February 1943, the wives of independence fighters from various groups joined hands to hold a rally to launch the Korean Patriotic Women's

Association in Zhongqing. Jeong was appointed training director of the association. Among other staff members were President Kim Sun-ae, Vice President Park Sun-hui, and Choe So-jeong, Kim Un-taik, Yeon Mi-dang, Kang Yeong-pa and Kwon Gi-ok, each named a division chief.

Under the slogan, "Let us build a new democratic republic to realize equality," the Korean Patriotic Women's Association proclaimed to be a women's national unification front. In its platform the association called on "all Korean women at home and abroad to be united to take part in the struggle to achieve national liberation and to build a new democratic republic where the equality between men and women will be realized." Then it waged a media campaign to raise national awareness among Korean women in and outside the country and called for their participation in the independence movement. It also collected cash and material donations and delivered them to the Liberation Army preparing for armed resistance.

The association took over Korean women POWs from the Allied Forces and educated them to take part in nationalist campaigns. At the same time it formed close alliances with Korean women's associations in various countries to encourage them to support the Provisional Government.

In May 1943, Jeong represented the association at the Free Koreans' Rally, jointly organized by various independence movement groups including the Korean Independence Party. The rally proclaimed that "Korea should duly become an independent country and the Koreans should duly become free citizens." It also adopted a letter to leaders of the allied nations urging them to support complete independence of the Korean nation and recognize the Korean Provisional Government.

Jeong was in Tuqiao near Zhongqing when Korea was liberated with Japan's surrender on August 15, 1945. After returning to Korea in January 1946, she supported the Korean Independence Party led by

Kim Gu who aimed to build a unified country. She never took part in politics after Kim's assassination. In 1982 the government awarded her the Order of Merit for National Foundation. In 1987 she wrote her memoirs at earnest suggestions from her family and friends. But she remained ever reluctant as indicated by her remarks: "Heroes are neither greedy nor vain; they aim high but never run wild. Like heroes, patriots also come and go like nature that never pretends. Much less, why did an ordinary woman, a common woman like myself, take up the pen to write about my own past? What do I have to pass on? It is deeply regretful and I wish so much to withdraw."

She hesitated so much to write her memoirs but her story proved to be a vivid testimony to important phases of independence movement, a vital page of the 20th century Korean history. Her clear and honest accounts give a useful glimpse into the real circumstances of the Korean Provisional Government and the true faces of its leaders.

Jeong was not a warrior who fought against the Japanese colonialists on the frontline of armed resistance. But her devoted service became a stepping stone to independence. The nation owes what it is today to the selfless sacrifice of numerous patriots like her.

The Ministry of Patriots and Veterans Affairs has to this date cited a total of 9,380 meritorious contributors to independence movement who struggled at home and abroad. They include only 149 women. Now the task we face is to discover the numerous nameless women who fought for independence and accord them due recognition and honors.

Helen Kim the First Female Ph.D. and University President

Korea's first woman Ph.D. holder was born during the dark years of colonial rule. Helen Kim (1899-1970) attained a doctorate in philosophy from Columbia University in the United States in 1931, giving hope to numerous Korean women alienated from society. Kim was a pioneer in modern education of Korean women and a living witness to the history of Ewha, a vanguard of women's education, and the school's symbol for many years. She was born when Korea's last monarchy was waning amid foreign aggression. She went through the tragic turmoil of modern Korean history and made distinguished contributions to the advancement of women's status, enlightenment of rural communities, national salvation, foreign relations, social service and Christian evangelism. She was a revered educator, feminist campaigner and religious leader.

Helen Kim was born in Incheon as fifth daughter among the eight children of Kim Jin-yeon and Park Ddora. Her childhood name was Gideuk, meaning "a child attained in the *gihae* year (by the Oriental zodiac)." Incheon was called Jemulpo at the time, a port city which actively accepted foreign civilization and Christianity. Helen's mother was an early Christian convert and devout believer. She led her entire family to be baptized when Helen was seven years old. Actually, Helen

Helen Kim (Ewha Archives)

was her Christian name and when she entered primary school, she was given a similar name in Chinese characters, Hwal-ran.

Kim entered Yeonghwa Primary School, the first school for girls in Incheon, at eight. But her family moved to Seoul the next year, and Kim and her two sisters enrolled at Ewha Haktang, the nation's first modern educational institution for women.

During its early years Ewha aimed at educating Koreans in accordance with Christian teachings. But its ultimate objective was to nurture "genuine Koreans" who would take pride in their own legacies. While a student of Ewha, Kim had the tragic experience of losing her country and also realized the deep-seated institutional barriers confining women. She was a brilliant student favored by her missionary teachers but suffered serious conflict in her soul as well. In particular, she recoiled from the beseeching of a pastor at the school's

1913 revival. "Repent and seek God's mercy," he ordered. "I haven't committed any sin to repent," she thought.

One day during her ardent nightly prayers she at last heard God's voice. God was saying to her, "Do you hear it? It is the crying of Korean women. How can you idly sit hearing their crying? You must save them. That only is your mission." She was thus assured that her mission was "paving the road for Korean women walking in darkness." She vowed to devote her life to women's education.

She advanced to the college department after finishing the high school course. During her college commencement ceremony held in March 1918 at Chungdong Methodist Church, she received a big applause for giving a lecture in Korean and English based on her graduation thesis about "Women's Higher Education and Family." On the day after graduation she began teaching pedagogy at the primary and middle school departments. With her goal set at the "humanization of women," she was convinced that Ewha should serve every Korean woman not only its students.

Kim was serving as a teacher at Ewha when the March First Movement of 1919 took place. She led a secret society for independence along with her colleague teachers, Park In-deok and Sin Julia, delivering campaign funds raised through schools, churches and women's organizations. Japanese police arrested most of her colleagues and Kim barely escaped with help from missionaries.

In June 1920 she organized the "Seven Evangelists" with her students, who shared her determination to "cultivate the spirit of self-sacrifice ready to die for the nation when necessary like Jesus who died for mankind." They toured around Pyongyang, Sineuiju and Anju, educating farmers and spreading the gospel to raise national awareness among the Koreans. But Japanese colonial authorities forced them to suspend their activity.

In April 1922, Kim participated in the conference of the World

Student Christian Federation, held in Beijing, along with Kim Pil-rye. They were the first Korean women ever to participate in an international conference. In June of the same year, as soon as they returned from Beijing, they brought together mostly women leaders of nationalist activity to launch the Young Women's Christian Association (YWCA) of Korea and served respectively as president and general secretary of the organization dedicated to improving the social status of women.

In July of the same year, Kim enrolled as a junior at Ohio Wesleyan University with recommendations by missionaries. She graduated as one of top students and advanced to the Philosophy Department of Boston University Graduate School. She returned to Seoul after completing her master's course and writing a dissertation on "Relations of Philosophy and Religion."

She returned to Ewha to teach English and religion, and as superintendent, participate in school administration and improve curriculums. At the same time she pursued theories and practical methods of improving women's position based on her conviction in the absolute worth of women.

Socialism was introduced to the Korean independence movement about this time, and many people, including Kim, became advocates of class liberation as well as national liberation. They coalesced around Geunuhoe, a women's organization founded in 1927 to promote women's status and join the struggle for national independence, injecting fresh impetus to various sectors of society not to mention the feminist community. As a founding member of Geunuhoe, Kim was on the forefront of women's liberation movement.

Kim also called for reform of rural communities through her book, *The Danish Rehabilitation* (*Jeongmarin-eui nongchon buheung non*), written upon returning from a trip to Denmark in 1928. She tried to educate rural leaders through the YWCA and social campaigns. In

The campus of Ewha Womans University in 1955 (Ewha Archives)

view of the fact that farmers accounted for 80 percent of the Korean population, she was firmly convinced that rural education and revival was the shortcut to national reconstruction. In her doctoral dissertation at Columbia University, "Rural Education for the Regeneration of Korea," she analyzed the situation of Korean rural villages and presented measures for their revitalization. Her theory drew favorable response as an advanced view of education.

Kim attracted spotlight when she returned after earning a doctorate in philosophy from the College of Education, Columbia University in 1931. She was the first Korean woman ever to achieve a doctoral degree but there weren't even many male Ph.D. holders in Korea at the time. She was a sensation and a challenge to Korean society. Much of the Korean society then regarded her to have accomplished an unthinkable

feat, while many young women found her a role model and an inspiration. She spread the conviction that women possessed the equal intellectual ability as men and proved the effects of women's education.

As U.S.-Japan relations deteriorated in the late 1930s, the Japanese government-general expelled all foreign missionaries and had Koreans replace them as school administrators. Therefore, Kim became the seventh president of Ewha College, succeeding Alice R. Appenzeller, in 1939. She shouldered the responsibility of leading Ewha through a tough period and at the same time took hold of an opportunity to show her ability as a woman leader of Korea. The loss of financial support from the Women's Foreign Missionary Society in the United States meant she had to work tirelessly to raise funds and organize a foundation to ensure financial security.

Kim held to a few principles as an educator: first, quantity education rather than quality education so as to give educational opportunities to as many women as possible; second, liberal education to encourage students to make decisions on their own with a sense of responsibility; third, humanitarian education for underprivileged women; and fourth, education based on Christian spirit. In her efforts to protect Ewha during the final years of colonial rule employing both harsh pressure and tenacious appeasement, however, she had to experience great ordeals and deep personal conflict and distress.

On October 1, 1945, amid the jubilant mood following national liberation, Ewha College assumed its new name, Ewha Womans University, and became Korea's first university officially recognized by the Ministry of Education. Kim pushed her school development plans under two principles — Korea needed a university for women and Ewha should explore new areas of specialization to keep pace with the world. Whenever anyone suggested that Ewha might turn into a coeducational institution, she countered with the same answer: "No. Not until the day women take half of the National Assembly seats."

Kim served as an advisor for women's education during the U.S. military rule from 1945 to 1948. She ran for the Constitutional Assembly ahead of the founding of the Republic of Korea in a bid to encourage women's political participation. But she lost the election, as did all of the 18 other female candidates. She attributed the devastating defeats to a lack of sympathy and unity among women. "I desperately felt the need to form closer links between women of the intellectual class and those at the common level."

During the Korean War of 1950-1953, Ewha conducted classes at its wartime campus set up in the southeastern port city of Busan. It was also at this temporary campus built of tents that Ewha opened its College of Medicine, College of Education and College of Law. Ewha actively supported its graduates to go abroad to continue their studies in the West and possibly return to Korea and join the Ewha faculty to help expand the school's curriculum.

In 1950 while the war was raging, Kim was appointed public relations minister. In order to promote international public relations in case the war would drag out, she organized a civilian diplomatic body named the "Wartime People's Union for Foreign Relations." She visited U.S. President Harry S. Truman to convey the gratitude of the Korean people for dispatching troops under the United Nations flag. She also founded the Korea Times, an English-language daily, to introduce Korean history and culture among foreigners. Beginning in 1949, she participated in the United Nations General Assembly seven times and successfully carried out her role as a cultural ambassador.

It was also during this period that Kim built infrastructure for women to work for the country and society. She spearheaded organizing the Patriotic Women's Association for Acceleration of Korean Independence in 1945, the Korean Association of University Women in 1950, and the Korean National Council of Women in 1959. She continued supporting the YWCA of Korea.

In 1961 she retired as president of Ewha Womans University but her service for Ewha continued as chair of its board of trustees. In the same year she and her colleagues in the ecumenical movement organized the Kumnan Evangelical Association to spread the gospel and promote rural evangelism.

Helen Kim devoted her entire life to the education of women and to the issues of the nation, society, religion and international relations. In recognition of her eminent contributions, she was conferred the Order of Merit for National Foundation in 1963. In the same year she also received the Ramon Magsaysay Award for Public Service and became the first Asian to receive the Upper Room Award given by the United Methodist Church Foundation in the United States to prominent church leaders.

She died in 1970 at the age of 72. She was posthumously awarded the Distinguished Order of Diplomatic Service.

Han Do-sin the Helpful Wife of an Independence Fighter

"I grew up looking at two huge mountain ranges — my father who fought for Korea's independence and my mother who accompanied him on his long, long journey with her pounding heart all her life. I never thought my father was greater than my mother. History is not created only by those who lead in the front. Looking back at the path my mother has trodden while compiling this book, I wondered how many nameless women served as the wheels of our history along its valleys."

— From the preface to *My Bloody Painful Tales from Dreamlike Old Days* by Han Do-sin, written by her son Kim Dong-su on her behalf.

Regardless of gender or age but with deep love for their country, countless Koreans struggled to regain freedom and independence by exploiting their maximum potential from all walks of life. Among them was Han Do-sin.

Han was born in 1895 at Goryeong, South Pyongan Province, and passed away in 1986 at the age of 92. In 1915, at the age of 21, she married independence fighter Kim Ye-jin and her life of endless suffering and ordeal began. Ahead of the March First Movement of

1919, she made Korean national flags, Taegeukgi, with a sewing machine to support her husband, who was to lead the anti-Japanese rallies. Her husband was placed under close surveillance leading to repeated arrest and imprisonment. With her "pounding heart," his wife accompanied him through all hardships.

Kim Ye-jin was from Daedong, South Pyongan Province. He was sentenced to six months in prison for taking part in the March First Movement. After serving his term, he went into exile in Manchuria, where he joined an independence corps. In March 1920 he returned to Korea to gather funds for armed resistance from counties around his home province. On the first anniversary of the March First Movement, he wrote a manifesto of independence and disseminated it around Pyongyang. He also organized a military corps for national salvation in cooperation with Yi Gi-yeong and Han Jun-gwan.

In July 1920 he discussed a bombing plot on local colonial government facilities with Jang Hye-geun and Jang In-gap. On August 3, around 9 p.m., they threw explosives at the South Pyongan provincial government's third office building, the Pyongyang Police Station and the Pyongyang City Hall. They only succeeded in destroying the provincial government building. While fleeing, Kim shot at police guards outside the city gate, Chilseongmun.

Later in the month, looking ahead to a U.S. Congressional group's visit to Seoul, Kim formed the Korean Ilsin Youth Corps along with some 20 colleagues and organized subversive activities to alert the visiting U.S. lawmakers to the need for Korean independence. In coordination with his fellow members of the Independent Assembly, Jang Deok-jin and An Gyeong-sin, he threw bombs at the South Pyongan provincial government headquarters. Then he fled to the French leased territory in Shanghai and served on the faculty of Inseong School run by independence movement leaders such as An Chang-ho and Yeo Un-hyeong.

In June 1925, Kim helped organize a security corps, headed by Na Chang-heon, assistant director of the Internal Affairs Bureau at the Korean Provisional Government, to protect the lives and assets of Korean residents. In December of the same year, Yeo Un-hyeong was attacked and beaten to raise awareness in stronger security across the Korean community. In January 1926, Kim joined the newly organized volunteer militia corps.

Kim was arrested on March 15, 1926 after throwing bombs at the Japanese Consulate in Shanghai and sent to Pyongyang for trial. Prosecutors asked for a 15-year prison term, but due to insufficient evidence to support charges for bombing the South Pyongan provincial government building, he received a two-year sentence. He was released in December 1928 and suffered from the residual effects of his prison life until he was shot to death by North Koreans during the Korean War. In 1962 he was posthumously awarded the Order of Merit for National Foundation, National Medal.

Han Do-sin suffered with her husband through their trying years. Severe torture by the Japanese brought her to the brink of death more than a few times, but her resolute courage never wavered, outshining most men.

In 1922 she went to Shanghai and served under leaders of the Provisional Government such as Kim Gu, An Chang-ho and Yeo Un-hyeong. Particularly, she continued to serve Kim Gu until his death by assassination at his home in Seoul in 1949. Widowed by the war, she worked odd jobs like sewing and working at a rubber factory to support her four children alone. In 1963 the Seoul city cited her as an exemplary mother.

Han wrote in her memoirs that she always regarded rearing her children well to be her primary duty. She embraced two important principles. First, she believed that Koreans should survive by all means to pass on the blood lineages of those who loved and struggled for the country. In order to do so, they should eat well to take sufficient nutrition under all circumstances. Second, she believed that everyone must study as much as possible and immediately put into practice what they have learned. Education is the most valuable asset of individuals. What one knows and how one lives is far more important than what one owns. In this context, she did her best to put into practice her belief that people need education to live properly.

With her amazing memory, precise writing skills and honest attitude, Han recorded her life story in notebooks over 15 years beginning in 1962. Her writings total some 1,200 manuscript pages. She made clear that she wrote candidly as a firsthand witness to history: "I have so far kept these stories to myself. Reading my accounts, some may laugh and some may slander, or some may sympathize. If 10 million people may sling mud at me, I am recording the real state of affairs exactly as they were."

Han did not fight on the forefront of armed resistance. However, with her yearnings for national liberation and her deep love and sense of duty toward her country and her family, she quietly and resolutely endured through hard times sacrificing herself to support her husband's struggle for national freedom. With her indomitable spirit and devotion, she joined the anonymous patriots who paved the way to a free and prosperous Korea today.

Numerous nameless women served the cause of restoring national sovereignty. Those mothers, wives and daughters of independence fighters need to have their proper places defined in history.

Part III

Historical Records and Sites Related with Women

Chapter 9

Korean Women as Seen Through Historical Records and Sites

King Sejong's Policy for Women as Seen Through Court Annals

Issues concerning women received more attention from King Sejong (r. 1418-1450) than any other ruler of the Joseon Dynasty. Certainly, the length of his reign and the fact the dynasty was still in the process of setting up its systems were factors. However, they would have been offset if King Sejong had been less receptive to rational social change. Most noteworthy among the entries to the Annals of King Sejong (*Sejong sillok*) were state measures that protected women's rights to property and inheritance, the lawful status of wedded wives, and humanitarian concerns about women's basic rights.

King Sejong wasted no time in staking out more civilized governance. In his first year on the throne, he issued an ordinance to sternly punish those who do not fairly distribute the assets of their deceased parents to their married sisters born to the same mother. Thus he made clear that the government assured the rights of married women to inherit their parents' assets. Joseon also guaranteed by law that land and slaves belonging to a wife who died without giving birth to an heir would be returned to her maiden family. If the assets had been bequeathed to her husband, he was supposed to revert them immediately to her family if he remarried. Women's assets were thus managed separately from their husband's property. Women's rights to equal inheritance of family property were recognized through succeeding reigns and manifested in the *Grand Code for State Administration* (*Gyeongguk daejeon*), the main statutes of Joseon, promulgated in 1471, the second year of King Sejongjong.

Property inheritance in Joseon was closely linked to ancestral rites, so women were likely to suffer disadvantages under a family system sustained through the male lineage. In actuality, however, when there was no male heir, daughters were allowed to perform ancestral rites during the early years of the dynasty. When a daughter died even her son could take over her role. Particularly, King Sejong said that he believed a daughter's son should make a more devoted heir than a nephew adopted to maintain the lineage of the eldest son.

Lawfully wedded wives in trouble due to their husbands' affairs with other women also appear in various entries to the annals of King Sejong. In 1440, the 22nd year of King Sejong's reign, the wife of a high-ranking official named Yi Maeng-yun beat her servant to death out of jealousy as her husband favored her. As she didn't even have a son, the royal advisors strongly insisted that she deserved a severe punishment as well as a divorce. Quoting from Chinese classics, King Sejong said, "While jealousy is common among most women, there are also the three reasons a wife should never be divorced. The lady showed jealousy and has no son, but she meets the three reasons that qualify her as the man's wife. Therefore, I cannot approve of their divorce. It suffices to withdraw her title as a courtier's spouse. Instead, the husband is guilty of mismanaging his family." Yi Maeng-yun was thus fired and sent into exile in Hwanghae Province. The divorce was not granted.

In the 21st year of King Sejong, in another case involving conflict between a wife and a concubine, an official named Yi Jung-jeong was given 90 lashes. He was charged with neglecting his duty as a husband because he had banished his wife to a farm and treated his slave concubine as if she was his wife.

In the eighth year of King Sejong, the government introduced a regulation providing a 100-day maternity leave to female servants at public offices who had babies. Four years later, the leave was extended so the expecting mothers could be freed from work a month earlier. In the 16th year of his reign, Sejong instructed, "Among female servants outside the capital, those who are in the last month of their pregnancy or within 100 days of delivery have been freed from work by law. But their husbands have been made to work as usual without a leave, so they cannot look after their wives after childbirth. It is not right if a husband and wife cannot help each other in times of difficulty. Therefore, some even lose their lives, which is truly pitiable. From now on, when a worker's wife delivers a baby, let the husband come back to work 30 days later." Thus, Joseon men were given maternity leave six centuries ago.

A series of policies for women was implemented during the years of King Sejong in an effort to reduce unnecessary social conflict and create a democratic environment based on humanitarian ideals. The policies harmonized the Confucian ideology of the newborn dynasty and time-old customs handed down among the people for realistic application. These policies should seem far short of today's standards of freedom and equality as intrinsic human values. But they represented notable advancement in view of the overriding barriers of Confucian ideology at the time. Some of King Sejong's policies continued to influence the life of Joseon people in later years, but some were short-lived. Yet the humanitarian spirit of the sage king, which served as driving force behind the creation of Korean script, Hangeul, and his numerous other cultural achievements, has significant implications to be reviewed in depth even from today's viewpoints.

Intellectual Activity and Self-Realization of Joseon Women

In spite of rigid gender barriers under Confucian social system, women of the Joseon period had far more extensive cultural activities compared with previous eras. Marvelous writings by distinguished female scholars can be found in Neo-Confucianism and Practical Learning (*Sirhak*), traditionally known to be all-male academic domains.

As we have seen, the prevalent thought in Joseon society was that women would grow arrogant and neglect their duties when they were educated too much. The only education deemed necessary was basic general knowledge, etiquette and home management. Accordingly, the government published a few textbooks for women, such as *Instructions for Women* (*Naehun*) and the *Four Classics for Women* (*Yeosaseo*, or *Nusishu* in Chinese).

Then how did Joseon women grow intellectually? Some women learned to read by themselves or by picking up bits of teaching from their brothers' home tutors. Some smart girls impressed their families enough to be given opportunities to take part in academic debate and to get education in more formal ways.

Ironically, Joseon women also benefited from practical thoughts of Confucianism, which defined the roles of a woman as a daughter, sister, wife, mother and daughter-in-law. They realized both the positive and negative aspects of their situation and on the basis of such a realization they tried to find the ways to express themselves and achieve self-development.

Women benefited from Korean script, Hangeul, created under the initiative of King Sejong, and also contributed to the preservation and development of the script. Some women conducted academic research and wrote poetry in Chinese characters. But a larger number of women wrote diaries, letters and literary pieces in Korean script. Their works were published to be read mostly among women. Thus women made significant contributions to Joseon's cultural advancement as both authors and readers.

We have noted the exceptional subtlety and dainty aesthetics of 16th century poet, painter and emroiderer Sin Saimdang, and the short-lived genius poet Heo Nanseolheon, who criticized reality and pursed a spiritual utopia a half century later. They made the most distinguished accomplishments among the many intellectual women of the Joseon period. Through their ceaseless efforts for self-cultivation and pioneering spirit, they added dynamics to Korean history. And there were other great women also worthy of attention.

Im Yunjidang (1721-1793) set a rare example as a prominent Neo-Confucian scholar. She reinterpreted such popular Chinese classics as the *Great Leaning* (*Daxue*, or *Daehak* in Korean) and the *Doctrine of the Mean* (*Zhongyong*, or *Jungyong* in Korean). She was as eloquent as any renowned male scholar of her days in expounding the essential Neo-Confucian theories of *li* and *qi* (reason and energy, or *i* and *gi* in Korean), and the Four Beginnings and Seven Emotions, i.e., the four virtues of benevolence, righteousness, etiquette and wisdom; and the seven emotions of joy, anger, grief, terror, love, hate and desire. In most of the 35 pieces of her academic writings that exist today she discussed her cosmic view on the supremacy of *gi* (energy) over *i* (reason) and human relations based on the principle of equality. She

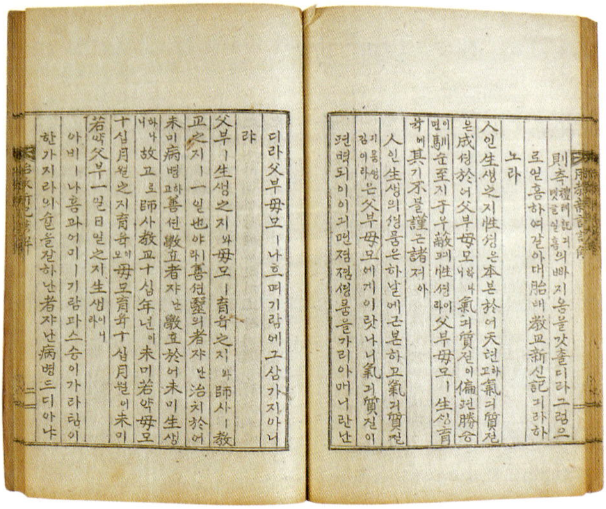

New Guidelines for Prenatal Care (*Taegyo singi*) written by Yi Sajudang
(National Library of Korea)

believed that there could be no difference between men and women in character development and mind cultivation. She insisted that men and women were equally essential for the universe as well as human society. She might not have departed completely from the conventional gender view but she propounded a fundamentally different view of women than the traditional Confucian position by remarking on women's intellectual ability and equality between man and woman.

Yi Sajudang (1739-1821), the author of *New Guidelines for Prenatal Care* (*Taegyo singi*), the first book of its kind in Korean history, devoted herself to the study of man all her lifetime. She realized that prenatal care is even more important than post-birth education for the character development of individuals. She put together the methods of prenatal care from ancient classics such as *Model Women* (*Yeobeom*, or *Nufan* in Chinese) and the *Lesser Learning* (*Sohak*, or *Xiaoxue* in Chinese) as well as her personal experiences and traditional techniques handed down among the Korean folks. Her husband praised her as an ideal wife equipped with feminine virtues and academic competence.

Two prominent female scholars earned fame in the field of Practical Learning (*Sirhak*): Seo Yeongsuhap (1753-1823), a mathematician who wrote hundreds of poems published in an anthology; and Yi Bingheogak, who authored *Women's Encyclopedia* (*Gyuhap chongseo*) in 1809. The book contains practical homekeeping knowledge on broad subjects such as foods, drinks, weaving, dyeing, dressmaking, handling utensils and stationary equipment, repairing household objects, and silkworm growing.

There are also numerous extant writings and artistic works left by nameless women. Whether known or unknown, Joseon women mostly achieved self-development through their quest for human nature and strong determination to overcome hardships in given circumstances. Despite a repressive social milieu, they showed great potential laying the foundation for the feminist movement to improve women's position in the ensuing eras.

Lady Hyegyeong's Political Stance as Seen Through Her Memoirs

Since she was chosen to marry Crown Prince Sado in 1745 when both were 11 years old, Lady Hyegyeong (1735-1815) lived amid endless factional struggle and political turmoil until her death at age 81. She spent her years in the palace as the consort to a short-lived crown prince, the mother and then the grandmother of two reigning kings, but she was never a queen consort or even a regent dowager. Therefore, she is probably best known as the unlucky wife of an ill-fated crown prince who never made his way to the throne and died brutally at the hands of his own father amid severe political strife.

Following her husband's death, Lady Hyegyeong desperately tried to avoid displeasing her fierce-tempered father-in-law, King Yeongjo (r. 1724-1776), the 21st ruler of Joseon. Obeying his orders to send her only son who was now grand heir (later King Jeongjo, the 22nd ruler) to live at the king's palace, she was commended and her palace awarded the name, Gahyodang, meaning the "Graceful House of Filial Piety." She cautiously steered her way amid the intricate power networks involving the royal relatives and in-laws. With those who posed threats to her son and her maiden family, in particular, she maintained amicable relations with some while keeping distance with others as necessitated by the circumstances.

In 1764, the 40th year of his reign, King Yeongjo decided to have the grand heir adopted as son of his deceased eldest son, Crown Prince Hyojang, who died in 1728 at age 10. The decision was aimed to lawfully sever the young grand heir's ties with his birth father, Crown Prince Sado, who had been charged for subversion. In July of the same year, Lady Yeongbin, the mother of Crown Prince Sado, passed away. Lady Hyegyeong was driven into even deeper grief.

King Yeongjo died in 1776 ending his long reign over 52 years. The grand heir ascended the throne and his mother was promoted from Lady Hyebin to Lady Hyegyeong. Also called Jagung (Lady of Benevolence), she reached the most powerful position among all royal ladies only next to the queen consort to the deceased king. In the very same year, however, she had to face another round of political upheaval in which petitions for punishment continued against her father, Hong Bong-han, and other members of her maiden family. Eventually her uncle, Hong In-han, was executed on charges of treason and her maiden family fell into disgrace.

Peace came to Lady Hyegyeong only with the banishment of Hong Guk-yeong, the powerful confidant of King Jeongjo, who conspired against her relatives, in 1780. With the consequent reinstatement of her family, except her uncle Hong In-han, she at last could lead a contented life. King Jeongjo's deep filial devotion made her life even more blissful. Under his profound considerations, she visited her husband's tomb, Hyeollyungwon, in the year of her 60th birthday. Many of her relatives were invited to her birthday party, held at the detached palace of Hwaseong. She recalled in her memoirs that the party was the happiest event in her life.

The sudden death of King Jeongjo in 1800 brought about another round of storm, however. With the ascension of Jeongjo's 11-year-old son Sunjo, Queen Jeongsun, the wife of King Yeongjo, began her regency and accepted petitions against Lady Hyegyeong's relatives.

Lady Hyegyeong's 60th birthday The party was held on the grounds of Bongsudang Hall in the detached palace of Hwaseong, as recorded by court painters. (National Museum of Korea)

Her family's reputation again was greatly tarnished and her younger brother, Hong Nak-im, was executed with poison. She lamented "feeling like a forlorn court lady with nowhere to go." She was utterly helpless with no power to prevent disastrous measures taken against her relatives. She was only able to defend her maiden family and criticize the relatives of Queen Jeongsun through her memoirs.

The Memoirs of Lady Hyegyeong (*Hanjungnok*, or *The Reminiscences in Silence*) were written on four occasions, each on different events for different motives, over a 10-year period.

The first memoirs were written in 1795 when Lady Hyegyeong marked her *hwangap*, or the 60th birthday, at the request from her nephew. In an autobiographical narrative she recalled her life, from her birth and childhood to her selection as the consort to crown prince, her wedding rites and her life in the palace over 50 years.

The second memoirs were written in 1801, the year after King Sunjo ascended the throne. Her younger brother Hong Nak-im had been killed and her father faced false charges of treason. Shocked and dismayed, Lady Hyeyeong recalled how Princess Hwawan, the favored daughter of King Yeongjo, schemed to alienate grand heir from her relatives in the wake of her husband's tragic death; defended her slain uncle and elaborated on how unfairly her younger brother was executed; accused Hong Guk-yeong of wielding unjust influence; and pleaded with the king for the reinstatement of her maiden family.

The third memoirs were written in 1802. She recalled how her filial son, King Jeongjo, had promised to reinstate her relatives. She emphasized the loyalty of her father, graphically and persuasively attested to the unfairness of his censure, and disclosed the treacherous intentions of Kim Gwi-ju, a brother of Queen Jeongsun, and his party.

The fourth and last memoirs were written in 1805 when Lady Hyegyeong was 71 years old. She retraced the background of her husband's bizarre death at the request from Lady Gasun, a concubine of King Jeongjo and the mother of King Sunjo.

Throughout her narratives Lady Hyegyeong revealed two explicit motives — giving her interpretation of the events that led to the death of her husband and defending her relatives.

Most of all, Lady Hyegyeong attributed the death of her husband, called "the incident of *imo* year," solely to his illness in a bid to keep it from turning into a cause of factional struggle. Next, she made a convincing case against the political opponents of her maiden family by efficiently protesting their accusations against her father, her uncle and her younger brother for conspiracy against the throne. She insisted that they had been victimized by bogus charges, particularly her uncle and brother who were both executed as traitors.

Lady Hyegyeong's memoirs demonstrate how thoroughly and precisely she understood the arc events that had claimed the lives of men of her maiden family. She knew exactly why they were charged and what all their political opponents said in their petitions to the throne. She refuted their accusations in detail. Considering her arguments did not depart a bit from the self-defense statements of the accused, she was certainly a smart woman who clearly grasped the political situation surrounding her and knew how to prevent further aggravation.

What is especially intriguing here is that Lady Hyegyeong's portrayal of Crown Prince Sado in her memoirs completely differs from King Jeongjo's assessment of his prematurely deceased father as presented in his posthumous profile and the record of his tomb. *The Memoirs of Lady Hyegyeong* consistently blame the mental problems of the crown prince. The official accounts compiled under the supervision of his son on the throne, "A Brief Biography of Crown Prince Sado" (*Sado seja haengjang*) and "The Record of Hyeollyungwon" (*Hyeollyungwon ji*) portray him as an able regent who only made wise decisions without a single remark on his mental state.

The contrasting depictions probably derived from different priorities of the authors. Lady Hyegyeong felt compelled to restore the reputation of her maiden family, while maintaining the dignity of his royal lineage was urgent for King Jeongjo. It may also be seen that conflict between father and son arising from their differing political positions was revived in conflict between mother and son pursuing different objectives.

Besides their significant political implications, *The Memoirs of Lady Hyegyeong* also contain important information about the lifestyle, language and customs in the royal palace, particularly those of women.

The Annals of the Joseon Dynasty (*Joseon wangjo sillok*) and other official historical records portray Lady Hyegyeong mostly as a woman subservient to men — a crown prince's wife, a king's daughter-in-law, a king's mother, or a king's grandmother — in accordance with the traditional Confucian gender view. From her memoirs, however, her personal agonies and frustrations as well as those of other royal consorts can be gleaned. Her marriage to crown prince brought about prosperity to her maiden family and political prominence of her father; and, thanks to her influence, the Hong family could also remove their obstacles in severe power struggles through the three successive reigns of King Yeogjo, King Jeongjo and King Sunjo. Her memoirs also shed light on the fierce confrontation between her family and the family of Queen Jeongsun, the second wife of King Yeongjo, who wielded enormous power as regent dowager.

Through her memoirs Lady Hyegyeong demonstrated her unusual political acumen. By delineating her position doomed with the specter of the tragic death of her husband, she skillfully defended her relatives in the endless turmoil of factional strife and wisely coped with possible trouble in the years ahead.

Women's Magazines during the Colonial Period

Women's magazines stood at the forefront of modernization of Korean women in the first half of the 20th century. It was a time of tight Japanese colonial rule. But it also was a period marked by conspicuous change in the life of women: access to formal education and jobs.

More than 35 women's magazines were published during this period. Although none of them lasted long, they managed to make an indelible impression on their female readership, changing the ways Korean women thought about themselves. That led to a different notion of their roles in society and in the nation and the formation of a new segment of the population.

Many topics covered in the women's magazines in the first half of the 20th century were not much different from today's issues. Among their most frequent topics were problems concerning marriage and divorce, the scant employment opportunities, gender bias in society and workplace, equal rights for both sexes, the heavy burdens of married working women, and school admissions. Their unanimous conclusion was that women could attain true liberation by cultivating their self-awareness and securing economic rights.

The first women's magazine in modern Korea appeared in June

1906. It was *Gadyeong Japji* (Home Magazine), a monthly of some 50 pages in pure Korean script. Yu Seong-jun was its president publisher, Yu Il-seon its editor and general secretary, and Ju Si-gyeong a proofreader. The magazine had part-time writers in provincial cities, and renowned journalists and national leaders such as Jang Ji-yeon and Yang Gi-tak were on its 15-member supporters committee. In response to the nationalistic movement triggered by the 1905 Protectorate Treaty with Japan, the magazine aimed at increasing knowledge and changing family life of the Korean public through introduction of new civilization. But it shut down in July 1908 after publishing only three editions.

Another women's magazine published in pure Korean script was *Yeoja Jinam* (Women's Guidance), founded in April 1908 by Women's Institute, an educational institution affiliated to the Women's Education Association. Yun Chi-ho was publisher of the magazine, which focused especially on women's education and gender equality.

Most of the women's magazines published after Japan's annexation of Korea in 1910 were published by the Japanese or Korean female students in Tokyo. Among these magazines were *Uri-eui Gajeong* (Our Home), *Yeojagye* (Women's World) and *Yeoja Siron* (Women's Current Views).

The 1920s saw more active publication of women's magazines. The rise in the number of educated women added to the female workforce in the publishing community as well as the readership of women's magazines. Japan also shifted its policy in Korea from military control to so-called "cultural rule" in the wake of the March First Movement for Korean independence in 1919.

Several nationalist magazines, including *Gaebyeok* (Great Beginning), *Sin Saenghwal* (New Life) and *Dongmyeong* (Eastern Light) emerged amid changes in Japan's colonial policy. Among women's magazines founded at this time was *Sin Yeoja* (New Women), which was founded in March 1920. The magazine closed after only four editions. Still, it had a significant influence on the feminist movement. Peggy Billings of Ewha Haktang was publisher and Kim Won-ju, a poet who later became a Buddhist nun, was chief editor. Famous childen's writer Bang Jeong-hwan and journalist Yu Gwang-ryeol served as advisors, and Rha Hye-suk, Park In-deok and Sin Julia also participated. In its inaugural message, the magazine proclaimed that it aimed at liberating women from their home and achieving equal rights for both sexes. Billings founded another magazine, *Sin Gajeong* (New Home), on July 15, 1921. The magazine was in a regular book size (21.8cm x 15.2cm) and each edition had some 60 pages. It contained home care and sanitation topics, literature and essays.

Gaebyeoksa, publisher of the nationalist magazine *Gaebyeok*, produced a magazine for general cultural education of women, titled *Buin* (Ladies), from June 1922 to September 1923. It had articles on the improvement of living, family life, children's education, promotion of good customs, and hobbies. Yi Sun-hwa was executive editor of the magazine. Gaebyeoksa was run by the headquarters of Chondogyo (Teaching of the Heavenly Way), a Korean nationalist religion rooted in the Eastern Learning (*Donghak*) peasant movement in the 19th century.

The magazine changed its title to *Sin Yeoseong* (New Women) on September 1, 1923, and published 38 editions before it closed in June 1934. It was the longest living women's magazine in Korea at the time and also the nation's first popular commercial magazine for women that carried advertisements. In a regular book size format, the magazine had about 100 pages in Korean mixed with Chinese characters, including some 10 color photo pages. It was made of white coated paper and relatively impressive in content and layout from the standpoint at the time. Aside from articles of general interest, the magazine had in-depth features on women's movement, female students and problems of rural women as well as editorials with socialist views. It contributed to progressive changes in women's ways of thinking to have jobs and strive for self-development to improve their own status.

More magazines were kicked off targeting at the growing market of female readers during the 1920s. They included *Bunyeo Jigwang* (Light of Women), founded in July 1924; *Hwalbunyeo* (Dynamic Women), founded in September 1926; *Bunyeo Segye* (Women's World), founded in April 1927; and *Geunu*, the organ of Geunuhoe, founded in 1929 in commemoration of the second anniversary of the women's association for nationalist movement.

Major media companies began to publish monthly women's magazines of fuller volumes in the 1930s. In February 1933, the Dong-a Ilbo founded *Sin Gajeong* (New Home), a regular book size magazine with some 190 pages. The magazine aimed at housewives and, as shown by the score of the song "Home Sweet Home" carried on a photo page of the inaugural edition, its motto was building a new style of homes. Yang Won-mo was publisher and executive editor of the magazine, a sister publication of the monthly *Sin Dong-a* (New Dong-a). The magazine gained popularity along with *Sin Yeoseong* (New Women), another magazine for housewives published by Gaebyeoksa. However, *Sin Gajeong* was forcibly closed on September 1, 1936 by the Japanese colonial government in the wake of the Dong-a Ilbo's removal of Japanese national flag from the photo of Korean marathoner Sohn Kee-chung winning gold medal at the Berlin Olympic Games. A total of 45 editions had been

Sin Yeoseong (New Women)
(Ewha Womans University Library)

published. It was revived in 1967 under its current title, *Yeoseong Dong-a* (Women's Dong-a).

Yeoseong (Women), founded on April 1, 1936 by the Chosun Ilbo, recorded the largest number of copies among all women's magazines published during the colonial period. It was in a larger size (25.8cm x 18.8cm) and had some 100 pages of well-organized contents and gorgeous color printing. In terms of overall quality, it deserves greater attention than any other women's magazine ever published in Korea. But it ceased publication in December 1940 after putting out a total of 57 editions.

In the wake of national liberation in 1945, various newspapers and magazines attempted to target women readers. Most notably, *Bunyeo Sinmun* (Women's Newspaper) began publishing in July 1946 and changed its title to *Yeoseong Sinmun* in April 1947. The *Gajeong Sinmun* (Home Newspaper), inaugurated in March 1946, changed its title to the Daehan Ilbo in July 1947. Another women's newspaper titled the *Buin Sinbo* (Ladies' Newspaper) was founded in May 1947.

The first women's magazine that appeared following national liberation was *Yeoseong Munhwa* (Women's Culture), which began publication in December 1945. It was followed by *Yeoseong Gongnon* (Women's Public Views) and *Yeohagwon* (Women's Campus) in January 1946; *Sin Sonyeo* (New Girls) in February 1946; and *Sae Sallim* (New Homekeeping) founded in January 1947 by the Women's Bureau of the Ministry of Health and Social Affairs. Few of these magazines lasted long either, but they enjoyed an enthusiastic response from women and now offer useful information about women's life back then. For example, they carried public opinion surveys on women's political activities, in-depth studies of new occupations for women and detailed stories about conflict among family members amid changing patterns of family life — all crucial material for study of women's life and ways of thinking in post-liberation Korea.

Historical Tours in Search of Women's Footsteps

It is regretful that stories about women have not been accorded due importance in discussing historical and cultural monuments. Looking through the eyes of a woman, however, numerous heart-moving episodes of ancient women can be rediscovered and new light shed on forgotten facts and spirit of the times. Historical tours can thereby become more complete journeys in time, facilitating a synthetic analysis of history and a fuller appreciation of the aesthetic value of ancient structures.

Among the royal palaces of the Joseon Dynasty (1392-1910) in Seoul, Changgyeong Palace, or the Palace of Prosperity and Felicitation, has the most traces of royal ladies. It was originally Sugang Palace, or the Palace of Longevity and Peace, a small residence constructed for King Taejong (r. 1400-1418), the third ruler, to reside after his abdication. It was drastically expanded in 1483-1484 during the reign of King Seongjong, the ninth ruler, and made a detached palace for three senior royal ladies. They were Queen Jeonghui, or Lady Yun, the grandmother of King Seongjong; Queen Sohye, or Lady Han, consort to posthumous King Deokjong and mother of King Seongjong; and Queen Ansun, another Lady Han, who was the second consort to King Yejong and aunt of King Seongjong.

"Picture of Eastern Palaces" (*Donggwoldo*) The painting depicts Changdeok Palace and Changgyeong Palace during the latter part of the Joseon Dynasty. (Korea University Museum)

The Joseon royal palaces typically consisted of four sections — the section for governance by the king, the residence of the royal family, the section for leisure and cultural activities, and offices of courtiers. While the other Joseon palaces were laid out to face the south, both the main gate and main pavilion, Honghwamun and Myeongjeongjeon, of Changgyong Palace face the east. The layout was probably intended to harmonize with the topography and make up for the weaker energy from eastern slopes.

Sometimes the kings handled routine state affairs at this palace, but

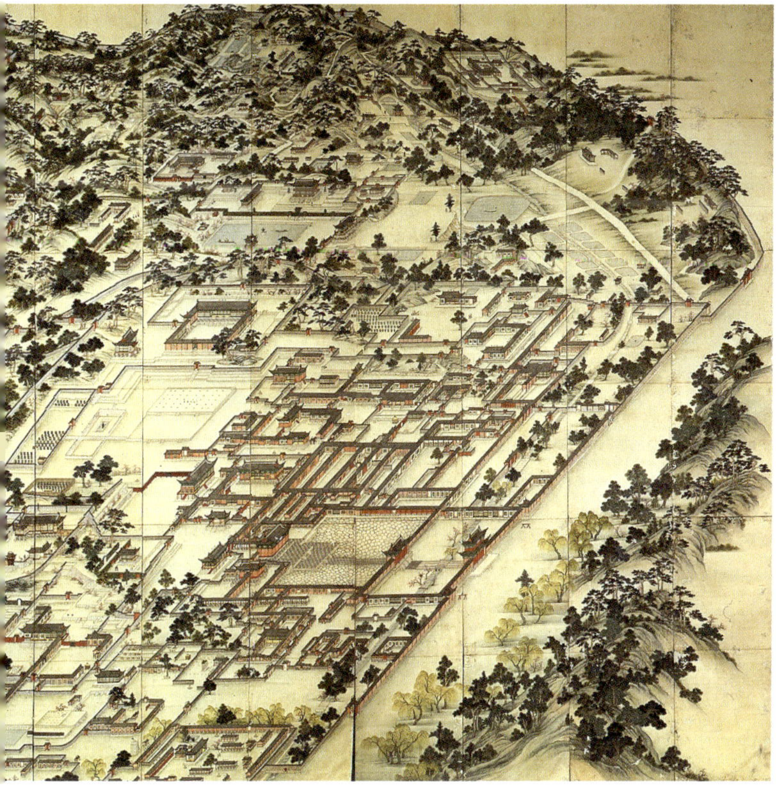

it was primarily the residence for queen consorts and dowagers. So its pavilions and gardens were the backdrops of palace drama — regent dowagers wielding formidable political power, queen consorts wisely and quietly assisting their husbands and sons on the throne, or suffering amid the turmoil of bloody power struggles. All these women, chosen as royal brides through meticulous screening procedures, had diverse dreams and aspirations. Blessed with outstanding family backgrounds and beautiful appearances as well as virtuous character, they also went through unusual trials and tribulations.

Queen Jeonghui (1418-1483), the first female regent of Joseon, resided at Changgyeong Palace only briefly but she was the most able regent dowager. Ruling on behalf of her son and then her grandson, who both ascended the throne in their teens, she effectively protected the throne and cemented the foundation of the dynasty by soliciting broad cooperation from power elites. A devout Buddhist, she prayed incessantly for peace and longevity of the royal household.

Changgyeong Palace in later years often turned into bloody scenes of jealousy and power struggle, however. Queen Sohye (1437-1504), consort to the prematurely deceased Crown Prince Euigyeong (posthumous King Deokjong) and the author of *Instructions for Women (Naehun),* met a violent death when her grandson, King Yeonsangun, knocked her down with his head. A notorious pleasure-seeking ruler, Yeonsangun was furious at her when she scolded him for taking revenge on courtiers who had banished his mother so she would die in disgrace.

In a more famous court scandal, the palace witnessed Lady Jang Huibin (?-1701), the favorite concubine of King Sukjong, taking poison following the king's decision to give her the death penalty. She was found to have held secret rituals to condemn the king's wedded consort, Queen Inhyeon. It was also at Changgyeong Palace that Crown Prince Sado (1735-1762) was locked up in a grain chest by his father, King Yeongjo, and died a week later. The ill-fated prince's son, King Jeongjo, later built a pavilion for his mother, Lady Hyegyeong, on the palace grounds. The pavilion has been destroyed, leaving its site testifying to the bizarre incident.

The palace suffered massive destruction in the 1900s when the Japanese removed many of its structures and built a zoo in their place. Hence the ancient pavilions, galleries and gardens disappeared and so did the traces of numerous nameless court ladies who served the dynasty behind the scenes.

Jongmyo, the royal ancestral shrine of the Joseon Dynasty, across the road from Changgyeong Palace and connected with an overpass, keeps the spirit tablets of 48 queen consorts and the wives of posthumous kings. The number exceeds those of kings, totaling 35 including reigning monarchs and posthumous kings. Throughout its 518-year rule, Joseon had 27 reigning monarchs and 41 queen consorts. The royal spirit tablets are enshrined in two memorial halls — 49 at Jeongjeon, the Main Hall; and 34 at Yeongnyeongjeon, the Hall of Eternal Peace.

The royal ancestral shrine was among the first state institutions built by the newborn dynasty of Joseon in its new capital, Hanyang, the present-day Seoul. Its construction began in November 1394 and completed in September 1395. The halls and courtyards of the royal pantheon symbolize the harmony of heaven and earth, the kings and their subjects, civil and military, and the past, present and future. They also envision the eternity and authenticity of the dynasty and the paramount moral value of filial piety, the roots of Confucian ideology.

The shrine grounds, surrounded by lush woods, are divided largely into three areas: the area surrounding the Main Hall, enshrining the spirit tablets of kings commanding greater respect and their spouses; the area surrounding the Hall of Eternal Peace, keeping the tablets of less important kings, posthumous kings, princes and their spouses; and the area for auxiliary facilities. The Main Hall compound has two smaller halls: Gongsindang, the Hall of Meritorious Officials; and Chilsadang, the Hall of Seven Deities. The former houses tablets of 83 officials who rendered prominent service to the dynasty, and the latter is dedicated to the spirits governing the grounds and buildings of the shrine.

Given that the shrine is among the primary state institutions of a Confucian dynasty, it may be somewhat unexpected that it houses memorial tablets of more women than men. It is because the kings remarried when their queens died. But it does not indicate that all formally wedded queen consorts were qualified to be honored by having their spirit tablets installed at the shrine. Some queen consorts were only admitted after disputes depending on the specific political situation or power structure at the time of their death. An outstanding example was Queen Sindeok (?-1396), or Lady Gang, the second wife of the founding monarch, King Taejo. She was accorded full prestige as queen consort while Taejo was alive but was demoted to concubine status after his death in 1408. She was reinstated as the first queen consort of the dynasty and her spirit tablet was installed at the royal shrine in 1669, the 10th year of King Hyeonjong, the 18th ruler.

The personal merit of individual consorts aside, their status was also determined by the position of their offspring. Queen Sohye and Lady Hyegyeong (1735-1815), both consorts to crown princes, failed to attain the status of queen consort while they were alive because their husbands died prematurely. But both women were posthumously promoted to queen consorts with the ascension of their sons to the throne. Their tablets are housed at the Hall of Eternal Peace.

Queen Sinjeong (1808-1890), or Lady Jo, who married Crown Prince Hyomyeong, was never the consort to a reigning king as her husband died at 20 before ascending the throne. She instead became queen dowager when her son, King Heonjong, ascended the throne in 1834. But King Heonjong died without an heir. She adopted a royal relative as her son and made him a king. He was King Gojong, the 26th ruler of Joseon. With Gojong's accession at age 12 in 1863, Queen Sinjeong briefly served as regent before passing on her power to the king's birth father, Yi Ha-eung, popularly known as Heungseon Daewongun. She was posthumously honored with the title of queen consort and her spirit tablet was installed at the Main Hall of the royal ancestral shrine. She set an example of a royal consort who smartly navigated her way around her fate to carve her place in history.

Epilogue
Korean Women: Past and Present

Introduction

It is my great pleasure to meet with you today at Harvard University with its most illustrious history of over four centuries. Above all, I would like to congratulate Dr. Drew G. Faust on her inauguration as the first woman president of your esteemed university.

I am especially honored to speak to you as president of Ewha Womans University. Founded 121 years ago in 1886, Ewha was the first modern educational institution for Korean women. Ewha has grown to become the world's largest women's university. On behalf of my school, I am here today to wish an even more splendid future for Harvard University.

I understand that your university has had extensive exchanges with academic institutions around Asia, mostly under the initiative of the Yenching Institute, which was founded in 1928. Korean studies have grown increasingly active since the first courses related with Korean subjects were opened in 1952. Recently, Prof. Carter J. Eckert and various other scholars have conducted active research to lead Korean

This is the text of a special lecture given by the author at the Center for Korean Studies, Harvard University, on October 10, 2007.

studies in the United States. As a researcher of Korean history myself, I am tremendously encouraged by all these significant developments. With hopes that Korean studies will gain even greater interests, I would like to share with you the history of Korean women and my views about their past and present.

Women have largely been alienated from mainstream activities throughout history. It means that history has been written mostly by men. Thus the history of humankind has largely been identified with the history of men. Political history has been at the center of historical research, while records about women that mostly concern living culture have been ignored or expressed with distorted gender views. More often than not, queens or the consorts to kings who had prominent abilities were disparaged with the illogical view, "when the hen crows, the family will go to ruin."

It is fortunate that women's studies are gaining momentum, bringing women to the front stage of history. Recognition of women as principal players of history gives balance to its two wheels. In Korea, Ewha Womans University has played a leading role in producing experts in women's history. We expect research in this area will continue to grow in quality as well as in quantity.

Women's Life and Activities in Traditional Society

Women were strongly repressed in the traditional patriarchal order of premodern Korean society. To understand their position, we should first look at the influence of Buddhism and Confucianism as the governing ideologies during dynastic periods, the nature of a centralized governing system and the socioeconomic conditions of an agrarian society.

Korean women's history may be divided largely into the Ancient

Period, comprising the Three Kingdoms Period (first century B.C. - A.D. 918) and the Goryeo Dynasty (918-1392); and the Joseon Dynasty (1392-1910). During both periods, Korean society operated under patriarchal order: men ruled over their family with absolute legal and economic rights. In this sense, Korea was no different than other countries in premodern times.

Let us compare the Ancient Period and the Joseon Period in Korea. They pursued different goals under their respective ruling ideologies, namely Buddhism and Confucianism. Women faced stronger pressures under the Joseon Dynasty which adopted a more rigid patriarchal system. It is vital to understand the different circumstances of women during the two periods since the governing ideologies had a profound impact on women's status and life patterns.

The Three Kingdoms to Goryeo Period

The patriarchal order was established in Korean society during this period. Men ruled in politics and economic affairs. Women were excluded. Men were allowed to have more than one wife as well as many concubines. However, wives were expected to be absolutely faithful to their husbands and not display any jealousy toward other women. If they did show jealousy, they were punished.

In contrast to their public standing, men did not have a paramount position in their families. Paternal and maternal relatives maintained equal importance in blood lineages until the Goryeo period. The balanced kinship with both sides had much to do with the time-old custom of post-wedding residence of married couples and popular practices in property inheritance. Until the Goryeo period, married couples lived at the bride's home for a considerable period following wedding rites, so the husbands maintained close relations with their wives' families. Family property was equally divided among male and female offspring, and women could manage and dispose of their assets on their own.

Buddhism was behind the relatively freer status of women. Buddhist tenets did not expect all women to marry but offered them broader opportunities for religious activities. Women were supposed to remain faithful to their husbands while they were alive, but once their husbands died or they divorced, they didn't face any social restrictions in remarrying. Besides, funerals and ancestral rites were usually performed at Buddhist temples. Monks oversaw the rites and the children of a family simply shared the expenses. In case there was no son, daughters or even their husbands or sons tended to the rites.

Korea had three female monarchs. All of them reigned during the Silla Dynasty (57 B.C.-A.D. 935). Their ascension was necessitated by the rigid class system and unique political circumstances. Silla was locked in a power struggle with the other two kingdoms, Goguryeo and Baekje.

Queen Seondeok and Queen Jindeok, who both ruled in the seventh century, laid the groundwork for unification of the Three Kingdoms. With their outstanding wisdom, diplomatic ability, forward-looking judgment and insight, they made correct assessments of the situation and had armies trained to defeat the other kingdoms. They also demonstrated remarkable diplomatic flexibility in forming alliances with neighbors when necessary, while achieving internal unity with tolerance and magnanimity. Thus they made monumental contributions to Silla's subjugation of rival powers and unification of the Korean nation.

The Silla queens set the precedent for female leadership in Korea. Therefore, during the succeeding Goryeo Dynasty, queen consorts could advise on state affairs, or queen mothers and grandmothers could participate in politics or perform regency to look after state affairs on behalf of young monarchs.

Goryeo society may be seen as a transitional period in the evolution of women's status from Three Kingdoms to Joseon periods.

The Joseon Period

The Joseon Dynasty, founded in 1392, established its governing systems on the basis of Confucian tenets. The founders of Joseon adopted Confucianism as their ruling ideology since Buddhism had caused trouble when monks grew too powerful during last years of Goryeo. They regarded Confucianism to be far more realistic with a logical system of thoughts.

The family served as the fundamental base for the Confucian institutions of the Joseon Dynasty. The founders of Joseon believed that they could stabilize society and cement the foundation of the dynasty by successfully governing families as the basic unit of society. To achieve their aim, they introduced laws and exacted moral discipline by teaching etiquette. In the process a patriarchal family system was reinforced and rules for gender segregation and women's chastity were introduced.

First, the Joseon government stressed the patrilineal order in the family in a bid to introduce Chinese-style weddings and ancestral rites as prescribed in Zhu Xi's classic, *Family Rituals* (*Jiali*, or *Garye* in Korean). The government emphasized the rite of the groom going to the bride's home and escorting the bride to his house to hold the wedding ceremony at his house. It was a shift from the age-old Korean custom of holding the wedding ceremony at the bride's home and the newlywed couple living there for a considerable period of time.

Joseon also changed the ancestral rites in accordance with the Confucian system of family rituals. The eldest legitimate sons were encouraged to shoulder the responsibility of ancestral rites. In the latter half of the dynasty, holding ancestral rites became a primary duty of the eldest legitimate sons. Thus the patrilineal family system became entrenched. The family lineage continued from father to son and women's share in property inheritance gradually decreased.

Second, the areas of activity for men and women were clearly distinguished and so was the physical space of activity under a law on gender separation. The law was intended to prevent possible changes that might occur to women's ways of thinking if they ventured outside their homes. Houses were clearly divided into outer quarters for men and inner quarters for women. And women were required to devote themselves solely to housekeeping and child rearing. Outings were strictly regulated and women were required to cover their faces in public. Those who went out to enjoy flowers in the field or visited Buddhist temples in the mountains were punished by the government.

Third, the government severely punished adulterers in order to stress women's chastity. Women who kept their chastity in adverse circumstances such as war were held up as models for other women. The emphasis on chastity only intensified and, eventually, widows and divorced women were forbidden from remarrying. All these measures aimed at keeping women within their family boundaries. The regulations did not only apply on women but their children as well. Children of remarried women were banned from sitting for civil service examinations, virtually the only way for men to join the bureaucracy and lead successful lives. No doubt this environment prompted stern regulation of women in their families.

Now, we may question whether the Confucian institutions of Joseon society only had negative influences on women's life. The answer is no. Joseon had queen mothers who ruled on behalf of their sons who came to the throne at a young age or while their sons were still training to become a king. It indicates that the mother's role was highly regarded in the Confucian family structure of Joseon. Its unequivocal emphasis on filial piety also helped to increase the mother's prestige.

Many Joseon women were active in writing or painting and not a few achieved excellence in their areas. It may be worthy of note that Joseon produced more women distinguished in academic and artistic fields than previous eras. They came from diverse social strata from royal ladies to women of lowly classes. This was possible because, though limited, women had opportunities for education within their homes.

Women of the noble classes, or *yangban*, received education in basic Confucian classics to acquire so-called womanly virtues. Some women overcame the social barriers to acquire high levels of knowledge and made their names known. Upper-class women and commoners alike achieved the means to read and write with ease when Korean script, Hangeul, was created in 1446 during the reign of King Sejong. Hangeul opened markedly broader opportunities for women to increase their knowledge and express themselves. Women turned out to be the primary readers and writers in the vernacular script, eventually making major contributions to its development and transmission.

There are always great mothers behind great figures. Mothers were eager to give their children a good education as a means to sustain the prestigious status of their families as well as to have vicarious satisfaction through the success of their children. At the base of such endeavors was also the women's strong desire for self-realization. The mothers' enthusiasm for education was indispensable for the development of human resources and cultural advancement during Joseon. The enormous potential of Joseon women displayed under restrictions laid the groundwork for the feminist movement to improve women's position in the ensuing eras.

Women's Self-Awareness and Social Activities in the Modern Era

The modern era dawned with enlightenment movement toward the end of the 19th century and continued through the Japanese colonial occupation which ended in 1945. During this era Korean women experienced considerable changes in their lifestyle and way of thinking. The oppressive social institutions persisted, but women began to realize societal inequalities and made increased efforts to eliminate them. Those who received modern school education began to have jobs and participate in various social activities. They organized interest groups and waged campaigns to increase women's rights, which often coincided with nationalist movement. Thus Korean women were reborn as principal historical actors.

Education and Changing Women's Awareness

Critical voices pointing out unfair discrimination against women began to be heard in the modern era. In the latter part of the Joseon Dynasty, the school of Practical Learning (*Sirhak*) criticized the institutional discrimination against women, and in the late 19th century, a homegrown religious movement called the Eastern Learning (*Donghak*) propounded equality between men and women. With the introduction of Catholicism and Protestant Christianity, these schools of thought were further stimulated by the Christian teaching that all human beings are equal before God.

Modern educational institutions for women, introduced in the late 19th century, also encouraged women's awareness in their situation. Ewha Haktang, founded in 1886 by American missionary Mary F. Scranton, was Korea's first modern educational institution for women.

Ewha Haktang had difficulty in finding students during its early years. The school opened with one student. But it gave hope and courage to young Korean women by educating them to demonstrate their potential and nurture their intellectual power. By attending the school, young women could break loose from home and social confines. The school offered momentum for women to be liberated from their repressive obligations as wives or daughters-in-law and to work in society. Women were awakened from the traditional patriarchal order.

The school helped to boost a new social atmosphere conducive to women's liberation from their conventional gender role.

Now, women realized their own value and dignity as independent human beings who can think and act on their own. Through education women attained the theoretical basis for their new thinking. Thus the new awareness in freedom and equality began to sprout in women, encouraging them to challenge the old order in their families and destroying bit by bit the oppressive norms that had confined women. Increasingly louder voices called for an end to legal and institutional discrimination against women. In response, the laws banning re-marriage of women and segregating men and women were finally abolished in 1894. Four years later, the first women's organization, named Chanyanghoe, meaning the "association for support and nurture," was founded. In its three-point platform, the association advocated equal opportunity in education, employment and movement for national liberation.

Women's Social Activity and Feminist Movement

The expanding educational opportunity and changing way of thinking opened the road for women to advance into society. By the 1920s, there were a fairly recognizable number of professional women, such as teachers, medical doctors, journalists and artists. They made their way into areas that had been traditionally considered men's professions. Thus women were empowered to wage efforts to improve their social position.

The early feminist movement mostly focused on demanding broader educational opportunities. The March First Movement of 1919, which sparked nationwide demonstrations for Korean independence, proved to be a major turning point in Korean women's movement. A large number of women joined the anti-Japanese campaign, expanding the popular base for women's movement.

The women's movement became more active in the 1920s. It had two goals. First, liberal feminism advocated free love, free marriage and nuclear family system, and improvement of social institutions to expand women's education and employment. These objectives were influenced by the Western feminist movement. The second goal was socialist feminism. It aimed at institutional reform with the notion that the oppressive social structure had caused sufferings of women. These two goals were pursued together under the colonial rule. At the time, women's movement was often combined with nationalist movement. Women struggled to resolve both the national and gender issues at the same time.

The movement not only helped to protect women's rights and improve their social position but also inspired women's self-awareness and enhanced the social perception of women's ability to expand opportunities for their social participation. These experiences were vital for securing better legal and social status after national liberation in 1945.

Women's Status Since National Liberation (1945-2006)

Contemporary Korean history since 1945 may be seen as a history of the advancement of women. Korean society has undergone rapid changes as traditional Confucian values and culture have wavered amid the surging waves of Western influence. Korean women came to realize the need for political participation and economic independence through their tough experiences in post-liberation chaos, war, industrialization and pro-democracy struggle. They have advanced institutional reforms to remove obstacles to the humanization of women and their social participation. At the same time, they have coped with their new roles demanded by the times.

As a result, women's status in Korea has greatly improved. Today, women are active in all segments of society and social perceptions of women's rights and roles have significantly changed. In a word, Korean history over the past six decades is an amazing record of the advancement of women to the forefront of history.

Changing Family Structure and Women's Legal Status

The family system in modern society has as much to do with women's life and status as in traditional society.

The Constitution of the Republic of Korea, introduced in 1948 with the founding of the Republic, provided gender equality and women's suffrage. Korean women thus achieved, legally at least, the equal status as men and the rights of political participation at the same time.

The Korean War, which broke out in 1950 and lasted three years, wrought the most profound change on the Korean family system. The war left numerous women widowed. They accounted for 16.1 percent of the female population in 1955, compared to 6 percent before the war. The tragic war forced an end to traditional gender roles. Single mothers had to protect their families and earn bread for them. Consequently, their role in the family grew important, triggering changes to their status.

The impetus to change also appeared in the progressive activities of women's organizations, which raised questions about women's status in the family and proposed revisions to concerned laws to the National Assembly. Their efforts began to yield fruit. The criminal code, promulgated in 1953, did away with impartial penalties for husband and wife in adultery cases. Instead the revised law prescribed equal duties on both parties to remain faithful to their spouse.

In the 1960s, the Korean family system underwent another wave of change amid rapid social transformation under state-led economic development. The family planning project, which was kicked off under a government policy in the late 1960s, had a decisive influence on the Korean family system and women's life.

The family planning slogan of the 1970s was "Son or daughter, let's just have two babies and raise them well." The slogan for the 1980s was "Given the small territory, let's have just one child and live young." The population control, however, backfired. In 2005, Korea's birth rate was 1.08, the lowest in the world. Now the government slogan is "Two are better than one, three will make you even happier." In addition, the government has adopted incentives for larger families, such as increased financial support for newborns.

The family planning of the 1970s and 1980s altered the traditional Korean family structure. Small families replaced the usual large households. Individual rights are respected in a small family. The husband and wife, not their parents, are the center of the family, both performing equal rights and seeking counsel from each other.

Though traces of the traditional patriarchal system still remain, the family system has obviously changed to upgrade women's status and broaden their roles. In 2005, the family register system was completely abolished as a result of persistent effort by the feminist circles. The family register had long been a major target of women's rights movement because only men could be the family head.

The legal revision was not a gift from the administration or the judiciary but the outcome of sustained efforts exerted by women individually and collectively. Through such endeavors women have been able to rectify unequal relations in their families to achieve an equal status.

Women's Educational Opportunities

The educational sector has had a more phenomenal growth in terms of quantity than any other sector in the last six decades since national liberation. The people's academic ability has continuously risen since elementary education became mandatory in accordance with the Education Act, which was legislated in 1949. Particularly, the rapid economic growth and social development in the 1970s brought about far-reaching changes to the educational environment.

Around 2000, the admissions rates at elementary, middle and high schools neared 100 percent and college admissions reached 86 percent. As of 2005, the proportion of women among university graduates increased to 43 percent. Since 1997 military academies have been recruiting female cadets.

Korea's economic growth and enhanced women's status and role resulting from the changing family system have helped to broaden women's educational opportunities and expanded areas of education accessible for women. Still, the outstanding zeal for education and earnest attitude of women themselves has been the primary factor in these developments. Korean mothers' globally famous enthusiasm for children's education, which already was notable back in dynastic periods, is now demonstrating its potential. Women's educational opportunities have expanded not only in public education but social education as well.

Social education has considerably improved in terms of both quality and quantity since the 1980s. The enforcement ordinance of the Social Education Act, announced in 1984, has led to a significant expansion of the areas of social education. In the same year, Ewha Womans University opened the School of Continuing Education, the first school of its kind in Korea. Other universities have also opened schools toward the same purpose, extending opportunities for re-education and contributing to the development of women's abilities and advancement into society.

With broader educational opportunities, women can take up more diverse careers amid diminishing social discrimination. Better educational opportunities have also improved women's social awareness and inspired them to engage more actively in political and economic areas.

Women's Economic Activities

Korean economy has made an amazing growth since 1945. Based on an economic development plan established in the 1960s, Korea's industrialization policy achieved dazzling results. As of 2007, its per capita national income is estimated at $20,000, a 200-fold jump from $100 in 1963.

Few would deny that a quality labor force, including that of women, paved the road to Korea's rapid economic advancement. Women's contribution to an economic miracle has changed the traditional notion of women's role confined to the boundary of home and marriage. A recent opinion survey shows that almost all female university students hope to have jobs upon graduation. It indicates that women place higher value on attaining economic independence as well as developing their ability and performing more successful roles in society rather than realizing their self-identity through their role in the family as a wife, a mother or a housewife. As of 2006, the ratio of women's participation in economic activity rose to 50.3 percent.

In the 1960s, Korea's industrialization put women in labor-intensive, light manufacturing industries such as textiles, foods and electronic components assembly. From the 1970s to the 1980s, heavy and chemical industries such as machinery and automobiles and electronic industry, including semiconductors, became Korea's core industries. At the same time, banking and insurance surged rapidly, demanding female work force, and so did the service sector, including the wholesale and retail distribution, and personal service businesses.

The 1990s saw transition to an information society, with technology and service industries assuming increasingly important roles. This shift required greater numbers of workers and significantly more employment of women.

The Equal Employment Act was enacted in 1988 to encourage women's employment by eliminating factors of gender discrimination in the job market. In spite of such a legal impetus, women still encounter various obstacles in economic activity. This is the reason women's promotion to higher, administrative and specialized positions needs to be addressed, apart from their numerical increases in economic activity.

Women's Political Participation

From the time of its promulgation in 1948, the Constitution of the Republic of Korea has provided the equality of man and woman as well as equal suffrage for women. When compared to other areas, however, women's political status has improved rather slowly. It is most glaring in the number of female politicians who are directly engaged in political activities.

Women's slow progress in political area has a lot to do with their conventional gender role. Korean society is still prevailed by the age-old prejudice that politics is a man's domain and women cannot properly perform their roles as politicians because they lack political training. Also, political parties pay little attention to cultivating women's political potential or securing women representatives. They are obsessed with coming to power and winning the majority of parliamentary seats.

Not a single woman won the election for the Constitutional Assembly in 1948. Up to 2000, or the 16th National Assembly, women had an average 3 percent of the parliamentary seats. The ratio of women lawmakers rose to 13 percent in the 2004 general elections for the 17th National Assembly.

Women's participation in the public service sector has been similarly lackluster. Since the systemic reform in the 1990s, however, the number of women serving in public posts has shown epochal increases. Above all, various committees affiliated with the government have the legal obligation to recruit a minimum of 30 percent women members. The Ministry of Gender Equality and Family also has pushed for greater women's participation in policy making so as to reflect women's needs in government measures.

Women accounted for 21.4 percent of public officials in 1983. The figure continued to increase to reach 35.7 percent in 2004. Women still tended to be assigned to women-related jobs or those popularly identified with the feminine image, such as family affairs, women's welfare, civil petitions, tax affairs or electronic data processing. Recently, the number of women assigned to so-called crucial positions in planning, personnel management, and audit and inspection has gradually increased.

More systemic improvements are in order for more women to join public service and increase the jobs accessible to women. Introduction of women's quotas in party nominations for election candidates, a women's political development fund and the target appointment of female public servants for managerial posts should be among the policies for consideration. A broader implementation of childcare leave, a homekeeping leave available for both sexes and flexible work hours also need to be settled to support women to reconcile their duties at home and workplace more smoothly.

Conclusion

The status of Korean women has improved as quickly as Korea's economic condition in the last six decades. Korean women have emerged from the dark lanes of the past to stand side by side with men on the front stage of history. However, Korean society remains largely under the influence of patriarchal order. There still are many tasks to be resolved before an equal society is realized, where both sexes are equally respected so they can fully demonstrate their abilities.

If Korea's rapid economic growth brought about the financial crisis of 1998, the fast progress in Korean women's status has resulted in a low birth rate when the nation stands on the threshold to an advanced society of the 21st century.

In the knowledge-based society of the 21st century, the development and use of human resources of women is an urgent national task. Women are sensitive, delicate, flexible and creative; women can maintain nice human relations. This is why women have come into the spotlight as potential creators of new civilization. In this regard, interest in the human resources of women cannot but be a matter of primary concern as a national development strategy.

The high level of education and potential of Korean women is the nation's vital growth engine. Compared to advanced countries, the economic participation rate of Korean women with higher education remains low. Universities, society and the state must join hands to lift the rate. I believe Korea's optimum preparation toward the 21st century is the realization that the level of public interest and state assistance to the higher education of women in producing excellent human resources of women determines the time needed for Korea to hone its competitive edge to join the ranks of advanced nations.

Looking ahead to the age of gender equality, Ewha's education program emphasized the humanization of women from its early days in the 19th century. And Ewha has since been the driving force of Korean women's development. Ewha's graduates played leading roles in breaking the lofty barriers to various professions that had been regarded to be men's realms in the 20th century. Ewha has produced numerous pioneers — the first woman medical doctor, the first woman lawyer, the first woman journalist, the first woman prime minister and so on.

In this 21st century era of women, Ewha has the mission to break more glass ceilings. Dr. Helen Kim, the seventh president of Ewha Womans University, said a long time ago that Ewha cannot give up its role as a women's university before women take half of the seats in the National Assembly.

In a similar context, I proclaimed "Initiative Ewha" when I was inaugurated as Ewha's 13th president last year. Under the "Initiative Ewha," I pledged to guide Ewha to fulfill its mission in leading university culture, realizing an era of gender equality in harmony, and contributing to a new civilization.

Ewha has thus far produced a total of some 170,000 graduates. Some 23,000 students are currently attending Ewha, the world's largest women's university with 11 colleges including colleges of engineering and medicine, and 13 graduate schools.

As a supreme intellectual community of women, which is truly humane, practically global and fundamentally creative, Ewha will put together the wisest wisdom and demonstrate enormous strength in the years ahead. Thus we will lead in opening a new era of true equality between men and women and realizing peace for humanity.

Index

A

B

C

D

E

F

G

H

I

J

K

L

M

N

O

P

Q

R

S

T

U

V

W

Y

Lee Kyong-hee

Graduated form the English Department, Hankuk University of Foreign Studies
Cultural reporter of The Korea Times
Managing editor of the ASPAC Quarterly of Cultural and Social Affairs
Cultural editor, managing editor and edior-in-chief of The Korea Herald
Executive director of the Seoul English Village
Editor of Korea Focus

Other works include:
Korean Culture: Legacies and Lore
World Heritage in Korea
Royal Costumes of the Late Choson Period (translation)
Royal Ancestral Shrine of the Choson Dynasty (translation)
Genre Pictures of Korea (translation)
Korean Mask Dance (translation)
Korean Travel Literature (translation)
Buddhism (translation)

Women in Korean History

Written by Lee Bae-yong
Translated by Lee Kyong-hee
Edited by Ted Chan

First published 20 October, 2008
by Ewha Womans University Press
11-1 Daehyun-dong, Seodaemun-gu, Seoul, Korea 120-750
Tel. (82-2)3277-2965, 2966 / 362-6076
Fax. (82-2)312-4312
E-mail : press@ewha.ac.kr
Online Bookstore : www.ewhapress.com

Price : 28,000 won
ISBN 978-89-7300-772-1 03910